THE CREATIVE MIND IN
COLERIDGE'S POETRY

By the same author

Sources, Processes and Methods in Coleridge's *Biographia Literaria*

The Creative Mind in Coleridge's Poetry

by

K. M. WHEELER

HARVARD UNIVERSITY PRESS
Cambridge, Massachusetts
1981

186093

Library of Congress Cataloging in Publication Data

Wheeler, Kathleen M
  The creative mind in Coleridge's poetry.

  Bibliography: p.
  1. Coleridge, Samuel Taylor, 1772–1834–
Criticism and interpretation. 2. Coleridge,
Samuel Taylor, 1772–1834—Philosophy. 3. Creativity
in literature. I. Title.
PR4487.P5W57   1981   821'.7   80–23543
ISBN 0–674–17573–5

Printed in Great Britain

Contents

Acknowledgments

My deepest acknowledgments are due to Dr John W. Wright, of Ann Arbor, Michigan, who several years ago suggested possibilities for reading romantic poetry and prose which have continued to work upon my mind in stimulating ways, and which I have far from exhausted at the present day. I owe thanks to Howard Erskine-Hill who gave advice in the early stages of the book which significantly affected the general plan. To John Beer I am always indebted for continuing advice and encouragement. I am also obliged to students at Girton and Jesus College over the last three years for patiently listening and responding to the ideas which form the basis of the book. Parts of the present study were given as a series of lectures at Cambridge University in the Michaelmas term 1979, in a somewhat altered form.

I am grateful to Jesus College, Cambridge, for a Research Fellowship which gave me the leisure in congenial surroundings to undertake the present study.

K. M. Wheeler
Cambridge
1981

Preface

Coleridge's life-long interest in philosophy and his active interest in the specific philosophical issues of his day are well known. To the dismay of his friends, his metaphysics eventually absorbed his attention and the 'metaphysical bustards' ousted the 'poetic partridges', as Coleridge himself once mourned. And yet, poetry and philosophy were ever entwined in Coleridge's mind, a connection that forms the basis of the integrity of the *Biographia Literaria*. As Coleridge insisted, 'a great Poet must be, implicitè if not explicitè, a profound Metaphysician' (*Collected Letters* II 810, and see *Biographia Literaria* II 19 for a similar statement). Clearly, finding the balance between the philosophic 'tact', as he called it, and the poetic inspiration that gave it life, was the difficulty which plagued him in later years. But in the years between the writing of 'The Eolian Harp' and 'Frost at Midnight', the difficulty was often overcome; a perfect interpenetration of ideas and images was achieved, and it is one of the distinguishing marks of Coleridge's poetry: the saturation of the poetry by philosophic reflection.

This study is an attempt to suggest some aspects of the extensive philosophic reflection and the self-consciousness permeating Coleridge's best poetry. Five poems are discussed, two supernatural poems and three conversation poems, always with the goal in mind of elucidating the poems in order to add to an understanding of how they may function within the reading experience as unified aesthetic wholes. This analysis is however limited and defined by the central philosophic preoccupation of the mind as essentially creative in its activity of organizing sensation into experience. Subsidiary issues also arise, such as the relation of mind and nature, the difference between ordinary perception and aesthetic perception, and the relation of art to reality, issues discussed not exhaustively but rather in terms of their function within the poetry.

The creative theory of mind is illustrated in the poetry from two perspectives; first, that of the poet and of the creative secondary imagination, and second, that of the reader and of the primary imagination. The reading process as a form of perception is shown to demand a creativity essentially similar to that of the poet. Thus a constant analogy between reading (perception) and composition (artistic creation) is alleged: reading, like perception, is creation too. The poem does not exist as an object external to and independent of the experience of it in any knowable sense. The exposure of the illusion of the reader that his reading is a passive receptivity of an already fixed and determined complex of meaning becomes one of Coleridge's prime objectives, as he exhorts his reader to join him, as author, in the shared labour of an imaginative response. This demand for reader participation breaks down the boundary between art and reality, the reader as subject and the object as text, and sets up the poem as a unity of opposites in a state of process and becoming, instead of as a product of independent status.

This study is further limited by the predominant interest in some of the chapters with the extra-poetical devices of prefaces, glosses, arguments, and footnotes, and with the way these devices impinge upon a creative theory of mind. For example, the chapter on 'The Ancient Mariner' is almost exclusively concerned with the function of the gloss in the poem, an issue constituting only one of the many fascinating areas of discussion about the poem. The chapter on 'Kubla Khan' is similarly concerned with the aesthetic function of the preface, to which little attention has been given; other matters do enter into the discussion, though, such as landscape imagery.

The method of analysis in the chapters varies somewhat according to the demands of the individual poems. 'The Eolian Harp' involves some mention of Coleridge's personal affairs in order to ascertain the tone and significance of the important third stanza. 'Frost at Midnight' offers an opportunity for some source-work in notebooks and letters, and suggests that while the conversation poems may have been inspired or conceived on specific occasions, the actual composition spanned a considerable period of time. 'This Lime-Tree Bower My Prison', on the other hand, invites a consideration of the final version of the poem with a significantly different manuscript version, and also provides the occasion for examining the relation of the supernatural poems to these, shall we say, more domestic writings. The intention, however, of each of these several approaches is to indicate how deeply the poetry is permeated by the philosophic issues which crowded Coleridge's mind, issues obscured sometimes by the effectiveness of poetic embodiment of these thoughts in sensuous form. Poetic elements must certainly predominate in poetry, but as Coleridge insisted, the best poetry is always philosophic. Indeed, Coleridge's best poetry seems to be philosophic.

Key to Abbreviations

AR	*Aids to Reflection in the Formation of a Manly Character.* Ed. Thomas Fenby. Edinburgh: 1905.
BL	*Biographia Literaria; or Biographical Sketches of my Literary Life and Opinions.* Ed. J. Shawcross. 2 vols. London: 1907.
CL	*Collected Letters of Samuel Taylor Coleridge.* Ed. E. L. Griggs. 6 vols. Oxford: 1956–71.
The Friend (CC)	*The Friend. A Series of Essays in Three Volumes. To Aid in the Formation of Fixed Principles in Politics, Morals, and Religion, with Literary Amusements Interspersed.* Ed. Barbara E. Rooke. 2 vols. Vol. 4: *The Collected Coleridge.* London and Princeton: 1969.
LS (CC)	*Lay Sermons.* Ed. R. J. White. Vol. 6: *The Collected Coleridge.* London and Princeton: 1972.
Lects 1795 (CC)	*Lectures 1795 on Politics and Religion.* Ed. L. Patton and P. Mann. Vol. 1: *The Collected Coleridge.* London and Princeton: 1971.
Misc C	*Miscellaneous Criticism.* Ed. T. M. Raysor. London and Cambridge, Mass.: 1936.
CN	*The Notebooks of Samuel Taylor Coleridge.* Ed. Kathleen Coburn. 3 parts in 6 vols. so far published. London and New York: 1957–
P Lects	*Philosophical Lectures of Samuel Taylor Coleridge 1818–19.* Ed. Kathleen Coburn. London: 1949.
PW	*Poetical Works.* Ed. E. H. Coleridge. 2 vols. Oxford: 1912.
Sh C	*Shakespearean Criticism.* Ed. T. M. Raysor. 2 vols. London: 1930.
TT	*Specimens of the Table Talk of the Late Samuel Taylor Coleridge.* Ed. H. N. Coleridge. London and New York: 1835.
BM *MS*	British Museum manuscript.

Introduction

The Struggle with Associationism

Any account of Coleridge's poetry of the 1790s from a philosophical standpoint should be concerned with the development his thought underwent during this period. For Coleridge was not a poet turned philosopher;[1] his philosophical interests are well known to have extended back to his schooldays at Christ's Hospital.[2] Nor is it possible to describe the development of his thought by a chronological list of the philosophers he took up with enthusiasm, as Southey implied in 1808.[3] For Coleridge was selective and did not hesitate to reject aspects of an otherwise esteemed writer, if he deemed them inconsistent with the whole. This is not to suggest that his philosophical attitude was syncretic; Coleridge had his own objections to such a patchwork job:

'Syncretism'; 'Adoption of the Best', and or by whatever other phrases the same process of intellect may be represented, is the Death of all Philosophy. Truth is one and entire, because it is *vital*. Whatever lives is contradistinguished from all juxtapositions of mechanism, however ingenious, by its oneness, its impartiability;—and mechanism itself could not have had existence, except as a counterfeit of a living Whole.

(*CN* III 4251, May 1815)

His marginal notes to Kant and Fichte are particularly revealing of his sophistication in this respect.[4] The tenacity with which Coleridge adhered to David Hartley, however, is one of the most difficult aspects of his thought to assess and understand.[5] For while he was throwing overboard nearly everything that had been associated with Hartley, including Priestley, Newton, and Locke, and while he spent perhaps years vaguely doubting Hartley's system (from 1796 as it seems), it was only in 1801 that Coleridge fully renounced Hartley's philosophy. Coleridge's reluctance to renounce Hartley is tantalizing because it seems to register in certain ways a conflict with the poetry being written during this period. And it also suggests a conflict with the commitment to Plato, Proclus, Baxter, Boehme, Cudworth, and Berkeley's esoteric philosophy, which characterized Coleridge's early tendencies in the late 1780s and early 1790s, and which, with the clear exception of 1794–5, seems to have been the predominant philosophy for the rest of his life.

This is clear from the letters and notebooks throughout the early 1800–1808 period. In *The Friend* of 1808–10, especially the early numbers, in the *Biographia Literaria* (1817) and the *Statesman's Manual* (1816), and in the *Lectures on the History of Philosophy*, Coleridge's 'Constructive Philosophy' is evident, developing, but rarely if ever changing substantially from its main direction. By 1801, this commitment had reasserted itself in the form of a 'completion' of the Kantian system by a modernized Platonism. For as early as the Wedgwood letters of February 1801 Coleridge was already mentioning the pregnant term 'constituent' ideas, which formed the basis of his 'completion' of the Kantian system (see *CL* II 696). An earlier letter also hints that Coleridge may have been seeing the relation of Kant to Plato very early, especially in view of the sophistication of the discussion about ideas in the Locke–Descartes letters. This following letter is important for its mention of Kant's correspondent, J. H. Lambert, whom Coleridge obviously had read by early 1801 at least. But it is especially notable for the attitude towards 'discoveries in metaphysics', and for the celebration of the ancients:

> But *I* take T. Wedgewood's own opinion, his own convictions, as STRONG presumptions that he has fallen upon some very valuable Truths—some he stated but only in short hints to me/& I *guess* from these, that they have been noticed before, & set forth by Kant in part & in part by Lambert . . . I have been myself thinking with the most intense energy on similar subjects/I shall shortly communicate the result of my Thoughts to the Wedgewoods/ . . . respecting Locke & DesCartes, & likewise concerning the supposed Discovery of the Law of Association by Hobbes.—Since I have been at Keswick, I have read a great deal/and my Reading has furnished me with many reasons for being exceedingly suspicious of *supposed Discoveries* in Metaphysics. My dear dear Poole! Plato, and Aristotle were great & astonishing Geniuses . . .
>
> (*CL* II 675)

Coleridge here seems to be placing Kant's and Lambert's observations firmly in an older tradition. Several of his marginal notes on

Tennemann indicate clearly that much of what was valuable in Kant, Fichte, Shelling, and others, could be traced to earlier philosophers, especially Plato, Aristotle, and Bacon. (For an account of Kant's main 'merit', see *CL* IV 852, April 1818.) A marginal note in Tennemann's *Geschichte der Philosophie* is a timely reminder that it would be a mistake to look exclusively to the German tradition as the heritage upon which Coleridge drew; the Germans, like Coleridge himself, owed much to a more ancient tradition. In this note Coleridge complained indignantly of this similar tendency in Tennemann to ascribe too much to Kant, *et al.*: 'Never, surely, was a Ph. History composed under a stronger *Warp* of a Predetermination, that the elder Philosophers *must have* been ignorant of Kant's Cr. d. r. Vernunft!!' (I 181).

Much in the poems of the 1795–8 period directly and consistently reflects Coleridge's philosophical preoccupations during this time. The inconsistency mentioned above arises not so much in the details, explicit materials, and language of the poetry, for they owe much to the specific issues of the moment. For example, 'The Eolian Harp' illustrates these philosophical elements in the allegedly mechanical image of the wind-harp and breeze as a metaphor for consciousness. The image is expressive of the mechanism, determinism, and necessity involved in Associationism and indirectly it is expressive of materialism, though at the time Coleridge did not see this as a consequence of the other three views (see *BL* I ch. vii 81 for Coleridge's reservations about the image if taken to represent consciousness). This apparently mechanical image contrasts with the images of growth and organicism that came to dominate Coleridge's poetry, and his later prose. They describe the mind as active and originating instead of passive and receiving influences ready-made from the external world. The use in this poem of the epithet 'Incomprehensible' is another detail reflecting Coleridge's preoccupations at the time, and having significance in his efforts to come to a satisfactory position with regard to certain theological issues preoccupying the minds of other philosophers. He wrote to the Rev. John Edwards in 1796 'Has not Dr Priestly forgotten that *Incomprehensibility* is as necessary an attribute of the First Cause, as Love, or Power, or Intelligence?' (*CL* I 192).[6]

'This Lime-Tree Bower' has its most obvious philosophical reference in the Berkeleian avowal at the end of Stanza II. The poem might also be taken as a reminder of the Priestleian cult of optimism, and of the belief that evil is only apparent, and essentially a hidden good. Such an attitude cropped up in the 1795 lectures on politics and religion, and in the letters of the two preceding years. For instance, Coleridge argued in a letter to John Thelwall: 'A Necessitarian, I cannot possibly disesteem a man for his religious or anti-religious Opinions—and as an

Optimist, I feel diminished concern.' (*CL* I 205, and see 168, 158, and *Lects 1795 (CC)* lxii). Both 'The Eolian Harp' and 'This Lime-Tree Bower' could be interpreted as illustrating the anti-Godwin position that general benevolence is not hindered by but deeply rooted in private attachments. Coleridge had insisted in the 1795 lectures that benevolence has its spring and source in the immediate personal circle of family and friends. This is an assertion of the 'concreteness' of our moral feelings, in contrast to Godwin's abstract and impersonal conception of virtue. The following letter extract is an early manifestation of Coleridge's anti-Godwin stance, consistent with his later philosophy in its relation of the individual to the generic. Coleridge wrote to Southey in 1794 'Philanthropy (and indeed every other Virtue), is a thing of Concretion—some home-born feeling is the center of the Ball, that, rolling on through Life collects and assimilates every congenial Affection.' (*CL* I 86; and see *Lects 1795 (CC)* 162–3.)

Thus the domestic setting of both poems and the personal attachments of wife and friends lead, especially in 'This Lime-Tree Bower', to a universal fellowship with life as a source of imaginative inspiration. In 'The Ancient Mariner', the blessing of the water snakes as a specific and concrete act of love and imaginativeness may also be an example of the commitment to the immediacy of the origin of moral feelings. The significance of Charles, the 'Friend', in 'This Lime-Tree Bower', can be further indicated by the comment in a letter to Southey in 1794: 'The ardour of private Attachments makes Philanthropy a necessary *habit* of the Soul. I love my Friend—such as *he* is, all mankind are or might be!' (*CL* I 86, and compare *Lects 1795 (CC)* 163.) Coleridge wrote in 1795 that 'Domestic Happiness is the greatest of things sublunary . . .' (*CL* I 58), and the foundation of all other virtue. Even the setting of 'Frost at Midnight' and the final stanza's evocation of a general domestic tranquillity suggest a gentle celebration of the domestic. The importance of the opposition between city and nature in all of these poems, like the concept of the concreteness of moral feelings, also has a source in Hartleian Associationism.[7] For as personal attachments lead, it is thought, by association, to general feelings of benevolence, so surroundings, whether city or nature, have by association profound effects upon the mind and heart.

What seems inconsistent in the poetry with the determinism and mechanistic theory of a passive mind inherent in Hartley's Associationism, to which Coleridge was attached in the 1790s, is the general commitment to the creativity of mind and to an organic view of reality suggested in the poems by virtue of their structure and unifying techniques, as will be discussed in detail in the following chapters. The poems of this period can readily be interpreted according to the Platonic theory of mind which Coleridge had temporarily set aside in favour of a Lockean–Hartleian passive theory. It is likely that he did not in fact see the issue in these exact terms at the time, but only somewhat later realized precisely what the nature of the empiricist–Platonist dispute was for a theory of mind. At the time, he may have thought in terms of a dispute, for instance, between the inexplicability of events, that is, chance, and necessity. What he later came to adopt was a more sophisticated argument whereby necessity and freedom were synonymous by virtue of the will, and the will originating and creative through its instrument, reason. But these possibilities and refinements seemed at the time obscure and distant.

Yet they were not as distant as they might first appear to have been. For Coleridge was deep into Cudworth already in 1796, as is clear from the notebooks (see *CN* I 200, 201, 203, 204, 208, 244n, 246n, 247n). Cudworth, as an expounder of a sophisticated interpretation of Platonism, cannot be underestimated as an influence at that impressionable time. More than anyone else, Cudworth would have been able to sophisticate Coleridge's naive attitude toward Plato, of finding Plato's dialogues 'gorgeous Nonsense', and would have helped Coleridge to discover in them an esotericism which demanded and repaid rigorous study.[8] Coleridge himself was prepared to be quite explicit about the irreconcilable commitments he was making, though he must have rationalized somehow so that Hartley could fit into an otherwise inappropriate slot. He wrote to Poole in November 1796: 'I do not particularly admire Rousseau—Bishop Taylor, Old Baxter, David Hartley & the Bishop of Cloyne are *my men*' (*CL* I 245).

Meanwhile, he was reading and taking notes from Cudworth's *True Intellectual System of the Universe*; he was planning an essay on Berkeley, in which he intended to expose 'Sir Isaac Newton & other material theists . . .', and to discuss the relation of corporealism, theism, and atheism (*CN* I 203 and n); and he was reading Plato's *Republic* on truth and illusion (*CN* I 204 and n). The rejection of Newton ought to suggest that Hartley's position was already becoming shaky, if not untenable, for Newton and Hartley were closely associated in Coleridge's mind (see discussion below). Furthermore, if corporealism was at that time associated with atheism, as it usually was later for Coleridge, this should denote another shaking of Hartley's position in Coleridge's estimation. It had been two years since Coleridge brazenly asserted the following avowal of complete adherence to necessitarianism, and two years would have been enough to see the foundations of this commitment begin to crumble. He wrote to Southey in December of 1794: 'I am a Compleat Necessitarian—and understand the subject as well almost as Hartley himself—but I go farther than Hartley and believe the corporeality of thought—namely, that it is motion' (*CL* I 137).

Coleridge's subsequent rejection of necessity in a notebook entry of 1795–6 also seems incompatible with an espousal of Hartley or Newton. But his interest in Berkeley in this same entry may also cause some wonder in the context of associationism, as for example his intention to include in one of his famous 'Hymns' a 'Bold avowal of Berkeley's System!!!!!' (*CN* I 174 f 25, 1795–6). For Berkeley's Platonic connections could hardly have remained obscure to Coleridge for long, and it seems more likely that this esoteric aspect of Berkeley appealed to Coleridge, rather than the scepticism of the writings; it may only be a device of irony in any case (see *CL* II 703, 1801). Berkeley's position is a highly problematic one, and a slightly broader interpretation of him may suggest how deeply Coleridge must have been involved, already in 1795–6, in a confrontation with traditional empiricism, i.e., Locke, Newton, and Hartley, since he was such an avowed Berkeleian. For it seems that Berkeley was anticipating Kant's formalizing of the subjectivity of space when he put everything 'in the mind', hence his preoccupation with distance in *A New Theory of Vision*. When he brought in the supreme mind to preserve the world, he was interpreted as introducing a crass hypostasization, when what he was surely trying to suggest was that space (the condition of outness, of externality) was subjective not merely for the human *qua* individual, but as generic percipient being. The external world was subjective because it was only appearance. Kant, on the other hand, was able to extend this subjectivity to time as well. Thus the 'internal world' of thoughts and sensations was equally of the status appearance, and Kant too talked of 'Mind' as more than merely the particular individual instances of mind. That Berkeley's 'Supreme Mind or Being' was precisely this sort of generic transcendent concept seems fairly plausible. To take Berkeley as merely a solipsistic, subjective idealist is to misconstrue his most important insights as anticipations of Kant, and to miss his method of ironically parodying two apparently irreconcilable points of view, as in *The Three Dialogues*.[9]

Coleridge explicitly announces Berkeley's connections with Platonism only much later, and this uncertainty as to how he read Berkeley adds to the confusion of his thought during these years of 1796–1800. For Coleridge's claims to be an immaterialist (*CL* I 192) may indicate that he was actually reading Berkeley as a sceptic and a subjective idealist, without perceiving until later the more sophisticated idealism implicit if not avowed in Berkeley's writings. Note the fascinating description of Berkeley's idealism in a notebook entry of August–September 1809:

Reason at farthest justifies us only in affirming the existence of a Cause out of ourselves adequate to the effect in ourselves: by no means, in the assumption that the Cause is a duplicate of that Effect, any more than it would justify us in attributing Suns, Planets, Moons, attraction &c &c to the Creator, or Cause of the Material World. Berkley's Idealism may be thus illustrated: Our perceptions are impressions on our own minds standing to the external cause in the relation of the picture on the Canvass to the Painter, rather than in that of the Image in the Mirror to the Object reflected.

(CN III 3605 f 120^v)

Nor was Coleridge's understanding of Plato without its ambivalence, as his well-known comment indicates: 'I love Plato—his dear *gorgeous* Nonsense!' (*CL* I 295 to Thelwall, December 1796). He was more positive in the lectures of 1795 when he explained 'But though Plato dressed Truth in the garb of Nonsense, still it was Truth, and they who would take the Trouble of unveiling her, might discover and distinguish all the Features . . .' (*Lects 1795 (CC)* 209). In 1801, the year of clearing up a number of uncertainties, it seems, Coleridge wrote to Poole that 'Plato, and Aristotle were great & astonishing Geniuses' (*CL* II 675, and see above page 2). Comments in the *Biographia Literaria* give us reason to suppose that Plato (and Platonism) was crucial during this time around 1796, when inconsistency between philosophical and religious principles may have had some bearing upon a continuing interest in Hartley. Discussing *The Watchman*, Coleridge mentioned this conflict: 'For I was at that time and long after, though a Trinitarian (i.e. ad norman Platonis) in philosophy, yet a zealous Unitarian in Religion' (*BL* I ch. x 114). Somewhat later in the *Biographia* he repeated the inconsistency between his philosophical principles and his religious conceptions, saying:

> A more thorough revolution in my philosophic principles, and a deeper insight into my own heart, were yet wanting. Nevertheless, I cannot doubt, that the difference of my metaphysical notions from those of Unitarians in general contributed to my final re-conversion to the whole truth in Christ; even as according to his own confession the books of certain Platonic philosophers . . . commenced the rescue of St. Augustine's faith from the same error . . .
>
> (BL I ch. x 137)

It might be that these same books of Platonic philosophers also in 1796 commenced the rescue of Coleridge's philosophy from Hartley.[10]

The account in Chapter Ten of the *Biographia Literaria* of Coleridge's changing philosophical and religious views gives yet more reason to suppose that Hartley was beginning to be doubted because of readings in Platonism, and that Coleridge did not wait until 1800 and Kant to have serious misgivings. For he claimed that 'there had dawned upon me, even before I had met with the Critique of the Pure Reason, a certain guiding light (*BL* I ch. x 137). He then implied that the Bible made him distinctly conscious of the role of the will and of the necessary distinction between the reason and the understanding, and of the distinction between ideas, concepts, and images. This position is the cornerstone of the 'Constructive Philosophy', while the denial of the distinction as Coleridge drew it is the core of associationism. But Plato's Socrates must have given Coleridge the admittedly important clue that from the same premises opposite conclusions could be demonstrated. Speaking of the 'sciential' reason he elaborated: 'it then becomes an effective ally by exposing the false show of demonstration, or by evincing the equal demonstrability of the contrary from premises equally logical' (*BL* I ch. x 135). Such an account might be a formulation of Socrates's own method of disputation, and Kant naturally relied upon it for his later account of the 'antinomies of pure reason'. That this discussion in the *Biographia* centres upon the ground for faith in a 'holy and intelligent cause' should not mislead us from seeing the application to a shaking of Hartley's credibility for Coleridge.[11] For in this more sophisticated position, Coleridge found the alternative to either the chance of atheism that he abhorred, or the blind determinism and passivity of mind resulting from Hartley's system.

Thus Coleridge himself seems to have been gradually evolving a new standpoint based on the Biblical and the Platonic distinction between reason and understanding, and between idea and image. At the same time Coleridge was stripping away the inconsistent elements in Hartley to try to take him along the new way. He may actually have believed for a time that he could still salvage something of Hartley, if, for example, he cleansed him of the corpuscular hypotheses or his 'hypothetical vibrations'. Indeed, as late as June 1803 he proposed the following: 'I would prefix to it [Search's Light of Nature] an Essay containing the whole substance of the first Volume of Hartley, entirely defecated from all the corpuscular hypotheses' (*CL* II 949 to Godwin). In the *Biographia* he later explained that Priestley himself had tried to omit the 'material hypothesis', but that this was the main support for the whole system and the 'motive which led to [its] adoption' (*BL* I ch. vi 76). Priestley's refinement of Hartley was entitled *Hartley's Theory of the Human Mind on the Principle of the Association of Ideas: With Essays relating to the subject of it* (London: 1775). In what way Coleridge's subtilizing of Hartley was supposed to go beyond Priestley's adaptation is not clear. This hope to cleanse Hartley may have been what kept him alive in Coleridge's mind up to 1801, and during the great confusions and uncertainties of 1796–1800, when perhaps a failure to recognize that the material hypotheses were the very basis of associationism (and a confusion about the consequences of associationism for a theory of mind) made it possible to cling to Hartley even while

Coleridge was progressing toward an opposing and more sophisticated philosophy.

Another clue to Coleridge's reasons for maintaining Hartley's philosophy is found in a notebook entry of 1796: 'Doctrine of necessity rendered not dangerous by the Imagination which contemplates immediate, not remote effects—hence vice always hateful & altho equally monotonous as Virtue' (*CN* I 156). In the *Biographia* (I ch. vii 84–5) Coleridge gave another reason why Hartley was not early rejected. Coleridge pointed out of Hartley that:

[in] the proofs of the existence and attributes of God, with which his second volume commences, he makes no reference to the principle or results of the first. Nay, he assumes, as his foundations, ideas which if we embrace the doctrines of his first volume, can exist no where but in the vibrations of the ethereal medium common to the nerves and to the atmosphere. Indeed the whole of the second volume is, with the fewest possible exceptions, independent of his peculiar system . . . no errors can be morally arraigned unless they have proceeded from the heart.

Coleridge then could have long continued to speak of the 'excellent and pious Hartley' without also continuing to hold his Associationism true.

The post-Germany reading of Kant in 1800–1801 must have added the final catalyst to an already fermenting mind, forcing a complete rejection of the imprisoning 'Mechanical Philosophy'. Coleridge said some years later: '[I] am convinced that Kant in his Critique of the pure Reason, and more popularly in his Critique of the Practical Reason has completely overthrown the edifice of Fatalism, or causative Precedence as applied to Action' (*CL* III 35). It would be rash, however, to rule out the effects Kant may have had in bringing about this earlier, gradual conversion to what one might term a modern form of Platonism. For Coleridge's acquaintance with Kant's philosophy is extremely difficult to date. It is known that by 1801 he was steeped in the 'Critical Philosophy' so deeply that he had already begun to formulate his objections to it as well as his enthusiasms. He objected especially to the stoic morality, but admitted:

There does not exist an instance of a *deep* metaphysician who was not led by his speculations to an austere system of morals—. What can be more austere than the Ethics of Aristotle—than the systems of Zeno, St Paul, Spinoza (in the Ethical Books of his Ethics), Hartley, Kant, and Fichte.
   (*CL* II 768 to Southey, October 1801 ; see *ibid.*, 706–7 and note four.)

But it seems probable that Coleridge was familiar with basic and important elements of the 'aller neuste filosophie' as early as 1796–7. He assured Poole in a letter of May 1796: 'I am studying German, & in about six weeks shall be able to read that language with tolerable fluency.' He then mentioned a plan to go to Germany to study, amongst others, 'all the works of . . . Kant, the great german Metaphysician'. He planned, upon his return, to 'commence a School' to teach, among other things 'Man as an Intellectual Being: including the ancient Metaphysics, the systems of Locke & Hartley—of the Scotch Philosophers—& the new Kantian S(ystem)' (*CL* I 209). In December of that year Coleridge. referred teasingly to 'the most unintelligible Emanuel Kant' (*CL* I 283–4, December 1796, a possibly tongue-in-cheek remark to irritate Thelwall?). In this letter Coleridge translated a German hexameter from Voss's *Luise* with reasonable accuracy; he also mentioned Mendelssohn, and then Kant, suggesting no small knowledge of German already.

Moreover, brief references to Kant occur in the notebooks by 1799, but, as it has been pointed out in the notes to the notebooks, Thomas Beddoes would have been an invaluable source of knowledge about Kant as early as 1795 (see *CN* I 249 n). John Thelwall, one of Coleridge's most frequent correspondents in 1796, belonged to F. A. Nitsch's Kantian Society in London, another major source of information on Kant perhaps. Indeed, the more we suspect Coleridge of knowing about Kant during this murky period, the more inconsistent his Associationism becomes.[12]

Coleridge's early disenchantment with Priestley also makes his extended adherence to Hartley surprising, or at least suggests that it must have been riddled with doubts roused by readings in Plato, Boehme, Berkeley, Kant, etc. He drew heavily on Priestley for the lectures on politics and religion in 1795, much of his enthusiasm probably stemming from Priestley's effectiveness as an antidote to Godwinism. But shortly after these lectures, in 1796, Coleridge had already begun repudiating parts of Priestley's doctrines in strong terms, as in the following criticism to the Rev. John Edwards:

How is it that Dr Priestley is not an atheist?—He asserts in three different Places, that God not only *does*, but *is*, every thing.—But if God *be* every Thing, every Thing is God—: which is all, the Atheists assert—. An eating, drinking, lustful *God*—with no *unity* of *Consciousness*—these appear to me the unavoidable Inferences from his philosophy—

(*CL* I 92)

By April 1799 Coleridge was branding Priestley's entire system Materialism, and saying, 'I confess that the more I think, the more I am discontented with the doctrines of Priestly' (*CL* I 482). Coleridge objected to the notion that God works by 'general laws', and he soon came to suspect that Priestley's method of defending Christianity by proofs, arguments, and evidences was altogether wrong-headed, as he later indicated in the *Biographia Literaria* (see *Lects 1795 (CC)* I xvi, and *BL* I ch. v 134–5).

It is noteworthy that Coleridge's two major criticisms of Priestley occur in relation to personal experiences of suffering, the first being the occasion of Sara's pregnancy. Coleridge's comments here precede those quoted above from the same letter of March 1796 to the Rev. John Edwards:

> Yesterday Mrs Coleridge miscarried—but without danger and with little pain. From the first fortnight of Pregnancy she has been so very ill with the Fever, that she could afford no nourishment to the Thing which might have been a Newton or an Hartley—it had wasted and melted away.—I think the subject of Pregnancy the most obscure of all God's dispensations—it seems coercive against Immaterialism—it starts uneasy doubts respecting Immortality, & the pangs which the Woman suffers, seem inexplicable in the system of optimism.

The 1799 criticism of Priestley partially quoted above is also occasioned by personal sorrow, namely the infant Berkeley's death. These personal experiences seem to illustrate Coleridge's rejection of the notion that God works by 'general laws', a position close to his avowal that personal attachments foster general benevolence (see discussion above). The linking of Hartley and Newton in the March 1796 letter to John Edwards is significant, for Coleridge's rejection of Newton's system, making the mind passive and a 'lazy Looker-on on an external world', is at the core of his ultimate liberation from the passivity and determinism of associationism (see *CL* II 709). This apparent praise of Newton and Hartley in March 1796 is in sharp contrast to the criticism of Newton in a November 1796 notebook entry.

These occasions of personal experiences forcing Coleridge to a re-examination of his philosophical principles suggest how thoroughly he sought to live according to his thought. His philosophy had to be grounded in his feeling; it could not contradict fundamental human feelings and experiences, otherwise he felt that philosophy must be false, or at least an inadequate account. Thus the unity of thought and feeling became the cornerstone of his own philosophical commitment.[13] Yet during these years he several times let slip his dissatisfaction with his adopted metaphysics, and complained of how little comfort it afforded in times of need: his metaphysical theories were, he complained, like toys beside the bed of a child deadly sick.[14]

The dissociation of thought and feeling must have been great during these years. Coleridge described his ideal as early as 1794:

> To perceive . . . and to assent . . . as an abstract proposition—is easy—but it requires the most wakeful attentions of the most reflective minds in all

moments to bring it into practice—it is not enough, that we have once swallowed it—The *Heart* should have *fed* upon the *truth*, as Insects on a Leaf—till it be tinged with the colour, and shew it's food in every the minutest fibre.

(*CL* I 115 to Southey, October 1794)

The personal experiences of his own creative mind, particularly during the extraordinarily productive period of 1797–8, could not have gone unnoticed by Coleridge in their application to a theory of mind. His experiences as a poet were hardly explicable on the associationist, necessitarian principles, as he must have begun to suspect early. He could by no means be described as a 'lazy Looker-on on an external world' when as a poet he wrote about his interaction with nature, as in, for example, 'This Lime-Tree Bower', or 'The Nightingale'. His mocking tone in the *Biographia* many years later explains the absurdity; when criticizing Hartley's account of the mind, Coleridge said: 'the will, and, with the will, all acts of thought and attention are parts and products of this blind mechanism, instead of being distinct powers, whose function it is to controul, determine, and modify the phantasmal chaos of association' (*BL* I ch. vii 81). He then criticized the mechanism of the breeze–harp image, with consciousness supposed to be the result, as a tune, applied to his own situation as a writer Hartley's views, and concluded:

Yet according to this hypothesis the disquisition, to which I am at present soliciting the reader's attention, may be as truly said to be written by Saint Paul's church, as by *me*: for it is the mere motion of my muscles and nerves; and these again are set in motion from external causes equally passive, which external causes stand themselves in interdependent connection with every thing that exists or has existed. Thus the whole universe co-operates to produce the minutest stroke of every letter, save only that I myself, and I alone, have nothing to do with it, but merely the causeless and *effectless* beholding of it when it is done.

(*BL* I ch. vi 82)

The absurdity of such a position and of such a man as Coleridge ever having adhered to it for long is well expressed by a comment of his own in 1794, during his hey-day of necessitarianism. In explanation of his Hartleianism he wrote to Southey the following lines, and it is difficult to be sure if the jesting tone does not also expose an uneasiness. That is, Coleridge seems at one and the same time to be defending and exposing his own absurd position:

Boyer thrashed Favell most cruelly the day before yesterday—I sent him the following Note of consolation.

I condole with you on the unpleasant motions, to which a certain Uncouth Automaton has been mechanized; and am anxious to know the motives, that impinged on it's optic or auditory nerves, so as to be communicated in such rude vibrations through the medullary substance of It's Brain . . .

(*CL* I 137, December 1794)

This is more like the joke of a schoolboy carrying to extremes the logical consequences of a position in order to show its untenableness. If Coleridge could have held such a position at all seriously, it is doubtful that it would have satisfied for long: it seems to have degenerated into 'toys' and 'playthings' before he was able to find the proofs he needed to show its weaknesses, and, more importantly, to find an alternative which was not still worse.

The final step in 1801 of completely rejecting Hartley is made verbal and public in a letter to Thomas Poole in mid-March: 'If I do not greatly delude myself, I have not only completely extricated the notions of Time, and Space; but have overthrown the doctrine of Association, as taught by Hartley, and with it all the irreligious metaphysics of modern Infidels—especially the doctrine of Necessity', (*CL* II 706, March 1801). The bragging tone may be a misreading. Coleridge may mean he has completely extricated *for himself* the notions of time and space. That is, he has resolved his own previous confusions. He is not claiming to have made 'discoveries in metaphysics', as is sometimes supposed.

This clarity is preceded by the February 1801 letters written to Josiah Wedgwood on the indebtedness of Locke to Descartes, Locke's errors, and the Berkeleianism of the Cartesian philosophy. All of the elements for a rejection of Hartley are contained in these letters. Hartley had always been closely associated with Locke and Newton, but both men are in these letters thoroughly criticized.[15] The long account of the correct meaning of 'idea' and its misuse through an identification with 'image' bases itself on a thorough-going Platonism, on the philosophy, that is, which makes ideas the 'original Faculties & tendencies of the mind, the internal Organs, as it were, and *Laws* of human Thinking' (*CL* II 682). The continuation of this passage throws some light on the way in which Platonism has been literalized by its followers, the result being to garb it in unrecognizable trappings; speaking of ideas, Coleridge comments:

the word should be translated 'Moulds' and not 'Forms'. (Cicero assures us, that Aristotle's Metaphysical Opinions differ from Plato's only as a Thing said in plain prose, i.e. worn out metaphors, differs from the same thing said in new & striking Metaphors—Aristotle affirms to the same purpose . . . —in respect of *Faculty* the Thought [Mind] *is* the Thoughts, but *actually* it is nothing previous to Thinking.) By the usual Process of language Ideas came to signify not only these original *moulds* of the mind, but likewise all that was cast in these moulds, as in our language the Seal & the Impression it leaves are both called Seals. Latterly, it wholly lost it's original meaning, and became synonimous with *Images* simply (whether Impressions or Ideas) and sometimes with Images in the memory . . .

(*CL* II 696)

Coleridge even went so far as already to propose the notion of 'constituent ideas' (*CL* II 696), and in these two ways he spoke out for the position that the mind, in its acts, *moulds* experience, and deduces knowledge not only from experience, as Locke maintained, but gains knowledge from those very acts: that is, it thinks about thinking. Or, as Coleridge quoted Leibnitz, there is nothing in the mind which was not first in the senses—except the mind itself (*AR* aphorism CVI, part eleven. See also *P Lects* 383–6).

The stimulus for these letters may have been partially the lectures of Mackintosh attended by Coleridge, on Locke, Condillac, ideas, etc. Coleridge took notes on these lectures of January 1800, some of which look almost like a brief for the main argument of the Wedgwood letters of a year later (see *CN* I 634, January 1800 and n). Several parts of these notes suggest that Coleridge was well on his way to adopting the position taken in the Wedgwood letters. For instance his comment that 'M's Explication of Likeness as only a species of Contemporaneity to me vague & Unmeaning' is a portentous statement. For it subtly suggests the distrust of the idea that time is the *law* of association, and not just the *condition*. Or as Coleridge explained:

These [paralogisms], it appears to me, may be all reduced to one sophism as their common genus; the mistaking the *conditions* of a thing for its causes and essence; and the process, by which we arrive at knowledge of a faculty, for the faculty itself. The air I breathe is the condition of my life, not its cause . . . Let us cross-examine Hartley's scheme under the guidance of this distinction; and we shall discover, that contemporaneity . . . is the limit and condition of the laws of mind, itself being rather a law of matter, at least of phaenomena considered as material.

(*BL* I ch. vii 85)

He then discussed likeness, contrast, and the role of the will. His other two criticisms of Mackintosh in the same notebook entry revolve around the problem of 'Ideas', the focal point of Coleridge's awakening. He wrote: 'M. asserts the old Tale of no abstract Ideas. Makes Idea (of course) mean Image'. Here Coleridge was hinting at the full development to be given to the 'Idea' issue in the letters to Wedgwood. A few months later he added to these hints (suggesting a questioning of Hartley) the comment about observing his children and not being 'able to derive the least confirmation of Hartley's or Darwin's Theory' (*CL* I 368).

Coleridge's realization in 1801 that 'any system built on the passiveness of mind must be false, as a system',[16] suggests the centrality of the dispute of mind as active or passive in his conversion from the 'Mechanic' to the 'Constructive Philosophy'. Furthermore, the issues discussed above indicate the possibility that by 1796, Coleridge was already beginning to be uneasy about the 'Mechanic Philosophy' with its necessitarianism and passive mind theories, owing to influences from Plato, Berkeley, Cudworth, personal sufferings, and experiences of creativity in poetry. Basil Willey may not have been altogether mistaken about Coleridge in concluding that 'the enthusiasms [for Hartley] of this period were largely froth upon his mind's surface'.[17] For although Coleridge's enthusiasm was at the time intense and committed, Hartley, Priestley, Locke, Newton, Condillac, etc. had no lasting effect upon him in a definitely constructive sense, however much they may have served as something to react against. Shawcross, writing in the introduction to the *Biographia*, may be correct in saying that the conviction of serious errors in Hartley 'had been long maturing in his [Coleridge's] mind', since 1796 perhaps.[18] But Shawcross's assumption that the conviction owed nothing to Kant is less plausible, for contrary to general belief, it seems that Kant was early influencing Coleridge through various channels mentioned above, and possibly even by 1795. It would be unwise therefore to conclude that Kant had no effect until serious study was commenced in 1800, after the return from Germany in the summer of 1799. For as has been pointed out above, Coleridge was excited enough about Kant to include the study of Kant in his reasons for going to Germany at all, and enough aware of Kant's influence to call him the 'great german Metaphysician'. It is unlikely that during the intellectually volatile period of 1795–1800, he would have underestimated the extraordinary things he must have been hearing about Kant from Beddoes, Nitsch, Thelwall, and from reviews and synopses or partial translations of Kant's works.

The philosophy of the 'Mechanists' may be said to have been 'froth' on Coleridge's mind, not in so far as it provided material for reflection and even matter for enthusiasm, but only because it was never assimilated at a deeper level. That is, Coleridge's feelings and intuition, his heart, were never touched by it. It neither expressed his temperament nor altered his intuition. His struggle from 1796 to 1800 involved the process first of appreciating fully the consequences of associationism for a theory of mind, and then of discovering why Hartleianism never satisfied and was never coincident with the feelings. The poetry of the period reflects this surface/depth anomaly. For while on the surface it illustrates the use of explicit materials from, for example, Priestley and Hartley, the organizing principles of the poems—their structure, design, and metaphorical levels—seem to be expressive of an idealism and a theory of mind as creative which Coleridge perhaps could not yet fully understand or prove discursively, but to which his feelings and intellect were always partially, and, gradually, wholly committed. Thus the poetry of this period is not only largely free of the constraining effects of the 'Mechanic Philosophy'; it is also a celebration of the dynamism of the 'Constructive Philosophy' soon to be articulated.

1

'Kubla Khan' and the Art of Thingifying

The Text

Kubla Khan:

Or, A Vision In a Dream. A Fragment.

The following fragment is here published at the request of a poet of great and deserved celebrity [Lord Byron], and, as the Author's own opinions are concerned, rather as a psychological curiosity, than on the ground of any supposed *poetic* merits.

In the summer of the year 1797, the Author, then in ill health, had retired to a lonely farm-house between Porlock and Linton, on the Exmoor confines of Somerset and Devonshire. In consequence of a slight indisposition, an anodyne had been prescribed, from the effects of which he fell asleep in his chair at the moment that he was reading the following sentence, or words of the same substance, in 'Purchas's Pilgrimage': 'Here the Khan Kubla commanded a palace to be built, and a stately garden thereunto. And thus ten miles of fertile ground were inclosed with a wall.' The Author continued for about three hours in a profound sleep, at least of the external senses, during which time he had the most vivid confidence, that he could not have composed less than from two to three hundred lines; if that indeed can be called composition in which all the images rose up before him as *things* with a parallel production of the correspondent expressions, without any sensation or consciousness of effort. On awakening he appeared to himself to have a distinct recollection of the whole, and taking his pen, ink, and paper, instantly and eagerly wrote down the lines that are here preserved. At this moment he was unfortunately called out by a person on business from Porlock, and detained by him above an hour, and on his return to his room, found, to his no small

surprise and mortification, that though he still retained some vague
and dim recollection of the general purport of the vision, yet with the
exception of some eight or ten scattered lines and images, all the rest
had passed away like the images on the surface of a stream into which
a stone has been cast, but, alas! without the after restoration of the
latter!

> Then all the charm
> Is broken—all that phantom-world so fair
> Vanishes, and a thousand circlets spread,
> And each mis-shape['s] the other. Stay awhile,
> Poor youth! who scarcely dar'st lift up thine eyes—
> The stream will soon renew its smoothness, soon
> The visions will return! And lo, he stays,
> And soon the fragments dim of lonely forms
> Come trembling back, unite, and now once more
> The pool becomes a mirror.
> [From 'The Picture; or, the Lover's Resolution', lines 91–100]

Yet from the still surviving recollections in his mind, the Author has
frequently purposed to finish for himself what had been originally, as
it were, given to him. Σαμερον αδιον ασω [Αὔριον ἄδιον ασω] 1834]:*
but the to-morrow is yet to come.

As a contrast to this vision, I have annexed a fragment of a very
different character, describing with equal fidelity the dream of pain
and disease.

KUBLA KHAN

> In Xanadu did Kubla Khan
> A stately pleasure-dome decree:
> Where Alph, the sacred river, ran
> Through caverns measureless to man
>   Down to a sunless sea.   5
> So twice five miles of fertile ground
> With walls and towers were girdled round:
> And there were gardens bright with sinuous rills,
> Where blossomed many an incense-bearing tree;
> And here were forests ancient as the hills,   10
> Enfolding sunny spots of greenery.

*Today I will sing a song [to-morrow I will sing a song 1834].

But oh! that deep romantic chasm which slanted
Down the green hill athwart a cedarn cover!
A savage place! as holy and enchanted
As e'er beneath a waning moon was haunted 15
By woman wailing for her demon-lover!
And from this chasm, with ceaseless turmoil seething,
As if this earth in fast thick pants were breathing,
A mighty fountain momently was forced:
Amid whose swift half-intermitted burst 20
Huge fragments vaulted like rebounding hail,
Or chaffy grain beneath the thresher's flail:
And 'mid these dancing rocks at once and ever
It flung up momently the sacred river.
Five miles meandering with a mazy motion 25
Through wood and dale the sacred river ran,
Then reached the caverns measureless to man,
And sank in tumult to a lifeless ocean:
And 'mid this tumult Kubla heard from far
Ancestral voices prophesying war! 30

   The shadow of the dome of pleasure
   Floated midway on the waves;
   Where was heard the mingled measure
   From the fountain and the caves.
It was a miracle of rare device, 35
A sunny pleasure-dome with caves of ice!

   A damsel with a dulcimer
   In a vision once I saw:
   It was an Abyssinian maid,
   And on her dulcimer she played, 40
   Singing of Mount Abora.
   Could I revive within me
   Her symphony and song,
   To such a deep delight 'twould win me,
That with music loud and long, 45
I would build that dome in air,
That sunny dome! those caves of ice!
And all who heard should see them there,
And all should cry, Beware! Beware!
His flashing eyes, his floating hair! 50
Weave a circle round him thrice,
And close your eyes with holy dread,
For he on honey-dew hath fed,
And drunk the milk of Paradise.[1]

The Preface to 'Kubla Khan'

An analysis of 'Kubla Khan' is complicated by its extraordinary preface,[2] and also by the way the verse seems to fall into two sections, or two separate visions, the 'body' of the poem (lines 1–36), and the last eighteen lines. For the sake of brevity one might refer to these final lines as the 'epilogue'.

The preface to 'Kubla Khan' acts to highlight specific formal aspects of the poem as opposed to the substantial content—the landscape descriptions and the Khan's activities—aspects such as the origins of the poem in subjective visionary experience, the nature of the composition processes, and the ultimate failure to complete the composition due to certain circumstances. The preface distances the reader from the specific imagery and content of the poem by explicitly focusing his attention upon the poem as an instance of poetic creation, while raising a host of subsidiary issues for the reader to grapple with: the relation of art to dream and extraordinary states of consciousness generally, sources of art in the unconscious, the relation of images seen with the inward eye and the correspondent expressions, the relation of the resulting poem to the original vision, and the role of memory in imaginative activity. In addition, there are more formal aspects of the *preface* to which the reader may attend, a shift analogous to the shift that the preface encourages with regard to the poem, away from factual details and concern for their accuracy, toward structural properties, narrative voices, and the relation of the preface to the verse.[3]

The preface, like the verse, seems to fall into two sections,[4] the first short paragraph (often left out in modern editions, and deleted from that of 1834), and the main body of the prose account. The first sentence reads somewhat like an advertisement to the poem, and makes two statements crucially affecting the reading of the poem: for it would never occur to a reader to approach the poem as a 'psychological curiosity', instead of for its poetic merit, unless he had been so instructed (see moreover the prefatory remarks to 'The Three Graves': 'Its merits, if any, are exclusively psychological'). Nor does it seem likely that a reader would have thought 'Kubla Khan' any more a fragment than any other poem, if he had not been told that it represented only a portion of a vision which inspired it.[5] The preface suffers from a somewhat similar over-determination: one assumes that it is separate from the verse in an absolute way, and not integrally related to the poem as a work of art; and one assumes the author to be Coleridge reporting directly his own views about the poem.

Two points militate against these assumptions; the preface is composed in the third person narrative, so that the writer of the verse and the author of the preface seem to be distanced aesthetically; a persona is created for the preface writer, an alternative authority responsible for the views presented, and this indirect discourse immediately alerts the reader to the possibility of irony. Such a gesture is not unknown to Coleridge readers: in his two other most important works, 'The Ancient Mariner' and the *Biographia Literaria,* he invents in the former a persona who glosses the poem, and in Chapter Thirteen of the *Biographia* he incorporates a letter 'from a friend' at a critical moment, also to explain a fragment, namely Chapter Thirteen. The friend is of course Coleridge himself, and the effect is an ironic detachment toward the content of the fragment in order to emphasize another level of content and another attitude. The existence of the preface persona in 'Kubla Khan' is further suggested by the sudden shift from third to first person in the last paragraph of the preface, and the statement of this persona suggests that he is meant to be taken as an editor: 'As a contrast to this vision, I have annexed a fragment of a very different character describing with equal fidelity the dream of pain and disease.' He refers to 'Pains of Sleep'. This last sentence is also frequently left out of the best modern editions, as for example I. A. Richards's edition for Viking Press, or John Beer's Everyman edition. One loses the shift from the third to the first person, and by this omission is lost the equally important comment about the 'Pains of Sleep'—namely that it too is called a fragment, and that it too is supposed to describe a dream. This puts a very different meaning on the use of the words 'fragment' and 'dream' in the early sentences of the preface, when the terms are used so broadly. For in what sense can one understand 'Pains of Sleep' as a fragment or as a dream poem?

Not only is a persona created in the preface by the third person narrative; the referent of this 'Author' is also not altogether clear. For instance, in the advertisement section of the preface, the persona uses the phrase, 'as far as the Author's own opinions are concerned.' But it is uncertain who 'the Author' refers to in this first occurrence of the phrase. The tendency to assimilate this referent to the referent of future occurrences of the phrase 'the Author' is admittedly strong, but not compelling. In the first instance it may mean 'that Author', referring to Lord Byron,[6] the 'poet of great and deserved celebrity'; it may mean the author of the advertisement, 'this Author'; or it may mean the author–poet of the verse lines. If we take seriously the idea that personas are important distinctions, whose perspectives are not to be confused with that of the 'omniscient', physical man to whose identity we ascribe poetic productions, such discriminations are not unimportant. Taking Coleridge to be this omniscient author we must nevertheless grapple with the problems he creates for the reader in creating his third person persona. That is, is his account to be taken seriously, or literally, and does *he* really believe that 'Kubla Khan' is a fragment, and important not primarily as a poetic production, but rather as a 'psychological curiosity'? Or does the ambiguity of 'the Author' not throw into question the authority of these 'opinions?'[7]

The creation of a persona (or perhaps more than one) in the preface lends the prose a literary–fictional quality which is not out of keeping with its general style; its Gothic evocation of summers, ill-health, lonely farmhouses on Exmoor confines, anodynes, travelogues, sleep and dreams, visions, and finally the extraordinary imagery of the last several lines before the lines from 'A Picture'. In comparison with the poem, the language is distinctly prose, and not as rich in imagery or as intensely compressed; but the wholly unnecessary detail of the description almost makes up for the imagery absent.

Such details are meant as, for example, 'lonely' farmhouse, the sleep of 'three hours', the '2–300 lines', 'pen, ink, and paper', the person 'on business from Porlock', being detained 'above an hour', the 'eight or ten scattered lines', and so forth. The informative detail is indeed more appropriate to the prose than a corresponding intensity of imagery might have been. A glance at the note attached to a manuscript copy of the poem raises questions as to the factual and fictional content of the longer account:

> This fragment with a good deal more, not recoverable, composed, in a sort of Reverie brought on by two grains of Opium taken to check a dysentery, at a Farm House between Porlock & Linton, a quarter of a mile from Culbone Church, in the fall of the year, 1797.[8]

With reference to the preface, the note adds some detail but leaves out much more than it contributes. The information in the preface conflicts with this cursory account in several respects, the most important perhaps being that the note reports merely a reverie of sorts, in which the poem actually was *composed*—there is no qualification on the idea of 'composition', 'images rising up in a dream with all the correspondent lines and no consciousness of effort'. Contrasting this relatively factual, literal, and dry account of the circumstances surrounding the birth of the poem with the actual published preface, one illustrates what the latter is not: it is not a literal, dry, factual account of this sort, but a highly literary piece of composition itself, providing the verse with a certain mystique. The preface itself is problematic in view of the extensive expansion from the note: to what extent are the additions to the preface mere interpolations and fanciful elaborations?

Although this question is probably unanswerable, it may not even be the important one to ask. Perhaps it is more pertinent to ponder why Coleridge chose to write a preface, and why he chose to include the details, facts or fancy, so minutely described.[9] For example, there may be some more profound significance to the statement that the poet fell asleep while reading the quoted lines from *Purchas his Pilgrimage* (lines closely related in factual content to the first lines of the poem), than merely that it was the occasion of the dream. Coleridge may be ironizing by playing on the tradition that the Khan fell asleep and dreamt the plan of the palace to be built.[10] Some connection between explicit sources and original transformation of those sources from other authors into new creations might be implied. Perhaps the chasm between such sources and the original use of them emphasizes the mystery surrounding the passage from ordinary consciousness into creative states.

Thus Coleridge himself would be giving the first hint that a tracing of the sources of his imagery would prove to be a fascinating way of becoming aware of the richness of the poem's meanings, as Lowes initially showed. But the problematic relation between the external world as stimulant, and inspiration, is being broached, as it is broached also in 'This Lime-Tree Bower'. Indeed the quotation in the preface of the lines from the travelogue relates to the first section of the poem as the manuscript note quoted above relates to the expanded preface. That is, the preface is a literary and poetic expansion of the manuscript note, dry and factual as it is, just as the quote from *Purchas his Pilgrimage* is expanded into the body of the poem. Did Coleridge then change 'a sort of Reverie' to 'a profound sleep, at least of the external senses', in order to emphasize and draw attention to the difference between *waking* consciousness and states of poetic vision, since the latter are more closely associated with the subconscious than mere reverie?[11] The connection between dream-consciousness and poetic vision is of course an ancient allegory which recurs in medieval dream poetry, and which Shakespeare and then all the Romantics take up. Of the Romantics, Keats most persistently relates sleep or dream and poetry.

Coleridge might also have qualified the notion of composition in order to suggest the problematic nature of composition and its mysterious connections with the will and memory, and with the original vision of images seen with the inward eye, but translated into linguistic expressions. The addition to the account of the 'person on business from Porlock'[12] may be a fictional personification of the inhibiting factors interrupting the recovery of the whole: the likening of this person to a stone in the last sentence before the excerpt from 'A Picture' may well cause a smile. The phrase 'Person from Porlock' could certainly be a designed alliteration of 'Purchas's Pilgrimage', the one marking the beginning, the other the end of the poem. The word 'business' also had for Coleridge a very special connotation at the time (see *CL* I 340–1); the 'business' has to do with the spying to which Wordsworth and Coleridge were subjected by the 'Aristocrats' (see also *BL* ch. x). This took place at the time Coleridge says he composed 'Kubla Khan', and at a time when he was trying to decide whether it would be wise to encourage John Thelwall to come to settle near him and Poole and Wordsworth. But the idea of spying might be applied to the faculty of reason as a censor of the imaginative faculty; thus the person on business personifies the spying, censorious reason interruptive of the imagination, the faculty uppermost in the minds of the 'Aristocrats' (see below Chapter Three on 'The Eolian Harp', for a similar personification of the censorious, repressive mind).

The Preface and the 'Epilogue'

Apart from the creation of personas and the addition of details which romanticize the account and lend to it symbolic associations which turn the preface into a literary prose, instead of a factual, direct communication, (a prose riddled with possible ironies and explicit metaphors), the second major factor suggesting that the preface is to be intimately associated with the poem in an aesthetic sense is its connection with the 'epilogue', that is, lines 37–54. In function, the preface and the epilogue exhibit strong similarities: both mention a prior experience in which some aesthetic activity is being described (the damsel sings and makes music, the poet dreams and makes a poem), and both make explicit reference to the loss of vision and the intense longing to revive it, and to build from it a 'dome in air' in one case, and the poem's remaining sections in the other. In both the preface and the epilogue the presence of a narrator is much more evident, as distinguished from the omniscient, unobserved narrator of lines 1–36.[13] The juxtaposition of seen images and heard sounds in the epilogue is very like the images and 'correspondent expressions' mentioned in the preface: in neither case is this problematic relationship explained. It seems correct to say that both preface and epilogue are distinct from the body of the poem in that both seem to refer to it; both are meditations upon visionary activity itself, whereas the body of the poem does not directly communicate these issues. It has a distinct and explicitly literary content. Neither the preface nor the epilogue contributes to the landscape description of the three sections of the verse which constitutes the body of the poem.

Some subsidiary complications arise from this comparison of the preface with the epilogue, and from the aesthetic distance of the epilogue to the body of the poem. When in the preface it is stated that 'the Author . . . wrote down the lines that are here preserved', as a consequence of a profound sleep, one may wonder whether the phrase 'these lines . . . here preserved' refers to all fifty-four lines of verse, or only to the first thirty-six, thus excluding the epilogue from the vision. In fact, it is only the first thirty-six lines which relate to the quotation from 'Purchas's Pilgrimage' in the preface.[14] There is no mention of an Abyssinian maid, a dulcimer or song, or a visionary and a group of frightened beholders.[15] But the mention of the dome and caves of ice in the epilogue suggests that the epilogue is not simply a second, separate vision, but that the music and song of the maid are connected in some mysterious way with the sunny dome of pleasure and the caves of ice. The intrusion of the narrative 'I' in the epilogue contributes to the disassociation of the content of the epilogue from the vision of lines 1–36 described by an omniscient narrator, and makes it almost impossible to include the last eighteen lines in that particular vision. On the contrary, the 'I' seems to take up where the preface left off, and to reiterate the concerns expressed there.[16] That is, the 'I' of the epilogue seems also to be the poet of the preface, but in a visionary state. In this reiteration, the vision mentioned in the preface seems to be mentioned again, but instead of describing the content of the vision, the vision is given a previously unacknowledged framework, a damsel with a dulcimer, who sings of Mount Abora, but also of Kubla Khan and the River Alph.[17] The visionary then repeats the desire reported by the preface persona for the poet to revive the vision, explaining that a revival of the maiden's song would make it possible for him to build 'that dome in air'. The connection of the song and the dome suggests that the song is the condition and inspiration for the dome, and 'dome in air' may be a way of symbolizing a poem, as 'articulated breath', or organized sound, as music itself is.[18] The omniscient narrator of the Khan's activities is not, then, the 'I' of the epilogue, or the 'Author' of the preface, but the damsel with the dulcimer, a design creating a dream-vision (about the Khan) within a dream-vision (about the damsel) within a dream-vision (about the 'I' of the epilogue). That is, the narrator is symbolically the imagination itself, or the ideal poet, the ideal creator, omniscient, mysterious, and unknown.

The absolute distinction between narrators is impossible to maintain, however. The visionary 'I' attributes a separateness to the character of the damsel by twice referring to the music as *her* song. He also intensifies her independence by inverting the word order of the sentence in lines 37–40, so that her existence is postulated as more objective than it would be if ordinary word order were preserved. By placing the object, the damsel, first, he foregrounds it and emphasizes her reality, de-emphasizing her visionary subjectivity and distancing her from himself. He 'externalizes' her to some extent. However, because she occurs admittedly in a vision, not only has she no independent existence apart from the persona of the 'I' in any absolute sense, but her song is equally his song: she is a mere intermediary between the visionary 'I' and the music. As an intermediate being, she is probably best understood as herself a personification of imagination, that 'intermediate faculty', as Coleridge elsewhere identifies it.[19] By creating such a separate, but not absolutely distinct persona, the poet manages to give poetic expression to the character of the faculty of imagination in its peculiar independence from his conscious control: his imagination is his and yet not his, as the song is his and not his. His control is tenuous at best, if not wholly illusory, and because of this lack of control, the faculty seems to have a will of its own, hence a personality or identity distinct from the poet.

It is precisely this independence and intermediary quality of imagination which Coleridge expresses in the preface. In the epilogue he has given the faculty a character of its own, but in the preface he does not dramatize in this way in order to express the nature of imagination. Instead he creates a dream allegory: he uses states instead of characters, and contrasts the waking state and the dreaming state. It might be correct to say however that although the dominant mode in the preface is the dream myth, characterization also takes place. The faculty interrupting or inhibiting imagination is characterized as the 'person on business from Porlock', a vivid and ironic counterpart to the Abyssinian maid as imagination in the epilogue. To liken the 'person . . . from Porlock' to a stone is to recall Blake's portrayal of 'Urizen' (Your Reason?) as a stony, inflexible authoritarian figure. In addition to this persona, the preface-writer persona is created as a characterization of, perhaps, a 'business-minded' or a censorious, literal-minded reader (see below, pages 28–9). In the dream state, the self has no conscious control over what it experiences; its creations, that is, its visions, seem 'as it were, given'. Things produced at the subconscious level almost always seem given, because the conscious ego is unconscious of any active role in their construction. Hence external nature, dreams, inspiration, etc., all seem to be independent of the self as known.[20]

Some independent reservoir or source for these images 'which . . . rose up . . . as *things*' is implied, analogous to the damsel in function, but not personified: a myth of mental topography is used instead. The waking self, when it does finally regain some control over the psyche, acts merely as an amanuensis to this other state of being. There is only an implied character in the idea of a being dictating to the waking self, and in fact this 'dictator' may best be *contrasted* with the imaginative, dreaming self or state, as memory. It may be in order to express this quality of imagination as beyond conscious control and the dictates of will and memory, and as having sources in the unconscious as suggested by the dream allegory, that Coleridge decided to alter the description of the state from 'a sort of Reverie' to 'a profound sleep, at least of the external senses', and to qualify the notion of composition as he did in the preface but did not in the manuscript note.

Both the dream allegory and the persona of the damsel act to split the self of the visionary or poet into an imaginative, inspired self, and a self that merely recollects the former self. Indeed a further, more removed stage is indicated, where the poet is neither visionary, nor textmaker (where the memory and imagination seem to act together) but merely a reader, a passive self in comparison to the other two stages. The third person narrative of the preface expresses precisely this latter distinction: the persona who wrote down 'the lines preserved' is not only distinct from the visionary self beyond the conscious control, in the persona of the Abyssinian maid; he is also distinct from the merely recuperative self who writes the preface. The aesthetic distance between the two would seem chasmic to the 'fallen' poet, and he would seek to represent the distance by the distancing devices of personas and allegories of states. Thus the poem is not only about inspired experience, but also about the fall back into ordinary experience, and the relation between the two.

A further correspondence between the preface and epilogue creates another perspective in the poem for the reader. The complexity of the poem has already been said to include a level representing the poet's consciousness of his process of creation. The level at which the poet is twice removed from vision is the level of the poet as reader of his own creations, his texts, themselves products of vision.[21] The suggestion in preface and epilogue is that the poet cannot remain contented with this relatively passive state, and seeks to become a maker again, or even a visionary. The present is always only a portion or a fragment of experience as long as it is uninspired by imagination. Without the imagination to perceive connections the mind sees not totality, but parts. Hence in 'unawakened' consciousness, in ordinary, 'third remove' perception, all of the productions of imagination seem only portions and fragments in comparison with what the mind is able to remember vaguely that it once knew: something whole and entire, a vision of eternity. The text is only a portion of that eternity. It is in this metaphorical sense that 'Kubla Khan' should be understood as a fragment: as an organic whole it is complete in itself; though, as a plant may grow to a larger size, lines may be added to increase it, but their additions do not imply that in its present size it is imperfect or incomplete in any aesthetic sense.[22]

The poet seeking to become maker again, and to raise himself from his merely passive state of reader or present spectator of past acts and visionary experiences, is a model for the reader who also dares not to remain satisfied with observing someone else's past acts. Thus the 'all' who cry 'Beware! Beware!', these observers of the poet, seem to be negative models of reading, as they refuse to participate in his activity, and refuse even to allow him to communicate with them. They seem to treat him as a 'psychological curiosity', and refuse to 'see' his visions of sun and ice. As an audience, referring to the poet–visionary as 'He', they repeat the perspective of the writer of the preface referring to 'the Author.' One must, on the basis of this analogy, wonder if the preface persona may not also be expressive of the limited perspective of a not altogether ideal reader. At the same time, the preface persona operates as ideal-reader, and this paradoxical superimposition, which also affects the 'all who cry' (who seem also worshipful), will be discussed below. It is this ambivalence which makes it possible also to relate the preface-persona and the visionary 'I', who is certainly *not* a negative model of reading. This 'I' is, on the contrary, as positive a model of a spectator–reader as one could imagine, so active as to threaten by his participation to become a poet as well. The preface persona becomes for the moment an example of a not wholly unimaginative, but nevertheless reductionist reader. It is *he*, not Coleridge, the ironical, detached creator of this persona, who believes that the origins of the poem mark it as a literal fragment, lacking in aesthetic wholeness. He cannot see that because the poem is a true part of a greater vision, that it is at the same time a unity, regardless of whether more lines might have been added. One might argue that more lines could always be added: there is no determined correspondence between images and words, and sounds and words. Images and musical sounds are not words, and hence are not exhaustible by them; this is surely why the relation between the two is left problematic in both preface and epilogue.[23] Moreover, the poem 'Kubla Khan' may also be understood to be a fragment in the sense that it lacks the correspondent images visible to the inner eye in an experience of eidectic imagery, as the dream-text lacks the wholeness of the dream experience of sights, sounds, and colours.

The literal-minded preface persona fails to see these ramifications of the notion of fragment. He views the poem as of interest primarily not as an aesthetic work, since it is a mere fragment, but as a psychological curiosity, as does the epilogic audience. Thus he not only fails to see the symbolic significance of the notion of fragment; he also fails to see the dream account as a metaphor of poetic creation. This reader allegory is posed in both the preface and epilogue as a model to the reader of how not to respond to the poem, a gesture all too familiar to Coleridge readers.[24] The analogy between poet and reader suggests on the other hand a model of a participatory, creative reading, and is illustrated in the lines from 'The Picture', included in the preface, in which it is clear that the poet's perspective and the reader's are analogous at certain times. Is the poor youth the poet or reader, or is he not both? Yet his role appears to be passive. But the stream mentioned in the preface as an allegory of the consciousness sets the stream of these lines in a similar allegorical relation with the consciousness. The passivity of the youth's posture may represent his stilling of the conscious self in order that the sources of genius may become accessible.[25] Thus he gives up any illusion of control over his faculty of vision, and adopts an apparently passive posture, while his active imagination takes over and creates according to principles normally inaccessible to the conscious self.[26] It is clear that the superficially active reader who reduces, paraphrases, chooses amongst ambiguities, decides about paradoxes, and judges, fails to activate his imaginative being, and never closes the gap between the poem and his perceptions of it. The poem remains an absolutely separate and distinct entity, whereas the breakdown of the boundaries of the poem as exhibited by the preface and the epilogue, and the intimate involvement of the preface in the poem, suggest, too, that the reader's 'preface', his account of the poem, is also not altogether distinct from some authoritative text, but actually contributes to the text as an entity. The account, then, is an integral part of the text.

In a sense, the preface makes it problematic to determine where the poem begins, and the epilogue prevents the determination of an end point. The epistemological claim being made is that one cannot decide the extent of the mind's contribution to the construction of objects of experience; hence the boundary between independent objects and mind is uncertain. The aesthetic claim corresponding to this epistemological one is that one cannot determine what is description and what is interpretation: the work of art as a work of art exists in the experience and response of the spectator to such an extent that when the reader thinks he is observing or perceiving the artifact purely or objectively, he is as mistaken as the philosopher who believes he can perceive a thing-in-itself. The challenging of the view that thought and thing are absolutely distinct entities is encouraged at both the aesthetic and epistemological levels of the poem. As Coleridge constantly insists, it is not necessary to divide in order to distinguish: thought and thing are different, but not essentially different. Moreover, they may only be facts of experience, not of reality, in the absolute sense (on the 'outness prejudice' see *BL* I ch. xii 177–9).

Because of the equally vague boundary between the 'vision in a dream', and the meditations about it, the certain line distinguishing

illusion and reality is dissolved: the border between art and reality has
already been shattered as the reader realizes that he mistakes his
responses for the text. The distinction between poet and reader erased
in the lines from 'A Picture', quoted in the preface, also emphasizes
this breakdown between art and reality; and the mixing up of Coleridge
and his ironic persona in the preface breaks down the distinction
between poet and reader, or at least makes it less than certain where
the boundaries lie and what exactly the distinctions in roles are. The
perception involved, for example, in reading, is suggested to be analogous
to the activity of creating artifacts, when reader and poet are mixed
up together, an analogy expressed by the distinction between primary
and secondary imagination. For in this distinction, Coleridge insists
that perceptual processes (such as reading) are fundamentally creative,
imaginative experiences.

The Perceptual 'Art of Thingifying'

Coleridge believed that the processes of construction involved in
artistic making were analogues of basic perceptual processes, but
operating at a secondary level. That is, art uses as its materials the
products of perception, and builds out of them new, higher order
cultural 'things'. Because art operates at a secondary level, it in effect
mirrors the primary level production of material things, or perceptual
objects, and can be a source of knowledge about those primary constructive modes indirectly through an analysis of artistic production.
When Coleridge investigates the artistic process of making, he is able
to draw an analogy to basic perception, and to psychological production. By adopting a transcendental idealist posture, he insists that
the mind is crucially active in the perception of the world, and is not
passively receiving already formed objects that impress their fixed,
stable and independently existing structures on the mind. Hence,
when the preface writer states that 'Kubla Khan' is of interest primarily
as a 'psychological curiosity', it is possible to understand that phrase
as an indication that the poem is not only interesting poetically, but
also as a source of knowledge about the mysterious processes of perception, which it mirrors as an artifact.

The productions of works of art, that is, the transformation of
subjective, internal experiences into external, public objects, is a
familiar experience, if not at first hand then at a removed perspective.
We do not easily forget that art products were not always things, but
results of mind externalizing subjective experiences. In 'Kubla Khan'

one of the most recurrent themes seems to be this process of 'thingifying', a word which Coleridge used to indicate the close relationship between thought and thing (and correlatively process and product, mind and nature, self and other).[27] The main interest in the preface is the process of making the dream or vision into a thing; in the epilogue the visionary wants to make the music into a more permanent 'dome in air' by reviving within him the Abyssinian maid's song; the damsel gives expression to her feelings about Mount Abora in 'symphony and song'; in the first half of the poem, Kubla Khan has a pleasure dome built according to his idea; and even in the second half of the poem, nature seems to be described as externalizing herself both by flinging up the sacred river on to the surface of the earth for a few miles before it sinks back into her inner world, and also by forcing great fragments, 'dancing rocks' into the air. In each case the objects made begin their existence by being 'flung forth' or externalized: they were not always there, but are products from another inner world. Not only works of art, but various objects are here presented as erupting from a subterranean world. Nature and culture are described as analogues. Indeed, it is not even clear in lines 1–11 which of the images are part of Kubla's design and which are nature.

In all of these examples there is an ambivalence between activity and passivity, an ambivalence central to a theory of mind as active or passive. Kubla Khan decrees the dome and gardens, but does he actively engage in the construction of it? Does the damsel act merely as the instrument performing an already composed music and song, or is she creating her song? Is the vision of the visionary in the epilogue a creation of his, or is he receiving it in a passive stance; and in what sense would he build the dome from the damsel's music, revived *within* himself? Would she somehow *give* it to him? Clearly this ambivalence is most explicit in the preface in the qualifications surrounding the notion of composition, and more generally in the dream allegory. It is repeated in the quoted lines from 'A Picture': for if 'now once more/The pool becomes a mirror', then the observer *makes* the image reflected, and thus his function is hardly altogether passive. In each case, the ambivalence between the active and passive roles seems to foreground once again the central mystery surrounding aesthetic creation: to what extent is art the result of inspiration, or forces beyond conscious control, and to what extent must the artist consciously guide this inspiration through decision, judgment, and technique acquired by practice?

The poem makes a gesture at a kind of solution, by seeming to indicate that whatever the degree of interaction, it is evident that the conscious ego must to a large extent remain in a state of stillness in order for unconscious sources of genius to awaken and begin to express themselves through the ego as instrument and not as source of the inspiration. Thus 'Kubla Khan' is not to be understood as an anomaly, but as a result of the ideal mode of production. That is, genius speaks so fully and coherently that no completing acts on the part of conscious man are needed. The author's genius is perfectly integrated with his conscious mind in this ideal production, and no arbitrary, merely conscious gestures are made; the conscious is always interpenetrated by an intuition of its appropriateness. By writing the preface, Coleridge emphasized the importance of the integration of the passive and active, of the conscious and the unconscious, and reversed the common notion of what constitutes activity in art.[28] The preponderantly active part must be given to the unconscious, while the conscious accepts a subordinate, though integrated, role. The presence of the preface, however, reaffirms the view of art not as a merely unconscious out-pouring of unreflective feeling, but as a highly self-conscious activity. The author is deeply impressed by his paradoxical position: his loss of self-control as he usually understands it; his subjection to this power seeming to be his, and yet more than him; his suspension of conscious intention at the same time that he is observing himself acting, yet not acting, or intending by means of intuition and not arbitrarily.

By bringing out this ambivalence in the meaning of 'active' in artistic processes, Coleridge implicates the reader's role as well, as the analogy so vividly expressed in the lines from 'A Picture' suggests. The reader as perceiver of the poem must participate and be active or the object will remain an entirely separate entity from him, never assimilated into his fabric of experience. Clearly it must be an activity guided by intelligence and creative response. And for this to occur, the conscious self must in reading subordinate itself to some intuitive guidance, to some genial stillness, while the artifact works upon him to awaken his imaginative faculty. Poet and reader roles are compared in order to emphasize this similarity in the kind of activity required for catching a glimpse of the vision that the work of art tries to embody.

If art mirrors perception, however, this analogy must be drawn out in its implications not only for reading as a type of perception, but for the production of things as products of perception. Coleridge explains that 'to think is to thingify'. But to perceive was also originally to thingify. When we think, we delimit the boundaries of concepts, and discriminate distinctions. But for Coleridge, culture, the world of thought, of art, of science, and all the objects of culture are no more dependent upon perception than the world of nature, as we know it. Objects perceived by the mind can never be known independently of the perception of them, and this general ontological point is enlighten-ing for an understanding of art from the point of view of both the spectator and the artist. Since there is no way of achieving certainty as to the nature of the object in itself, its familiar objectivity must be understood as a purely inter-subjective independence. Primary imagination, that is, perception, reveals its principles of organization and construction in its products because, like art, it constructs them according to those inner principles.

Landscape and the Imagination

The analogy between art and perception or poet and reader is expressed by the distinction between primary and secondary imagination, and this distinction may be seen to be functioning as an explicit metaphor in the body of the poem, while in the preface and epilogue it is only implied. For in the preface and epilogue the problem foregrounded is the relation of the artist and the spectator to the work of art. In the body of the poem this relationship is generalized to include perception through the metaphor which the landscape provides. The landscape has two contrasting aspects. But in 'Kubla Khan' the contrast between the Khan's architectural and landscaping gestures in lines 1–11 and the natural, wild, and unencompassed scene of the 'deep romantic chasm', its fountain, and so forth, in lines 12–30, suggests the distinction between the secondary activities of art and culture, which use the materials of nature to create new materials, and the primary activities of perception. The Khan, like the artist, builds out of nature. But the labours of the earth, her flingings of huge *fragments* into air, and her forcing up of the fountain as the source of the river, are analogues of the unconscious mind creating its nature for itself.

An alternative allegory to account for the contrast in landscape presents itself, however, as the distinction between fancy and imagination. Coleridge had not yet articulated either the fancy/imagination distinction or the distinction between primary and secondary imagination. They can only be said to be implicit in the poem, a fact which suggests how much his experiences as a poet must have affected his thinking about art, reality, and the faculties of mind or 'powers of knowledge'.[29] The Khan's measuring and counting, his erecting of walls, and his decrees suggest a more mechanical construction relying on fancy as its faculty of direction. As a contrast, the natural imagery of Stanza II combines both the idea of the truly artistic mode of construction according to organic principles, and the idea that art mirrors nature as an organically unified and naturally produced whole. It also suggests the metaphorical implications of the idea of fragment:

not only artifacts, but natural objects are fragments in the sense that they participate in a greater whole: 'dancing rocks' is an effective image to combine the two oppositions of culture and nature, and the idea that every part may be both a unity and a fragment of a larger unity. 'Dancing *rocks*' may relate to 'stony reason' as well, and may imply a theory of language and art as inevitably degenerating through familiarity (as will be further discussed below). Shelley's 'dead metaphors', or Coleridge's 'worn-out metaphors', would seem to express a similar idea. The image of the earth labouring in 'fast thick pants' suggests childbirth, the birth of ideas or works of art, and natural production as all interrelated experiences contrasted with more deliberate, mechanical productions.[30]

The overlapping of these two allegories in the landscape imagery suggests no accidental ambiguity. It suggests that the activity of secondary imagination has a further, ominous aspect to it. It can degenerate from the creation of new metaphors and symbols into a faculty manipulating fixities and determinates, or it can be mistaken for such a faculty. Shelley expressed this sinister aspect when he pointed to the degeneration of metaphors into dead metaphors;[31] Coleridge pointed to truths so true as to lose the power of truth.[32] Thus the ambivalence of the landscape actually seems to function to express this further side of imaginative experience and its gradual change into fancy, and indeed memory. Perception even more than art seems to suffer the degeneration which results in a chasm between thought and thing. Indeed, art is the corrective to the degenerate perceptions of 'single vision'. The only corrective to degenerate art is art that revitalizes the lost associations. The representation of the cessation of imagination or its change into fancy and memory is a repetition of the preface and epilogue; both bemoan the loss of vision in a much more explicit way, though perhaps less demonstrably, since here we actually have an instance of the difference: the Khan measures and decrees and walls and girdles. He shuts out nature and imagination, and art degenerates.[33]

The preface encourages such a procedure of internalizing the landscape, or making it a topographical metaphor of mental processes.[34] The stream of consciousness of the preface both in the extended metaphor of images on a stream and the lines from 'A Picture' provides a model for interpretation of the landscape. The use of landscape as the content to be internalized suggests two applications: first, the landscape we know as nature is revealed as an externalized projection of mind, and secondly the topographical imagery acting as the surface or landscape of the *poem* is equally projected. To understand either nature or art correctly, we must understand them as things, but as things not absolutely external and independent of perception. For as the poem has suggested in preface, epilogue, and body, and in several allegoric levels of all, things originate in the life of the mind and are projected according to its principles and categories of organization. The 'prejudice of outness' almost obliterates this awareness of the origins of things: art can remind us of it, and give us a truer view of experience: what is 'given' and 'external' seems so because its production originates at unconscious levels.

The poem depicts the tremendous desire of the human psyche to create objects and send them out into the world. And it shows nature in the throes of the same intense productivity. The Khan, the damsel, the visionary, and the poet are all making, and nature is making rivers, fountains, and fragments of 'dancing rocks'. But at the same time as the poem expresses the force and primacy of this making instinct, it also seeks to understand its origins, its conditions for success, its degeneration, and its recurrence. It seeks to analyse the relation of the product made to the maker, and to the experience that inspired the maker.[35] It shows how the familiar devices of personification of forces (e.g. the Abyssinian maid as imagination and the 'person on business from Porlock' as ego—two figures additionally effective in their contrast with each other), and the creation of personas either to split the self of the author or to make a caricature of the 'sleeping' reader, are instances of 'thingifying'. But by demonstrating the process of making, things are 'dethingified': their origins are shown to be in the creating mind, not in an external substance.

The myths of dream and vision, and the invitation to internalize the landscape as a psychological topography, further act to depict the art of thingifying and the tenuousness of the border between art and reality, mind and nature, creation and perception. The writer makes distinctions between dream and reality, creates distinct characters in the vision, distinct parts to the poem, distinct landscapes, distinct objects, but then builds an uncertainty around them all so that closer examination reveals them to be striving toward a dissolution of distinct selves or boundaries. For example, the maid's song and Kubla's dome are distinct, but are then mysteriously brought together both when we realize that the 'second' vision may imply that the song of the maid is about the dome, and when the visionary says that he will build the dome with the song of the maid. The visionary and the damsel are not altogether distinct, as we realize she occurred in a vision; and even Kubla and the visionary are identified in the visionary's claim that *he* will build the dome in air: he takes over Kubla's distinct role.[36]

Nor can we be certain in the landscape and architectural imagery what is built and what is there already as nature, what is part of the enclosure and what is excluded from it. Are we given a description of what was enclosed or of that which does the enclosing?[37] The 'forests ancient as the hills' enfold 'sunny spots of greenery' but do the walls enclose all, or are they enclosed by the forests? Is the deep romantic chasm within or without the walls? Is it part of or an alternative to the Khan's gardens, and has he surrounded it or walled it out?

The landscape models, and thus enriches, the indeterminacy of the poem's boundaries. Does the epilogue contain the body of the poem as an embedded vision, or is it contained in the Khan's landscape vision? The ambivalence is effectively expressed by the detail of contrasting 'here' in line 10 with 'there' in line 8. Moreover, the narrator's perspective is subtly indicated as 'here', in the ancient forests, as opposed to 'there', in the gardens (the 1828 and 1829 editions ignore the distinction; 'here' is repeated in line 8). The narrator seems to be located in the natural scenery looking down upon the artifice of the Khan. He might be understood to be singing of the dangers and limitations of uninspired art: of imposing form instead of discovering it. Or he may be emphasizing the important relation of nature to art, thus suggesting the integration of inspiration and intention: art must be produced naturally, but with skill or artifice. This is precisely the dilemma suggested by both the preface and the visionary of the epilogue. In the preface, 'the Author' is tempted apparently to try to fashion what he cannot regain from the muse: 'Yet from the still surviving recollections in his mind, the Author has frequently purposed to finish for himself what had been originally, as it were, given to him . . . Σαμερον [Αὔριον] ἄδιον ἄσω [tomorrow I will sing a song]: but the to-morrow is yet to come.' This is at least the view of the persona, but perhaps 'the Author' is too wise to attempt such an artificial work. Likewise, the visionary knows that his 'vague and dim recollection of the general purport of the vision' of the damsel is not enough to build the dome in air (the rest of the poem?); only a *revival*, not a memory, but a genuine imaginative reproduction of the lost vision, will achieve the completion desired: a genuine repetition.

The most extraordinary ambivalence occurs in the last part of the body of the poem, lines 31–6, in which the *shadow* of the dome of pleasure seems to be the referent of 'it' in line 35, rather than the dome itself. And both lines 36 and 46 suggest that the miracle is not the dome of pleasure, but a unification of the dome and the caves of ice. But the caves of ice are nature's child; only the dome is Kubla's creation. We tend to forget this distinction and read the lines as if the Khan had created this synthesized miracle 'That sunny dome! those caves of ice!' But it seems to arise from the musings of the narrator about the shadow of the dome floating upon the waves midway between fountain and caves.

Lines 31–6 suggest further clues to the perspective of the narrator of the body of the poem as an observer seeking to portray the limitations of 'decreed' art. The ambiguous reference of 'it' in line 35 to either 'the shadow of the dome' or 'sunny dome with caves of ice' has Platonic undertones of relations of shadow to substance with the correspondent reversal of the reality of each. The 'miracle of rare device' referring either to shadow or to the fusion of dome and caves is something more than the mere dome of the Khan it would seem, and the narrator, by introducing these lines, strangely disconnected from the landscape of lines 1–30, seems to be trying to propose some solution to the opposition between art and nature. The use of the word 'measure' to mean song or music contrasts with the literal measurings of the Khan for his garden, and sets up a tension since the source of this 'mingled measure' is the 'caverns measureless to man', and the fountain. The implication might be that imagination most faithfully captures the nature of human experience not by measuring it deductively or quantitatively; it measures by expressing that nature in outward forms but according to inner principles, and thereby best captures its 'dimensions'.

Concluding Remarks

A model of ambivalence occurs in the epilogue and is mirrored in the preface. The reported speech of lines 49–54 is attributed to an unidentified group of observers, the 'all'. But the speech is not direct report, it is the interpolation of the visionary: the words are *his*, the symbols and images are his representations (as the damsel's song was his also). And although this audience at first appears hostile, it is not really clear whether they are ostracizing the poet or worshipping him, and it is far from clear which attitude the visionary is describing. For the revived music heard by the 'all' also will enable them to see the dome and caves of ice.

The persona created in the preface suffers the same reversal. His perspective seems limited and narrow, as he brands the poem fragmentary and a 'psychological curiosity'. He believes the author intends to finish the poem, but is unable to. Indeed there is no limit to the interpolation from the manuscript note that we may ascribe to him. The extraordinary intrusion of an 'I' in the last sentence of the preface seems to give further reality to the persona of the preface writer as a mere editor of the poems, and not the author of them. Whatever the author may have told him may have been meant ironically, and he may have taken it all literally. But even this naïvety is transcended when one realizes that the persona, as long as he is not distinguished from Coleridge, is the literal-minded reader projecting his own notions of fragment (as literally a fragment) and psychological curiosity (as hence not of poetic merit) on to Coleridge. He assumes Coleridge means the preface literally because the reader cannot see it imaginative- ly. But the moment he 'thingifies' a persona, sees the possibility of indirectness and irony, and takes the hint from the third person narrative and the conflicting 'I' in the last line ('I have annexed a fragment of a very different character'), he has actually 'thingified' or made an object of awareness his own unimaginative response to the poem, distanced himself from it, and thereby overcome it. He too, then, must personify, as does the artist, his 'person on business from Porlock', who restricts his view.

The process comes full circle as the reader realizes now the importance of personification as a model, and the importance of the symbolic and mythic meanings of the dream, the fragment, and so forth. For as he does, he sees that there is no longer a need to maintain the preface persona, with Coleridge as the ironical detached creator of him. The very terms of the preface: the 'dream', the 'fragment', and the 'psy- chological curiosity', all were meant symbolically anyway. They are not pejorative terms but simply characterizations which identify the nature of all aesthetic products. That is, all poems are fragments, in the sense that they are 'portions of one great poem'; all originate in dream-like states or 'sleeps of the external senses'; and all are psychologi- cal curiosities because all are expressive of the mind's mode of per- ception by 'thingifying' experience into outward forms. Thus Coleridge achieves an aesthetic representation of his philosophy of art: he is not content with mere discursive rendering. He embodies his theory in the practice, and this may partially account for the richness of his poem.

Thus, just as the apparent irreverence of the speakers in lines 49–54 is changed to worship, so the criticisms and belittling comments of the preface are changed into descriptions of what art should be. The persona is dropped when we read the preface as written by Coleridge the genius, who had confidence in his poetry and had the ability to devise every conceivable mode of helping the reader to see its richness, including the risk of making himself a 'laughing-stock' in order to make available to the reader the tool of irony and indirectness if meta- phor and symbol proved too difficult in the first stages. To sacrifice his right of authorship to the muse and the poem's claim to meaning by originating it in a dream, in order that the reader may be stimulated to a kind of authorship by interpreting the dream, is a gesture of incalculable generosity.[38]

The myriad ambiguities and possibilities discussed throughout this chapter result from the effort to represent the complex, contradictory and multivalent nature of both aesthetic and perceptual experience from several different perspectives. Thus the visionary 'I' of the epilogue may be seen as a model reader, striving to respond appropriately to the work of art, the Khan's productions, by means of the damsel, a personification of imagination or inspiration. In this respect the structure of 'Kubla Khan' is much like that of 'The Ancient Mariner', the Wedding Guest serving a similar function as a model spectator. But the visionary 'I' is then complicated by representing, as well as the reader's or spectator's perspective, the act of composition from the poet's point of view. Indeed he has usually been understood only in this way, as ideal poet, though it is arguable that his spectator function is still more interesting and adds a dimension to the poem, for his role as poet is only a repetition of the Khan's representation as a poet. This dual role of the visionary 'I' helps to emphasize the essential similarity of the poet's and the reader's roles.

Further complications arise in an effort to grasp the significance of the Khan's activities. For he has been seen to offer an equally contradictory duality like the visionary 'I'. The Khan's paradoxical nature is slightly different: he offers a split in the artist's nature, rather than a split between artist and spectator. He represents the artist as too purposeful, as conscious, and as uninspired, that is, as talent and artifice, in distinction from genius. And he represents the true artist and his essential integration with nature and natural forces, the word nature drawing on all its other connotations as well, of human nature, the natural, and nature as imagination. The ambivalent relation of the garden to the natural scenery contributes to this paradoxical duality. But this duality further represents the way even true art can become degenerate, through familiarity, habit, and acquiescent approbation, or, for example, unthinking acceptance of certain works as of classic stature. This possibility immediately creates another split, analogous to the split in the artist's nature. That is, the reader is subject to such a split, and he too can be represented as inspired or only artificially responsive. This ambivalence in readership is iterated in the portrayal of the 'all who cry', where it is not clear whether the attitude is worshipful or censorious.

But the reader split seems most effectually represented in the preface, and in this, 'Kubla Khan' once again repeats the technique of 'The Ancient Mariner', with its gloss persona (as will be discussed in Chapter Two). For the preface persona seems to offer the identity of a reductive and naïve reader who fails to see the importance of the artifact as self-imaging. The 'person on business from Porlock' may be, like the damsel, a personification of a faculty of the mind, but in this case the faculty personified is not the one instrumental in creative response. That faculty represses and censors, and therefore properly belongs to the reductive reader persona as his habitual state; it belongs to the poet only as an interruptive agent. The complication in the preface persona, not repeated in the gloss persona in 'The Ancient Mariner', involves another level of self-awareness; the preface persona as a reductive reader turns out to be a projection caused by the failure of the reader to take the elements of the dream, the fragment, and 'psychological curiosity' as metaphors. If taken as metaphors, these elements imply a persona who is not a reductive reader, but who is ironizing that sort of reader.

One final set of complexities must be considered, involving the relation of the epilogue to the body of the poem, and the preface to the verse. It has been pointed out at length that the relation of the last eighteen lines to the first thirty-six is problematic in the extreme. This uncertainty could be taken to represent the obscure relation of the reader to his text and the poet to his creation. The omniscience of the narrator of the first thirty-six lines implies that there is no question of conscious control or volition in this relation. And the contrast of omniscience with first person narrative in the epilogue seems to highlight this difference between conscious and unconscious selves or states. This last section of the verse, like the final stanza of 'The Eolian Harp' and the last stanza of 'This Lime-Tree Bower', and like the Wedding Guest framework in 'The Ancient Mariner' or the ambivalence of the imagery of frost in 'Frost at Midnight' in the last stanza of that poem, adds a level of self-consciousness to the poem and without this level the verse would be incomplete, ending at an arbitrary point. An experience would have been portrayed, but without any level of reflection about that experience, and without any reflection about the possibility and nature of communicating it. It would have remained at a remove, as an external object never assimilated, never 'seeking echo or mirror of itself', never 'making a Toy of Thought'. Without such a level of reflection, the poem would have been a literal fragment; but with its epilogue, like all the poems mentioned above, it becomes a complete, rich work of art.

The preface acts as a link between the reader and the poem and as such its relation to the verse is as problematic as is the relation of art to reality or of spectator to art. It is appropriately ironic, as is the gloss, because it thereby renders the inherent irony of the spectator's situation. It gently caricatures the delusion of literal-mindedness, and gives metaphor as the solution to that imprisoning language. And since it engages the reader aesthetically and not discursively, it is proper to consider it as an integral part of the text, not merely as an external prose commentary, though of course it seems to be only that to the unimaginative, reductive reader parodied in the persona. Perhaps it would be correct to conclude that such a negative model of reading as is offered by the preface and the gloss of 'The Ancient Mariner' must always appear to be outside the formal structure of a work of art initially. For its function can only be apprehended after a level of critical reflection on the work has been achieved. A positive model, on the other hand, such as the visionary or Wedding Guest, or the speaker in other poems such as 'This Lime-Tree Bower', can always be understood as the poet. This viewing of someone else's experience does not require self-conscious reflection, but it should never be mistaken for aesthetic response. As most artists realize, superficial non-integration may be a great stimulus to reflection, enabling the reader to discover the profound unity of a work: it can act as a stepping stone to an understanding of the full implications of the more integrated aspects. Thus the preface helps to lead the reader to see the possibilities of the epilogue and its relation to the body of the poem. The apparent non-integration of the epilogue to the body of the poem reflects the schism in experience between the conscious and the unconscious, or the conscious and the self-conscious. The poem will appear as fragmented and incomplete as the understanding of its readership is; but its beauty, that is, its intuited unity and truth to aesthetic experience, has preserved it as a compelling enigma, and will surely continue to do so.

The Gloss to 'The Ancient Mariner':
An Ironic Commentary

In spite of its many differences, 'The Ancient Mariner'[1] nevertheless shares with 'Kubla Khan' certain structural and narrative features. Landscape is effectively used as a crucial feature in the internalization of the poem for the reader, in so far as it acts as a metaphor for mental landscape.[2] While the specific context of dream is absent,[3] unlike in the other poem, and while the bizarre supernaturalism of the poem itself sets up the tension between reality and illusion that the dream context achieved elsewhere, the gloss provides the main context for a tension between reality and illusion. It does this not by invoking a dream metaphor, as in 'Kubla Khan', but by setting up an aesthetic context. In 'The Ancient Mariner', the distance achieved by the glossing technique makes it possible to reflect the primary observer in art: the reader. At a higher theoretical level of analysis these distinctions coalesce and both reader and poet must be understood as observers as well as makers. By destabilizing reality in this way, that is, by setting up a rival reality within the context of aesthetic illusion that so closely resembles the reality of the observer's situation as to shatter the ordinary boundary between the two, the formal distinctions between mind and nature, external and internal, thought and thing, are questioned as real or illusory. Indeed, they are exposed as absolute distinctions characteristic only of an illusory reality.[4]

The gloss, the most interesting structural feature of 'The Ancient Mariner', was added in 1816 to the text of the poem as published in *Sybilline Leaves* (1817), though it may have been written much earlier; this same year (1816) Coleridge published 'Kubla Khan' with its preface. The preface may be profitably examined as functioning in similar ways to the gloss, as will be discussed below. The present analysis will approach the poem from three points of view: the 'Wedding Guest Framework', the 'Argument', and the gloss.[5]

The Wedding Guest Framework

Before examining the gloss, the reader may notice that within the verse text of the poem, a frame highlighting the communicative act is brought into sharp focus and is contrasted with the basic core-content of the poem—the journey in the ship. The framework, the narrating of the tale to the Wedding Guest, another instance of the 'aesthetic situation' of author and audience, mirrors the reading situation and breaks down the fixed boundary between art or illusion and reality.[6]

The importance of the framework to the poem as a whole can be appreciated if one considers how vastly different the poem would be without it.[7] Two elements in the poem draw our attention to this difference—the 'Argument', and the narration of the tale to the hermit. For the 'Argument' focuses essentially only upon the journey in the ship and the experiences occurring therein. It explicitly excludes any reference to a time before or after the journey (in both its versions), though the boundaries of this core-content are explicit only for its beginning. Nor can one be clear as to how the narration of the tale to the hermit would have finished. It would seem to have been quite different from the version given to the Wedding Guest, and subsequently given to the gloss writer and future readers by the narrator–poet. For the first twenty lines, numerous interjections, and the final 160 lines (a full quarter of the poem) would not belong to the version heard by the hermit. The first twenty lines and the interjections belong to a later time, and the last lines include him in the drama of events so that he would not need to be told what he himself had participated in. Nevertheless we cannot know how the ending of the hermit version might have gone, since his point of view is different enough from that of the Ancient Mariner to allow for considerable explanation of the final events even though the hermit was present. One might ask, for instance, whether the moralizing verses toward the end of the poem would have been included in the hermit's version. Nor is it obvious how the section from lines 542 onward would have been dealt with. The narrative intrusions in lines 514–22 create further complexities for determining a core-content or the hermit's version, or a version corresponding to the 'Argument's' description.

The story narrated to the hermit as an alternative version of the

Ancient Mariner's experience is interesting for critical reflection primarily because it seems unfinished in two senses, the one being in the sense of the indeterminate ending discussed above, and this applies as well to the 'Argument' version. It is also unfinished since at the time of the Ancient Mariner's narration to the hermit, the Mariner was unaware that the experience of the journey on the ship had far from played itself out. One of its most disturbing and fascinating consequences was yet to make itself manifest: the necessity for telling about the journey again and again throughout the Mariner's life. This necessity for repetition means that the Mariner is never to be free of the past; it recreates itself each time he tells the tale, with a vividness and reality that no merely voluntary memory could evoke.[8]

The 'strange power of speech' comes upon the Mariner unpredictably, and suggests that he becomes a visionary of sorts, caught in a spell. Not merely memory, but imagination as well speaks through him, yet in some mysterious association with memory. Many of the features descriptive of the process of narration seem to emphasize that the narration is definitely not a mere remembering of a past experience. The narrative is a product of an involuntary and irresistible force taking the form of 'agony' until it is released to express itself by this 'strange power of speech'. The Ancient Mariner is *compelled* to tell his tale. This contrast of memory with imaginative recuperation of past experience into a present reality thus becomes an issue in the framework of the poem, just as it has been in 'Kubla Khan'.

Furthermore, it is not only the Ancient Mariner who is caught in some spell-binding, involuntary activity: the Wedding Guest 'cannot choose but hear' (line 8), and is held by the 'glittering eye' of the Mariner. Just as the narrative is not a product of a passive memory, the narrative as heard is not assimilated in a passive way. That is, it is not to anyone that the Mariner tells his tale; he chooses his listeners instinctively, only those who will be so deeply aroused by the tale as to be taught something 'stunning' in its import. The listener, it seems, will often be unwilling to listen, but then unable to refuse, as the Mariner 'hath his will'. The ambiguity of the phrase, turning upon the uncertain reference of 'his', heightens the emphasis on the suspension of the will. The emphasis on the suspension of the voluntary power, the sense that some greater force is compelling *both* listener and narrator, and the indirect references to entrancement all suggest that memory and passive perception are being infused by an imaginative force that makes past experiences become vividly present and real, though the external events initiating them are over. Thus the act of telling becomes tantamount to the recomposition of a narrative on each occasion, and a narrative motivated by imagination, not merely by memory. The Ancient Mariner becomes a poet at each telling; however it is the telling of not altogether the same poem.

The Hermit version and the 'Argument', while seeming to assert a core-content version of the tale, actually show the difficulties of such a version both by being unfinished and by drawing attention, by contrast, to the framework version. The most interesting difference is the fact of highlighted narration in the framework version. The act of telling and of communication becomes important as it functions in two ways. First, as an effective mirroring of the reading situation it forces the reader to assess the role of the Wedding Guest and the nature of his participation, as a 'recipe' for reading and aesthetic response. Secondly, the framework narrative situation is a theoretical gesture about the nature of poetic composition, its mode of production, its sources in personal experience, the role of the faculty of the will and the conscious and sub-conscious, the relation of memory to imagination, the transience of imagination and its unpredictable return, and the problems both of the relation of the text as imaginative product to the experience which inspired it, and the possibility and nature of the communication of the experience via the text. The Wedding Guest framework, like the preface to 'Kubla Khan', provides then substantial hints towards a theory of art in a dramatic, structural feature of the work of art, as opposed to a discursive account analytically expressed; and the work of art, at the same time as it expresses the theory, demonstrates through the reading experience those theoretical assumptions asserted dramatically and metaphorically.

The indeterminate, unfinishable character of the two alternative versions of the 'Argument' and the Hermit calls into question the viability of the notion of a core-content free of the interpretative effects of narration, that is, an objective set of facts. Their lack of an end boundary has a counterpart in the unending repetition of the tale creating the framework text. Since the verse text as a whole is explicitly about both the tale and the telling, it becomes itself tainted by the never-ending repetition: the telling is never finished, and, as a result, neither is the verse text. The end of the verse is practically the beginning of the search for a new listener. The gloss writer may act as an example of such a continuation.

This feature of the verse seems to suggest another characteristic of works of art and of aesthetic experience, expressible in a paradox: in its unity the work of art is at the same time a fragment. It is a fragment in many senses, for example, in its relation to the experience it purports to express; in the need for completion by the reader; in its relation to its literary context; in the fact that no one reading can exhaust the whole possibility of meanings latent in it. The notion that art is always fragmentary draws attention to the fact that language can never express the whole of experience or replace it. That is, the translation process from experience and perception to linguistic expression involves distortion, compression, generalization, abstraction, subjective (unconscious) selection, habit, and so forth. The narrative does *not* correspond in a determinate way to an experience somehow described by it. The framework technique seeks to expose this erroneous assumption by revealing the relation between text and reality as indeterminate, since the core-content cannot exist apart from the telling of it: the latter essentially alters the content. Perception and expression, two modes of internalizing and assimilating the external, rob the external of its pure independent status with respect to the possibility of knowledge: 'Some experience in a ship occurred, but what?' Art, then, does not correspond to reality: it creates a new reality, or offers a rival account of reality to the account given by memory and the understanding. Art may, paradoxically, offer itself as that reality, or at least as a more complete account of reality than ordinary perception. The reader, analogically, is instructed to see the narrative not as the end in itself, as the repository of the facts of an adventure, or even as a repository of metaphors and images about the facts of an adventure. The narrative is rather a threshold, not an end, where the reader must remain poised.

The characterizing of reading and aesthetic response generally as a threshold is encouraged by the specific circumstances of the framework. The Ancient Mariner and the Wedding Guest are poised on the threshold of the bridegroom's door as the tale is narrated. This poising on the threshold is a metaphor for the way the verse is meant to function in contrast to the gloss, for the gloss is constantly disrupting the balance and pushing the reader into one specific response or meaning.[9] The threshold is a symbol of imaginative experience; with it, there is no illusion of passing into definiteness. At the threshold one is kept hovering amongst possibilities. If the Wedding Guest is correctly understood as representative of the ideal reader, just as he is the chosen listener for the Ancient Mariner, his position on the threshold would also be a description of the appropriate reading and response to art. The gloss, on the other hand, would be a caricature of the irony of conventional perception, where the threshold experiences are constantly resolved into certainties:[10] the heightened awareness and the tension that something is about to happen—features of the threshold experience—are dissipated into the familiar, relaxed state of resolved tensions. The sense of the extraordinary is lost; but art, and specifically the verse text of this poem, seeks to restore precisely this intense expectancy of being about to move into a new or different state. The sense of being poised or balanced on the boundary of two worlds (a familiar world perhaps, and an unfamiliar one) is one of the primary features of the suspense that an imaginative narrative can induce. It can be related to the anxiety in ordinary life of border crossing. It can also provide a definition of metaphor, as the mode of moving the mind to the border of the familiar by inducing a connection with the unfamiliar, or of causing changes in consciousness from unimaginative to imaginative perception. Certainly this change of state is suggested by the spells, trances, and swounds mentioned in the verse, and by the description of the Wedding Guest: 'He went like one that hath been stunned,/And is of sense forlorn . . .' (lines 622–3). He is forlorn of his outward senses only; his inner awareness has been so aroused and deeply affected that his outward senses are left passive as his inner sense is activated. He is reduced to silence, unlike the glossing persona who is prepared to interpret, articulate, and determine fixed meanings at every turn of the narrative. Thus the threshold metaphor suggests yet another theoretical gesture about the nature of art and aesthetic experience. Art involves a balancing, poising activity. This activity contrasts both with the resolution of meaning or tension characteristic of ordinary perception and discursive thought, and with the loss of distance, or detachment, which characterizes sentimentality and illusory objectivity.[11]

The balancing or poising upon the boundary between two states achieves a metaphysical significance as well, for it suggests that the apparently absolute boundaries between thought and thing, self and world, and mind and nature are overcome in imaginative experience. Imagination exposes these distinctions[12] as conventions or mental expedients and not characteristics of reality, though of course they are facts of experience which must be reckoned with. But the notion of a stable reality depends precisely upon such stable distinctions. The framework further threatens the boundary between art or illusion and reality by incorporating the reading situation metaphorically into the dramatic structure of the text, offering a programme for effective reading. The gloss too threatens this boundary, but by offering a typically unimaginative reading: it depicts an overlaying of a facade of conventional meanings to explain the tale and incorporate it into a body of accepted belief (as will be shown in detail below). The Wedding Guest on the other hand spreads no obscuring veil of interpretation over the deeply affecting action: he is rather stunned into silence, a silence that is not vacancy, but the generative condition of wisdom. This deep involvement may be the experience to which the wedding scene is meant at some level to correspond metaphorically. The wedding inside might be seen as a mirror of the aesthetic union taking place on the far side of the threshold: the successful communication of imaginative experience between author and reader by means of the text. On the other hand, the wedding scene could reach the reductionist reader, who by observing conventional form, only *seems* to be achieving a union. The wedding genuinely allows for these two contradictory interpretations, and such ambivalence suggests that our interest is not in setting up allegories, but in exploring possible expansions of ordinary boundaries. It also emphasizes the duality of experience (as opposed to some reality), which results from looking at the 'same' situation from differing perspectives, especially moral perspectives.

The model of this fusion of identities is given in the poem through the blurring of distinct speaking voices at the end of the verse text. The narrative voice, at the outset of the poem clearly distinguished from the voice of the Ancient Mariner, merges with the latter precisely at the moment when the Ancient Mariner begins to explain the necessity of his telling the tale over and over again to a specific, intuitively chosen listener. Thus not only is the past experience in the ship suddenly united with the narrative present, but the (for the reader) past telling of the entire tale, including the repetition syndrome, is united with the present account by the narrator–poet. The third stanza from the end most precisely illustrates such a blurring of voices, as one realizes the uncertainty of the authority for the further interpolation of the moral expressed by lines 612–13. The quotation marks added in many editions obscure the effect preserved in E. H. Coleridge's text. Lines 591–6 present an equal difficulty, since the narrator–poet has consistently spoken any lines descriptive of the interruptions from the wedding, and would seem now to be speaking these lines, except for the personal pronoun in 'Which biddeth me to prayer' (line 596). As the narrator–poet assimilates the dramatic persona of the Ancient Mariner back into his own identity through the ambiguity of speakers, as if the Ancient Mariner is his visionary self, the speaker is provided with a model for assimilating his dramatic persona, the Wedding Guest, and thus overcoming the chasm between himself and the text. For if it is not clear who is speaking at what aesthetic level, it is also not clear who is spoken to, Wedding Guest or reader. The presentness of the narrator, intensified by the 'Now' of line 620, and the '*is* gone', increases the vividness of the ambiguity of voices. The reader is further included in these last few stanzas by the strict appropriateness of narrator–poet and Ancient Mariner *both* seeming to speak lines 614–17, if the analogy of Wedding Guest and reader is noted.

The 'Argument'

Coleridge first published 'The Ancient Mariner' in the *Lyrical Ballads*, in 1798, without the gloss and with substantial variation in the text from later versions modernizing the archaic diction, and thereby despecifying somewhat the genre and narrative perspective. The gloss seems often to be read as if it were an indivisible part of the verse, with an identical authorial persona, and such an uncritical view obscures both the functioning of the gloss and its relation to the verse. It is therefore useful from the outset to emphasize that the modernized text of the poem falls into two distinct elements, the gloss and the verse. Their interaction is of primary concern for analysis, and not simply to be taken at face value. The tendency to identify the persona of the gloss and the narrator–poet of the verse may account for the casual treatment of the gloss as simply an extension of the verse with no significantly different character or role.

It is not known when the gloss was composed, but it does seem to arise from a perspective similar to that of the 'Argument', though expanding the latter out of all recognition. The 'Argument' was included in the first published version of the poem in 1798, was altered significantly in 1800, deleted in subsequent editions, and 'reappeared' as the gloss in 1817. The 1798 *Lyrical Ballads* version of this peculiar element in the poem is as follows:

ARGUMENT

How a Ship having passed the Line was driven by storms to the cold Country towards the South Pole; and how from thence she made her course to the tropical Latitude of the Great Pacific Ocean; and of the strange things that befell; and in what manner the Ancyent Marinere came back to his own Country.

The 'Argument' confines the focus of the poem to the sea journey, leaving the reader completely unprepared for the necessity of retelling the story. The necessity for repetition keeps that past perpetually present and is one of the most fascinating aspects of the 'strange things that befell'. The two features most distinctive in the 'Argument' are its specifications of geographical locations and its concern with time sequence: it seems to have no other function than to place the drama of the verse in a completely clear space/time grid. The authorial persona of the 'Argument' mentions 'the Line', 'the South Pole', 'the tropical Latitude', and 'the Great Pacific Ocean', details far more specific than any geographical information given in the verse. The persona similarly treats the sequence of events with a precision and exactness, in effect reductive. He divides the action into four sections, no doubt accurate in some sense, but arbitrary in the divisions, and indeed, even misleading in its time placement of the 'strange things that befell'.

The 1800 version of the 'Argument' contrasts markedly with the version above:

How a Ship, having first sailed to the Equator, was driven by Storms to the cold Country towards the South Pole; how the Ancient Mariner cruelly and in contempt of the laws of hospitality killed a Seabird and how he was followed by many and strange Judgements: and in what manner he came back to his own Country.

This version sacrifices geographical information for the sake of moral commentary, with the exception of one detail: 'the Line' becomes 'the Equator'. This preciseness adds to the sense of a modernized viewpoint, further attested to by the modernized spelling of 'Ancient Mariner'. The 'strange things that befell', a somewhat primitive and, more importantly, altogether uncritical generalization, is replaced by the sermonizing and accusing tone of the second version: cruelty and contempt are attributed to the Ancient Mariner, and not 'strange things' but 'strange Judgements' *followed* him (not 'befell' him). The moral tone and causal connections are much more pronounced, as the killing of the seabird is directly posited as the cause of the things which followed, while in the former version no such connection is alleged.

These changes having been made in 1800, the next edition in 1802 omitted the 'Argument', and it was subsequently omitted from all the editions published in Coleridge's lifetime. What function the 'Argument' was supposed to serve is itself a puzzle. But why it should have been so important as to be revised and then deleted is even more teasing. It seems correct to view the 'Argument' as an early effort at a gloss-like commentary, deleted perhaps because the effect desired was not altogether satisfactory. The desired effect was achieved in the much more elaborate form of the gloss, it seems, since the gloss was then kept in all subsequent editions. This relationship of 'Argument' to gloss is somewhat obscured by the fact that most modern editions include both the 'Argument' and the gloss as if complementary elements, when actually it seems more correct to see the gloss as superseding the 'Argument'. The 'Argument' might be placed more appropriately in a note (in both its versions) than in the body of the poem beneath the title. Only E. H. Coleridge gives enough information on the 'Argument' to make such a theory viable; even his presentation, however, is misleading, since he places the 'Argument' at the head of the poem, and most modern editions follow this model, omitting the information which clarifies the function of the 'Argument'.

This view of the gloss as growing out of the 'Argument' is substantiated both by the changes in the first and second versions and by the similarities of gloss to 'Argument'. For the gloss takes over both of the features of the two versions of the 'Argument', the geographical over-specification and the tone of moral over-determination. Gloss and

'Argument' both focus distractingly upon sequence of action, both act as commentaries or reductions of the poetic verse into a prose narrative account, and both create an authorial persona distinct from the narrator–poet. The archaic spelling of the 1798 version, the naïvety of the account suggested in the tone, and the phrases 'Great Pacific Ocean', 'the cold Country', and other peculiarities of diction or style all contribute to an authorial persona. The voice of the 1800 version is even more marked, and more similar to the gloss persona in its moralizing. The persona of the 1817 gloss, while most clearly distinct from the narrator–poet by virtue of his moralizing tone, is also distinguished by the more specific information he gives and by the extraordinary reference in the gloss facing lines 131–4:

A Spirit had followed them; one of the invisible inhabitants of this planet, neither departed souls nor angels; concerning whom the learned Jew, Josephus, and the Platonic Constantinopolitan, Michael Psellus, may be consulted. They are very numerous, and there is no climate or element without one or more.

It is tempting to see the persona of the 1798 'Argument' version as close to if not indeed identical with the narrator–poet, though this assimilation would seem to offend the sense of chasmic difference between the discursive, reductive, and time/space specificity of the former and the poetic freedom from any constraints of that sort of the narrator–poet. It is probably better simply to view the personas of both versions of the 'Argument' as well as that of the gloss, as separate from the narrator–poet, but undergoing increasing distinction from the narrator–poet as the persona is developed from the less definite character of the 1798 version, through the moralizing tone of 1800, and finally to the full-blown Neo-Platonist commentator of the 1817 edition. The modernizing of the archaic diction of 1798 may have been an effort to universalize the narrator–poet by further distinguishing him from the Ancient Mariner, and from the gloss persona.

The Gloss

This interpretation of the 'Argument' as an embryo gloss, important for an understanding of Coleridge's attitude to the gloss and its development, also suggests three characteristics to look for in the fully expanded gloss: a persona, a moral tone toward the 'strange things that befell', and a time sequence of the action with geographical and spatial over-specification. These three features of the 'Argument' in both versions are also probably the most important elements of the expanded text of the gloss for determining the relation of gloss to verse text.[13] The primary difference between the gloss and the 'Argument' is the sustained effect upon a reading of the verse that the extensive gloss achieves. The effect is beyond anything the short 'Argument' could conceivably accomplish. The second difference is the highly poetic language of the gloss (which will be discussed below). This poetic style of the gloss often obscures for readers the distinction in speaking voices between the verse narrator–poet and the gloss writer. Nevertheless, however poetic the gloss may be, even at its most intensely poetic level it has a very different effect upon the reader from the verse: it never is 'saying the same thing' as the verse.

The two most characteristic elements of the gloss setting it apart from the verse are its geographical specifications and its technique of streamlining the narrative so that the sequence of events and their causal connections are made more clear. The verse is correspondingly vague on these three categories of time, space, and causality. The effect of the additional specification in the gloss is to externalize the action of the sea-journey, thereby firmly locating it outside the subjective experience of reader or poet. But one might want to argue that sufficient 'thingifying' has already occurred in the verse, and that what is now needed is a reassimilation of these external events so that their representative value and metaphorical dimension as mental landscape gradually dawns on the reader. To externalize further as the gloss does is to miss the landscape metaphor of a psychological or spiritual journey;[14] in epistemological terms, it is to see 'a thing' and to fail to know it as also 'a thought' (thus the relation between thing and thought becomes a primary focus for theories of perception and artistic creation). The preoccupations in the gloss with time sequence, causality, and spatial determinations seem contrary to the imaginative spirit explicitly free of the ordinary laws of time, space, and causality, both as it is exemplified in the verse's imaginative language, and as the imagination is described elsewhere by Coleridge.[15]

For in commenting on 'the poetic effect of Spenser', Coleridge makes the following remark, and draws attention to the level of internalized action and mental landscape identical with the imaginative level of 'The Ancient Mariner':

You will take especial note of the marvellous independence and true imaginative absence of all particular space or time in the Faery Queen . . . It is truly . . . of mental space. The poet has placed you in a dream, a charmed sleep, and you neither wish, nor have the power, to inquire where you are, or how you got there.

(*Misc. C.*, 36)

Such a remark indicates that the imaginative process for the reader must be one of internalizing the action of the poem, so that the drama, located literally in natural space, is relocated into mental space and thereby assimilated imaginatively into the experience of the reader. 'Thing' becomes 'Thought', and the drama of the poem becomes also the drama of the reading mind as it seeks metaphors to identify the literal actions in the poetic context with mental actions in the drama of the mind's struggle to apprehend some reality.

The association of imagination with an absence of particulars of time and space makes possible a sharp distinction between the verse text and the gloss. The marked contrast between the two seems to function as a poetic and structural embodiment of the distinction between imagination and understanding. Coleridge's distinction between the symbol[16] and the allegory further points out the importance of the freedom from 'particular time or space' in imaginative discourse:

> It is among the miseries of the present age that it recognizes no medium between *Literal* and *Metaphorical*. Faith is either to be buried in the dead letter, or its name and honors usurped by a counterfeit product of the mechanical understanding, which in the blindness of self-complacency confounds SYMBOLS with ALLEGORIES. Now an Allegory is but a translation of abstract notions into a picture-language which is itself nothing but an abstraction from objects of the senses; the principal being more worthless even than its phantom proxy, both alike unsubstantial, and the former shapeless to boot. On the other hand a Symbol (ὅ ἐστιν ἀεὶ ταυτηγόρικον) is characterized by a translucence of the Special in the Individual or of the General in the Especial or of the Universal in the General. Above all by the translucence of the Eternal through and in the Temporal. It always partakes of the Reality which it renders intelligible; and while it enunciates the whole, abides itself as a living part in that Unity, of which it is the representative.
>
> (*LS (CC)* 30)

This passage is architectonic of a Platonic ontology in its four-fold schema, and the latter part is further explained by the following passage from a notebook, having peculiar relevance to the poem under discussion:

> . . . and this leads us at once to the Symbolical, which cannot perhaps be better defined, in distinction from the Allegorical, than that it is always itself a *part* of that of the whole of which it is representative—Here comes a *Sail*—that is, Ship, is a symbolical Expression—Behold our Lion, when we speak of some gallant Soldier, is allegorical—of most importance to our own present subject, that the latter cannot be other than spoken consciously/ while in the former it is very possible that *the general truth* represented may be working unconsciously in the Poet's mind during the construction of the

symbol—yet proves itself by being produced out of his own mind, as the Don Quixote out of the perfectly sane mind of Cervantes—& not by outward observation or historically—/. [The advantage of symbolical writing over allegory, that it presumes no disjunction of Faculty—simple *predomination*]

(*CN* III 4503 f 134, March 1819)

But the gloss seems frequently to veer dangerously toward allegory, and more specifically, toward a moralizing allegory (as will be detailed below). The following distinction between the understanding and the reason is an apt expression of the difference in effect between the gloss and the verse:

That hidden mystery in every, the minutest, form of existence, which contemplated under the relations of time presents itself to the understanding retrospectively, as an infinite ascent of Causes, and prospectively as an interminable progression of Effects—that which contemplated in Space is beheld intuitively as a law of action and re-action, continuous and extending beyond all bound—this same mystery freed from the phenomena of Time and Space, and seen in the depth of *real* Being, reveals itself to the pure Reason as the actual immanence of ALL in EACH.

(*LS (CC)* 49–50)

One of the most exemplary attitudes of the gloss is to make gestures at reducing the lines glossed by an immediate act of abstraction from the poetry, so that although information is not actually added or specified more precisely, it is presented in abstract categories avoided by the verse. The gloss reduces happenings to *things* standing in relation to one another and thus externalized, while the verse holds them in an immediate apprehension or perception. Specific examples of these differences are necessary for a full appreciation of the gloss in relation to the verse text. For instance, an early gloss passage exemplifies this more subtle reduction from the immediacy of sensations in the verse to the more categorized, 'reduced' reportage of the gloss:

| The Mariner tells how the ship sailed southward with a good wind and fair weather, till it reached the Line. | The ship was cheered, the harbour cleared, Merrily did we drop Below the kirk, below the hill, Below the lighthouse top. | 21 |
| | The Sun came up upon the left, Out of the sea came he! And he shone bright, and on the right Went down into the sea. | 25 |

> Higher and higher every day,
> Till over the mast at noon   30

A comparison of the gloss with the verse reveals the remarkable difference in the effect of each text. The verse speaks in concrete and sensuous images which appeal directly to the mind and have a correspondingly direct effect of communicating sun, sea, brightness, and movement of the ship through the changes in its relation with the sun. An outward, forward, southward movement is not sensed at all. Yet precisely this linear, outward movement is expressed by the gloss. Such movement is expressed otherwise in verse lines 22–4: one feels as if the ship is dropping backward away from the known world of civilization into the unknown of nature, of vast seas and sun, or correspondingly, into the vast sea of the subconscious. Note too in lines 25–8 that the passing of a day is communicated by images and movements of the sun. It is never reported that 'a day passed', though this is what our gloss writer might have said about these lines. Lines 29–30 imply that many days pass, and that the ship is sailing toward the equator, but this is not how the information is expressed. The *effect* of sun and water, of the intensity growing as the sun moves higher and higher, is described by the verse. Though of course the conclusions the gloss writer reaches are 'correct', the objection is simply that they are conclusions and deductions for the sake of information and discursive treatment, thereby stripping the sensuous imagery of its mysterious power of arousing the mind. The most obvious deduction is 'with a good wind'; and of course the verse descriptions imply 'fair weather'; also when the sun is over the mast at noon the ship probably *is* close to the equator. But here the gloss is in spirit at cross purposes with the symbolic and imaginatively evocative power of the verse.

The next gloss but one achieves a similar closure as the ship is made to progress 'toward the south pole'. Not only does the geographical specification destroy the wonderful sense of moving into an unknown, unlocatable region of intense cold, ice, and snow; it also inhibits the gradual awakening of the spiritually and mentally metaphorical level of a psychological journey, and the confrontation with supernatural or sub-conscious forces, found in the physically powerful and concrete imagery of the ice and snow and alienation from civilization. Objects, in the gloss, are definite, external things, in explicit relations to one another, such as the ship, the storm, the south pole. In the verse there is a freedom from naming; the storm is not a thing, but a blast of energy, personified to increase the poetic effect. The ship is not just a ship but a heaving mass of effort to keep afloat, 'sloping masts and dipping prow', also a person, a chased victim, who 'forward bends his head', and ship and storm are caught in a human context of combat and pursuit. The naming of these elemental forces in the gloss seems to deplete the energy and intense openness of the verse.

The gloss continues its naming and generalizing gestures in the next passage; they have the effect of externalizing the action and distancing it altogether from the mind. It describes the 'land of ice and snow', which suggests, in 'land', a fixity and stability, and a 'thingness' which the verse seems to defy: the ice is in motion, there is no sense of land at all: 'And ice, mast-high, came floating by,/As green as emerald.' The 'fearful sounds' and 'no living things' of the gloss are categorizations *par excellence* of the verse lines, as for example: 'It cracked and growled, and roared and howled,/Like noises in a swound!' The presence of the gloss is a constant reminder that the poetry communicates not information of a time/space/causality sort, but effects of a metaphorical and imaginative sort that must indeed avoid such informative gestures if they are to succeed in arousing more than the mere understanding.

The albatross then appears through the fog 'as if it had been a Christian soul'; this simile and the mystery surrounding its appearance in the icy, lifeless realm makes it possible to focus on the symbolic and poetic function of the albatross, at least until the gloss intrudes with 'Till a great sea-bird, called the Albatross . . .'. 'Sea-bird' directs the attention to a literal, external animal, and then depletes the symbolic aspect, whereas in the verse the thing which comes is first and only an 'Albatross', *like* a Christian soul, and not a sea-bird at all. In the gloss it is first a sea-bird, and only *called* an albatross. But the gloss thus calls attention to its method by this line, when it calls the thing, that is, names it. The verse seeks to evoke associations and connotations, and not confine the albatross to being a mere sea-bird, but seeks to heighten its symbolic connections.

A further example of the orientation of the gloss toward information gestures comes in the gloss passage to lines 103–10. The gloss explains that 'the ship enters the Pacific Ocean, and sails northward, even till it reaches the Line.' It thus places the drama in the actual, external world while the verse says 'We were the first that ever burst/Into that silent sea.' Which sea is left unnamed by the verse; nor is it at all clear that the ship has once again returned to the 'Line'. While the gloss seems to chart a linear, forward movement, the verse suggests a bursting into a new realm of experience, a completely different movement.

Part III begins with a fascinating example of the technique of the gloss to over-determine and specify. The Ancient Mariner says 'When looking westward, I beheld/A something in the sky.' (lines 147–8). This 'something' is then vaguely referred to as 'a mist', 'a speck', or 'a shape'. The gloss superstitiously refers to this as a 'sign', and in the next passage it becomes explicitly a ship. Yet in the next fifty lines,

the verse never once calls this 'something' a ship, while the gloss
constantly determines it as such. Indeed, the 'something' is as much
not a ship as a ship; it is a mysterious thing inadequately referred
to as a ship. For a ship is a known, and this is an unknown, mysterious,
and supernatural something which cannot be constrained by natural
laws of movement and space: 'Without a breeze, without a tide,/She
steadies with upright keel!' (lines 169–70) This unearthly, unreal
quality, the very presence of which is appalling, is dissipated by naming
it a ship; the inadequacy is even indicated by the gloss writer posing
the question 'For can it be a ship that comes onward without wind or
tide?'

The personifications of the next few lines contrast too with the dry
and factual impersonality of the gloss, and colour the verse with a
primitive, mythical tone. The 'something' in the sky has now become a
'strange shape' and then a 'she', while in the gloss the references are
to a ship, and 'it'. The sun 'peered/With broad and burning face'
as if through a dungeon-grate; in the gloss this lively metaphor has
turned into a cliché: 'the face of the setting sun' is a mere surface with
no genuine personifying aspect.

The closely following gloss to lines 195–8 now interpolates the
action in an audacious and aggressive way. The verse is almost annoy-
ingly unclear about the stakes or the winner, but the gloss happily
establishes the 'facts'. The uncertainty of the winner is revealed in the
wording of the gloss, as '(the latter)' is added to clarify what is far from
clear. The connections moreover between the game, the subsequent
events, and the two deathly women are quite uncertain in the verse.
The gloss offers only one possible interpretation, and ends Part III
by continuing its references to 'Life-in-Death' working on the Ancient
Mariner. The verse makes such causal claims and agents much less
obvious.

The last few gloss passages of Part III also aptly illustrate the technique of abstract description and conventional diction of the gloss,
as contrasted with the evocative, sensuous imagery of the verse. The
gloss reports 'No twilight within the courts of the sun'. The verse
appeals to detailed perceptions: 'The Sun's rim dips; the stars rush
out:/At one stride comes the dark.' Then, 'His shipmates drop down
dead' is a gloss translation of 'Four times fifty living men,/(And I
heard nor sigh nor groan)/With heavy thump, a lifeless lump,/They
dropped down one by one' (lines 216–19).

In Part IV one of the most interesting of the gloss passages is the
poetic reverie affixed to lines 263–70, a passage often called upon as
an argument against the gloss writer as an ironized, reductive reader.
Yet by giving the character of the gloss persona a poetic sensitivity,
Coleridge can imply how pervasive and deeply rooted the tendency

and habit of reductive response to nature and art is.[17] It seems to infect the most intelligent and sensitive of minds at times, for it is a fact of perception that response degenerates with time, and must be revitalized. But even at this moment of high poetry in the gloss (rare enough to count as a marked exception), the social and cultural associations imposed here by the gloss upon the verse are out of place and obtrusive, however poetically expressed they may be. In the gloss the reader never feels the naked power of the pantheistic elemental forces that the verse, in spite of references to Christianity, constantly affirms, as for example in the contrast between gloss and verse texts of lines 271–81.

Part V opens with a characteristic effort in the gloss to establish connections and causal relations. In the verse the connection between Mary and the sleep, lines 291–5, seems at most rhetorical, and yet this reference is taken up, and the connection in the verse of dreams of rain during this sleep is telescoped into 'By grace of the holy Mother, the ancient Mariner is refreshed with rain.' Thus the quite indirect and completely unexpressed relation of Mary to rain is directly established by the gloss. The gloss then generalizes the extraordinary imagery of lines 309–26 into 'sounds and . . . strange sights and commotions', and it is at moments where the contrast of gloss and verse is so ominous that the reader must wonder why such superfluous narrative reduction has been added to the poem at all. When the gloss is often no more than a facade distracting the reader from the beauty of such lines as 'The upper air burst into life!/And a hundred fire-flags sheen', it seems to expose itself as the ironic, reductive paraphrase of ordinary perception, as contrasted with the imaginative awareness inspired by the verse.

The next few gloss passages establish with disturbing clarity the narrative sequence of events, reassert the Neo-Platonic orientation in the text facing lines 345–9, report the return of the ship to the 'Line', and identify the speakers as the fellow demons of the Polar Spirit. In the verse they are only 'two voices in the air', discerned '*in my soul*', not positioned outside the Ancient Mariner's psyche at all, as the gloss implies.

The gloss of Parts VI and VII continues with abstractions, generalizations, and over-determinations of the sort encountered in the first four parts. Most strikingly, it reduces the verse in these last two parts of the poem to a dry narrative sequence of events almost unrelieved by any poetic gestures. Each gloss passage seems to try to isolate a single event, and the resulting short, choppy sentences destroy any of the immediacy and open fluidity of the verse. Note the contrast, for instance, between the details and immediacy of the impressions described as happening in the verse lines following, as opposed to the generalized deduction of the Gloss:

And the ancient Mariner beholdeth his native country.	Oh! dream of joy! is this indeed The light-house top I see? Is this the hill? is this the kirk? Is this mine own countree?	464

Similarly the following contrast:

The ship suddenly sinketh.	Under the water it rumbled on, Still louder and more dread: It reached the ship, it split the bay; The ship went down like lead.	546

Because in these two sections of the poem the most obvious character-istic of the gloss is the sequential presentation of events, the selectivity of the gloss is also most evident. The gloss presents only some of the isolable events, a fact which further exposes its very restricted point of view. For instance, in Part VII, it seems strange that the gloss should make no mention of the events of the Pilot's fit or the boy's madness. Nor does it mention that the Mariner has arrived upon land, line 570, an obvious event to catalogue in the gloss. The gloss writer also fails to note that the Mariner tells his tale to the Hermit; and it falsely puts the emphasis in lines 580–90 on travelling from land to land, instead of on being 'wrenched' to narrate the tale.

The most notable contrast between the gloss and the verse is prob-ably not the specification of particular space, time, and causality in the gloss; its moralizing, exhibited everywhere, is a still more perva-sive feature of the gloss. While the former three features act as elements in a theory of perception (and subsequently of reality) as bounded by these organizing categories of mind, the latter takes the reader to a higher level of experience and presents a theory of culture.| This cultural theory asserts that nature is as much bounded by cultural categories as it is by space, time, and causality. Culture to some extent determines our concept of and response to nature. Nature is therefore not the opposite of culture, but a product of it.

The gloss moralizes by interpolating guilt, blame, remorse, super-stition, omens, cause and agency, sin, and retribution into the action of the poem, while in the verse moralizing is specifically and markedly excluded. Nor is this conventional moralizing in the gloss consonant with Coleridge's own insistence, in reply to a comment by a reader that the moral was not emphasized enough, that, on the contrary, it intruded too far (note the irony about the 'probability'):

Mrs. Barbauld once told me that she admired the Ancient Mariner very much, but that there were two faults in it,—it was improbable, and had no moral. As for the probability, I owned that that might admit some question; but as to the want of a moral, I told her that in my own judgment the poem had too much; and that the only, or chief fault, if I might say so, was the obtrusion of the moral sentiment so openly on the reader as a principle or cause of action in a work of such pure imagination. It ought to have had no more moral than the Arabian Nights' tale of the merchant's sitting down to eat dates by the side of a well, and throwing the shells aside, and lo! a genie starts up, and says he *must* kill the aforesaid merchant, *because* one of the date shells had, it seems, put out the eye of the genie's son.

(*TT*, 31 May 1830)

Unless one sees the gloss within an ironic context of a caricatured, reductionist, and moralizing reader, it is difficult to understand why it would have been included in the poem at all. Coleridge's description of the faults of Bowles's poetry in a letter of 1802 to William Sotheby is strikingly applicable to the technique of the gloss writer:

Bowles's Stanzas on Navigation are among the best in that second Volume/ but the whole volume is woefully inferior to it's Predecessor. There reigns thro' all the blank verse poems such a perpetual trick of *moralizing* every thing—which is very well, occasionally—but never to see or describe any interesting appearance in nature, without connecting it by dim analogies with the moral world, proves faintness of Impression. Nature has her proper interest; & he will know what it is, who believes & feels, that every Thing has a Life of it's own, & that we are all *one Life*. A Poet's *Heart & Intellect* should be *combined*, *intimately* combined & *unified*, with the great appearances in Nature—& not merely held in solution & loose mixture with them, in the shape of formal Similies. I do not mean to *exclude* these formal Similies— there are moods of mind, in which they are natural—pleasing moods of mind, & such as a Poet will often have, & sometimes express; but they are not his highest, & most appropriate moods. They are 'Sermoni propiora' which I once translated—'Properer for a Sermon'.

(*CL* II 864)

The gloss also seems to exhibit this 'perpetual trick of moralizing every thing', and certainly is aptly described by the lines, 'never to see or describe any interesting appearance in nature, without connecting it by dim analogies with the moral world'. A much later rejection of moralizing comes in the *Biographia*, when Coleridge explains that 'the communication of pleasure is the introductory means by which alone the poet must expect to moralize his readers' (*BL* II ch. xxii 105).[18]

Thus the description of Bowles in the letter extract above might also be said to describe the persona represented by the gloss writer, but in relation to a reader rather than to a poet. The letter continues by comparing fancy and imagination, and contrasts Greek with Hebrew poetry; it ends by discussing Milton's depths of meaning and the religious implications of his poetry. The entire letter helps to understand what Coleridge meant by rejecting 'moralizing' in art. It is not that he is being pantheistic or rejecting moral implications in art.[19] He is attacking rather the moralizing of a direct, dogmatic, and hence ineffective sort in art. Art and nature responded to imaginatively will, in their characteristic, appropriate ways—by means of beauty and pleasure—activate the moral feelings much more effectively from within than any imposition of allegorical or analogical moral meanings. This is immediately illustrated by the success of the verse lines 270-90 in communicating and making us deeply feel that 'every Thing has a Life of it's own, & that we are all *one Life*.' The gloss on the contrary is only able to present a cliché which neither makes us feel nor communicates anything when it says, 'And to teach, by his own example, love and reverence to all things that God made and loveth' (lines 610-14).

The gloss, however, does indeed allegorize and 'moralize every thing', and contrasts with the vividness of the impressions effected by the verse. The 'trick of moralizing' begins at the end of Part I, when the gloss describes the albatross as a 'bird of good omen' on two separate occasions (lines 71 and 80), and later refers to it as a bird of 'good luck' (line 94). The gloss also connects the bird as the cause of the strong wind which springs up and moves the ship out of its ice-bound stillness, while the verse only indicates an unknown conjunction of events (lines 69-72). When later, the sailors aver the connection, they then promptly reject it to aver the opposite. Their claims are made to seem both superstitious and unfounded, just as the gloss writer's moral claim that the bird rewards the mariners with a good wind should be understood.

The gloss in Part II then introduces 'justification', 'crime', and 'accomplices' into the drama, while the verse simply charts the change in attitude of the mariners to the slaying of the albatross, with no moral suggestion. This introduction of words charged with cultural significance to interpret the events directly connects the gloss with the second version of the 'Argument'. For it mentions 'cruelty', 'contempt', 'Judgements', and 'laws of hospitality'. It is not at all clear from the verse that the killing is a 'crime'; the event of killing is kept in the verse utterly mysterious and unexplained. There is no hint of motivation or intention whatsoever. An inability to appreciate the distinction between killing as an event and killing as a crime only exposes the thickness of the moral spectacles through which the world is interpreted.

In the gloss to lines 120-3, the ship's having been becalmed is interpreted as a sign that the albatross is avenged, but this vengeance is only another example of the 'dim analogies' with the moral world that even good poets sometimes connect with natural events. No such connection is made in the verse between the killing of the albatross and the becalming of the ship, until the mariners themselves hang the dead bird around the Ancient Mariner's neck. But the mariners themselves have already been exposed as intensely superstitious and opportunistic: *their* interpretation of the events can hardly be taken as a model of sophistication. The verse does not by any means preclude such a connection, but it does not directly offer it as the 'explanation': it leaves the possibility open for a much more complex and cosmic interpretation of the significance of the events.

The gloss immediately following the passage on vengeance exhibits more precisely than on any other occasion the Neo-Platonic perspective of the persona, and even connects him with the criticism of Greek poets made by Coleridge in the same letter quoted above. Coleridge contrasted Greek poetry with the truly imaginative poetry of the Hebrews, and with the truly imaginative spirit of Platonism, in contrast even to Neo-Platonism.[20] The gloss describes several levels of spirits, or 'invisible inhabitants of this planet', from departed souls and angels to spirits of some other kind, which 'no climate or element' is without (line 135). Coleridge best described this animation of the natural world with spirits in his letter to Sotheby:

> It must occur to every Reader that the Greeks in their religious poems address always the Numina Loci, the Genii, the Dryads, the Naiads, &c &c—All natural Objects were *dead*—mere hollow Statues—but there was a Godkin or Goddessling *included* in each—In the Hebrew Poetry you find nothing of this poor Stuff—as poor in genuine Imagination, as it is mean in Intellect —/At best, it is but Fancy, or the aggregating Faculty of the mind—not *Imagination*, or the *modifying*, and *coadunating* Faculty . . . In the Hebrew Poets each Thing has a Life of it's own, & yet they are all one Life.
>
> (*CL* II 865–6)

The moralizing of the gloss continues in Part IV with imputations of 'horrible penance' (line 231), and then describes the Mariner's response to the water snakes as hate and envy. But the verse lines are rich with detailed acts and sensations, and these never move the reader to the conclusive judgments characteristic of the gloss:

He despiseth the creatures of the calm.	The many men, so beautiful! 236 And they all dead did lie: And a thousand thousand slimy things Lived on; and so did I.
And envieth that they should live, and so many lie dead.	I looked upon the rotting sea, 240 And drew my eyes away; I looked upon the rotting deck, And there the dead men lay.

The reader may never feel that the gloss is actually wrong; what he feels is the sense of a constant determination of meaning from the detailed, concrete sensations and acts reported in the verse. This closure itself, not whether it is reasonable or unreasonable, is the point at issue. The demand for openness made by the verse, in virtue of its freedom from any generalizations or reductions to discursive codes of meaning, sets up a standard of imaginative response as the aesthetic context demands. It contrasts it sharply with the tendency toward the unimaginative, deterministic closure that causes only one of many possible levels of significance to emerge. Art must broaden our horizons, not simply confirm our prejudices and codes of organizing the world, but the gloss uses the verse only as confirmation, while the Wedding Guest has seen beyond his ordinary borders of experience into a profoundly shaking depth of unfamiliarity.

The gloss in Part V creates moral agency in lines 345-9, when it attributes the troop of spirits to the invocation of the guardian saint, and in the last gloss passage of this section the 'voices in the air' heard 'and in my soul discerned', are made entirely external by the gloss, their internal, subconscious, and spiritual existence completely lost. The gloss then mentions that 'penance long and hard for the ancient Mariner hath been accorded to the Polar Spirit, who returneth southward', but this is entirely a fabricated interpretation of the gloss writer in its particulars about the penance.

The moral at the end of the poem is the occasion on which the bias of the Mariner himself intrudes most obviously. And it reminds the reader that he also from time to time has interpolated according to certain cultural and religious preconceptions. But these interpolations which occurred, though only very occasionally in comparison with the constant preoccupations of the gloss, quite clearly establish a personality and limited perspective for the Ancient Mariner, whereas the gloss seems implicitly and by its very nature to make claims for omniscience and authority. Yet the preconceptions and moral categories into which it fits the events of the poem seem to demand that the gloss writer also be seen as a personality of limited perspective, and furthermore even as an ironized reader. Such a reader, far from being the model and standard of response, as a gloss might seem to suggest, is a model of the wrong approach to reading, doubly effective in its contrast with the Wedding Guest and the narrator–poet.

The gloss then functions as a stark contrast to the method of communication of the poem. Coleridge's own statements quoted above about moralizing seem to suggest that the gloss was not added as a Christianizing, constraining commentary on an otherwise pantheistic, imaginative speculation. The contrast here is not between pantheism (verse) and Christianity (gloss), but between a falsely moralizing response to art—equally false to the real spirit of religion and morals—and a genuinely aesthetic, imaginative participation in experience at its most unfamiliar and unknown outskirts. The gloss presents a persona of the Bowles type described above, a model not only of moralizing art, but at a more general level a parodying of the process of perception as it unreflectively classifies, categorizes, and names too quickly. The mind closes in upon impressions and sensations and organizes them according to habit and custom, so that only selected aspects of the total significance are perceived. Other possibilities of meaning, context, and relationship are simply filtered out by the perceiving mind and never known.

The response of the Wedding Guest, his final stunned state, and his silence show that the tale has done far more than simply to teach him 'love and reverence to all things'. He seems to have undergone a genuine transformation of his ordinary view of human experience and its possibilities. But the world view of the gloss writer has not been altered; he has succeeded in incorporating all that has happened into it, unchanged. That the Wedding Guest is the model of an audience is suggested by the fact that he is one of the elected listeners: 'That moment that his face I see,/I know the man that must hear me:/To him my tale I teach' (lines 588–90).

The gloss has left the poem untouched, though it purports to 'gloss' it. But for Coleridge the word 'gloss' had ambivalent implications: he wavered at one time between 'gloss' and 'feign' and 'paint'.[21] As in the preface to 'Kubla Khan', Coleridge has 'feigned' an attitude that seems to provide an occasion for the sketching out of an inadequate response, in order to awaken the reader to the typical ways of misreading and misperceiving. A glimpse of one's own incomplete reading of the poem by means of the gloss, along with an alternative model of reading, builds up an ironic or self-conscious context around an aesthetic experience and renders it more completely accessible.

3

The Radiating Imagination and the Censorious Reason in 'The Eolian Harp'

The Text

The Eolian Harp

Composed at Clevedon, Somersetshire

My pensive Sara! thy soft cheek reclined
Thus on mine arm, most soothing sweet it is
To sit beside our Cot, our Cot o'ergrown
With white-flower'd Jasmin, and the broad-leav'd Myrtle,
(Meet emblems they of Innocence and Love!)   5
And watch the clouds, that late were rich with light,
Slow saddening round, and mark the star of eve
Serenely brilliant (such should Wisdom be)
Shine opposite! How exquisite the scents
Snatch'd from yon bean-field! and the world *so* hush'd!   10
The stilly murmur of the distant Sea
Tells us of silence.

        And that simplest Lute,
Placed length-ways in the clasping casement, hark!
How by the desultory breeze caress'd,
Like some coy maid half yielding to her lover,   15
It pours such sweet upbraiding, as must needs
Tempt to repeat the wrong! And now, its strings
Boldlier swept, the long sequacious notes
Over delicious surges sink and rise   20
Such a soft floating witchery of sound
As twilight Elfins make, when they at eve
Voyage on gentle gales from Fairy-Land,
Where Melodies round honey-dropping flowers,
Footless and wild, like birds of Paradise,

Nor pause, nor perch, hovering on untam'd wing!   25
O! the one Life within us and abroad,
Which meets all motion and becomes its soul,
A light in sound, a sound-like power in light,
Rhythm in all thought, and joyance every where—
Methinks, it should have been impossible   30
Not to love all things in a world so fill'd;
Where the breeze warbles, and the mute still air
Is Music slumbering on her instrument.

And thus, my Love! as on the midway slope
Of yonder hill I stretch my limbs at noon,   35
Whilst through my half-clos'd eye-lids I behold
The sunbeams dance, like diamonds, on the main,
And tranquil muse upon tranquillity;
Full many a thought uncall'd and undetain'd,
And many idle flitting phantasies,   40
Traverse my indolent and passive brain,
As wild and various as the random gales
That swell and flutter on this subject Lute!

And what if all of animated nature
Be but organic Harps diversely fram'd,   45
That tremble into thought, as o'er them sweeps
Plastic and vast, one intellectual breeze,
At once the Soul of each, and God of all?

But thy more serious eye a mild reproof
Darts, O belovéd Woman! nor such thoughts   50
Dim and unhallow'd dost thou not reject,
And biddest me walk humbly with my God.
Meek Daughter in the family of Christ!
Well hast thou said and holily disprais'd
These shapings of the unregenerate mind;   55
Bubbles that glitter as they rise and break
On vain Philosophy's aye-babbling spring.
For never guiltless may I speak of him,
The Incomprehensible! save when with awe
I praise him, and with Faith that inly *feels*;*   60
Who with his saving mercies healéd me,
A sinful and most miserable man,
Wilder'd and dark, and gave me to possess
Peace, and this Cot, and thee, Heart-honour'd Maid!

*L'athée n'est point à mes yeux un faux esprit; je puis vivre avec lui aussi bien et mieux qu'avec le dévot, car il raisonne davantage, mais il lui manque un sens, et mon ame ne se fond point entièrement avec la sienne: il est froid au spectacle le plus ravissant, et il cherche un syllogisme lorsque je rends une action de grace. 'Appel a l'impartiale postérité,' par la Citoyenne Roland, troisième partie, p. 67.

'The Eolian Harp',[1] probably the most successful of Coleridge's early poems, seems to illustrate in a number of ways both the struggle with associationism and an attitude toward the mind as fundamentally creative in perception. Most obviously, the poem establishes a relationship between the speaker and the surrounding landscape in Stanza I by a gradual progression through the imagery from a state of relative passive observation to a highly responsive, articulate level of appreciation.[2] The active and passive alternatives are further contrasted in the characters of Sara and the speaker, offering the related analogies of types of readers or types of mental faculties, though this finally becomes clear only in Stanza IV. The complexity of the conflict between an active and a passive theory of mind is drawn out in Stanza II, with its references to language as music and the paradoxical relation of silence to 'telling'. For both suggest that the nature of communication is problematic and possibly indirect, so that what appears to be passivity, silence, and solitude, may actually be the generative conditions of creative activity, while the apparently active may be a distraction to imagination.

Once Stanza I has introduced the problematic nature of the mind as creative or passive in perception and observation, and after Stanza II has developed the paradoxical relation of the active to the passive through the idea of the language of silence and music, or of language with crucial non-verbal significations, Stanza III seems actually to delineate that which constitutes creative activity. The speaker is made to achieve an explicit identification of the external 'object Lute' with himself as subject consciousness, or as 'subject Lute'.

A similar empathic identification takes place when Coleridge compares the harp to a bird in a notebook entry, some years later. The entry is interesting as an example in prose of the empathic identification which plays an important part in the romantic aesthetic:

O that sweet Bird! Where is it?—it is encaged somewhere out of Sight—but from my bedroom at the Courier office, from the window of which I look out on the walls of the Lyceum, I hear it, early Dawn—often alas! then lulling me to late Sleep—again when I awake—& all day long.—It is in Prison—all its Instincts ungratified—yet it feels the Influence of Spring—& calls with unceasing Melody to the Loves, that dwell in Fields & Greenwood bowers—; unconscious perhaps that it calls in vain.—O are they the Songs of a happy enduring Day-dream? has the Bird Hope? Or does it abandon itself to the Joy of its Frame—a living Harp of Eolus?—O that I could do so!

(*CN* III 3314, 16 May 1808)

After he empathically identifies himself and his thoughts with the lute and its melodies, the speaker then sweeps all of nature into the comparison and makes the lute–mind a symbol of all organic life.

The initial assimilation of the external into the internal individual experience is thus balanced by that further expansive movement outward toward something higher than the individual, but not necessarily external to it. This two-fold imaginative movement is enriched by a still more immediate level of response for the reader. The poem gives signs that the poet recognizes an analogy between the lute as object of attention and of empathic identification, and his poem as object, an analogy having a corresponding significance for the poem in relation to the reader.

Finally, 'The Eolian Harp' may be described as another one of those poems of Coleridge's exhibiting a framework. The speaker's relation to Sara and to his cot constitutes this hypothesized boundary in the structure of the poem. Sara begins and ends the poem, with its very domestic setting, and with the single exception of line 34, 'My Love ...', she does not intrude from line 6 to line 48. Like the frameworks of the gloss and the preface, a censorious, reductionist, literal-minded, and pre-eminently passive observer seems to be contrasted with the creative perception of the speaker. The contrast may be seen as a characterization of the conflict within the mind between the reason and the understanding, the active and the passive faculties. For a creative theory of mind does not deny that the mind is often passive, or, as Coleridge says, degenerates through custom and familiarity. It rather asserts that this degenerate passivity is insufficient to account for all the mind's acts. Fundamentally, the mind is creative even in its perception, and experience is the outcome of that initial activity. Passivity is merely the result of a long familiarity with a product that itself originates in creative perception, not independently of it; hence the conflict between the active and the passive.

The Spectator as Creative Participant

As in all the conversation poems discussed here, the opening of each is characterized by an effort to establish either intense silence, a trance-like stillness, or a mood of solitude, as the atmosphere surrounding the speaker of the poem. The ordinary, busy consciousness is lulled, while the metaphorical use of landscape as mental terrain heightens the intensity of the mood and acts to help the reader to begin the process of internalization. Arising at the beginning of the poem, this deep and almost mysterious silence seems to be the posited condition for the awakening of the creative perception about to emerge gently out of the hush until it gradually swells into a floating and wild melody.

Coleridge explained in the following letter extract the primary mode in which nature and landscape, when fully internalized, produce profound effects upon the psyche. The process here described is an analogue of the way in which landscape in poetry can act:

It is melancholy to think, that the best of us are liable to be shaped & coloured by surrounding Objects—and a demonstrative proof, that Man was not made to live in Great Cities! Almost all the physical Evil in the World depends on the existence of moral Evil—and the long-continued contemplation of the latter does not tend to meliorate the human heart.—The pleasures, which we receive from rural beauties, are of little Consequence compared with the Moral Effect of these pleasures—beholding constantly the Best possible we at last become ourselves the best possible.

(*CL* I 154 to George Dyer, 10 March 1795)

The silence and hush that enthralls the speaker's mind is first felt upon his emerging from the cot, when he turns away from the 'Jasmin and broad-leav'd Myrtle', these 'emblems of Innocence and Love', toward the expanse of the sky and nature all around him, rich with changes in light and colour. The last trailings of brightness from the clouds and the first emergence of the brilliant star of eve announce the end of the day, but prolong the moment of twilight before the night closes round. Twilight trembling between the two extremes of light and darkness becomes a point of internalization of the mood as the metaphor for consciousness is perceived. Twilight is like the moment of perfect balance between the conscious and unconscious mind. Placed at the outset of the poem, it suggests that this balance is yet another of the generative conditions of imaginative response, as were the silence and tranquillity. Twilight, as a metaphor for a state of mind, suggests the rare moment when the consciousness is stilled but not yet totally overpowered by the unconsciousness as in sleep or madness. In this 'trembling equipoise' or this 'hovering on untam'd wing' between two opposite states, the conscious side of the mind is alerted to or discovers some external element to which it attends, while the imagination slips through the crevice of the twilight world and infuses that element with symbolic and mythical associations all its own. This element, thus enriched with imaginative value, becomes the focal point whereby it then unfolds itself in an extension of the symbolic imaginative power it was lent. Twilight also becomes an expression of the paradox of the active/passive dichotomy: when the mind is passive at the conscious level, it may be most active at an unconscious level, a level finally erupting into consciousness only after the period of apparent passivity.

Already before the lute has been focused upon as the element in the surroundings most apt for metaphorical elaboration, the humanizing and internalizing processes of the faculty of imagination are at work, flitting from cloud, to star, to bean-field, to sea, until the lute is centred upon; but the imagination leaves its traces on these other less central elements. And throughout the first stanza the gradual emergence of the spectator's creative response is charted through these lesser images. The first genuine example of the imagination at work is seen in the gentle shaping touch which it leaves on the 'clouds, that late were rich with light,/Slow saddening round' (lines 6–7). The clouds are darkening, but in the speaker's imaginative awakening they are 'saddening', a humanizing qualification that, in the context of the beauty of the twilight, suggests a close association of deep delight and pain. This poignancy marks the turning point from simple sweetness of domestic peace to the profound feelings of awe inspired by the next images. The phrase 'slow saddenning round' also manages to move firmly from any sense of the passive, 'to be sad', into a sense of active progression; even 'the clouds sadden round' would not be as effective for movement and activity as is the progressive immediacy of the participial form. 'Round' then suggests a focusing of some coming event, as the whole of the heavens seem about to swing around to centre upon the next increment.

The 'star of eve' becomes temporarily the centre of this gradual change, and indeed the clouds, as well as the speaker, 'mark the star of eve/Serenely brilliant'. For the clouds have given up their last rich light, by which they had obscured the star, to its predominance, and it seems to gather its brilliance from them as they slowly sadden round it, marking it, by the contrast of dark and light, as the central splendour of the sky. The star also, like the clouds, is 'humanized': for it is admired as the perfect symbol of wisdom. Its natural beauty is enhanced by the conscious assimilation of star as a metaphor for the highest of human values. Its appropriateness is apparent on so many different levels that its integrity as a metaphor seems assured, no matter how conventional it may have become, as long as it is used in close intimacy with its surrounding imagery. The star is perhaps most effective as a symbol of imagination through its light as radiation, as a 'centre without a circumference' but with a shape nevertheless. For, paradoxically, the light escaping from the bounds of a circumference is what gives the radial form its indistinct and pulsating shape.[3]

The next four lines reveal a movement downward toward the earth once again, but still outward and away into the expanse rolling out before the speaker. The humanizing process continues,[4] as the 'exquisite scents' are *snatch'd from yon bean-field*. The world is *'so hushed!'* and the distant sea's 'stilly murmur' . . . 'Tells us of silence' (lines 9–12). The movement downward is completed by a return toward the speaker and the lute close by, and the lute takes over now as the germinal point for the next thirty-six lines.

The first stanza is notable also for its progression of verbs, for the verbs seem to chart the movement from passivity to a state of alertness and, finally, intensity, while the subjects of the verbs create an interesting pattern. The stanza begins with the speaker using the impersonal and passive 'it is' as the anchor for the next few infinitives. First, 'to sit' is introduced, and the next verb, 'to watch,' is still passive compared to the succeeding verbs, though apparently more active than 'to sit'. Finally, the speaker 'marks', another progression in the alertness and creativity of his perceptions: he seems, by marking, to isolate an element from the background and colour it with meaning. The last verb in this sequence is furthest removed from the 'it is' clause, but surpasses all the dependent infinitives that preceded it by its power, as 'the star of eve/ . . ./Shine opposite' (lines 7–9). The syntax of this long progression is actually quite complicated. 'Shine', uninflected, still seems to function as an active verb. In a strict sense it probably ought to be the participal form, 'shining'. The requirements of the main verb 'mark' on dependent verbs is not clear. Though the grammatical structure, then, seems to demand an adjectival form of the verb, the effect of preserving the infinitive (without the 'to' indicator) is to heighten the intensity of the action and make it more immediate. The next two lines depend again on an elided form of the verb 'to be', a momentary regression; but the last verb, 'tells', independent of any 'it is' clause, reaches an apex of articulate energy for the entire stanza.

The subject of these verbs is often less easy to determine than the progression from passivity to activity, or from receptive to creative perception; and such uncertainty of authority in action has become, as has been discussed above, a touchstone for subject–object dissolution, reversal of author–reader roles, and imaginative transcendence. In the case of the first verbs, it is difficult, and perhaps not very important, to distinguish Sara from the speaker as subject, though doubtless the speaker is himself a subject even if we must be uncertain of Sara's participation. 'It is sweet' for him (and her?), he sits (she seems to also, vide 'reclined'), but as the poem progresses, her contribution seems less and less certain. This contrast between Sara's and the speaker's participation in the imaginative perception of the beauty around them, and in the active appreciation of it, may act as a model for the active versus the passive mind. The speaker watches the clouds, she perhaps only sees them: certainly it is he who makes the observations of lines 6–7; the clouds are 'saddening round' for him, and they are lately 'rich with light' for him. These much more subjective observations begin to suggest that he is moving out into a world of contemplation all his own. By the time he marks the star of eve, he certainly seems alone: she may notice the star, but by means of a metaphor he marks it as 'serenely brilliant (such should Wisdom be)'.

Surprisingly, a new claimant for the subject authority of 'mark' has arisen, namely the clouds, as was mentioned (in passing) above. But the act of marking by the clouds is much more obviously active than the marking, or observing, of the speaker is likely to seem. This greater activity of the clouds in making the star the centre of the sky, in 'marking' it, by contrast, with their own diffused and fading light, lends a connotation of greater activity to the speaker's 'marking'. That is, it becomes an alternative model to the meaning of 'marking' as merely passive observation. By analogy with the clouds, the speaker's marking becomes not only a seeing and noting of the star, but a gesture of imbuing it with a centrality and significance in the natural heavens as well as in the intellectual universe: thus he marks it as a symbol of wisdom, and in doing this he himself emits a spark of imaginative symbol-making. He articulates a metaphorical relation that might only have made itself vaguely felt, but not known, in the response to the star's serene brilliancy. It may be that all such immediate awareness of beauty is the truth of imaginative relations only vaguely felt but unarticulated and unhumanized. The ambiguity of the grammatical subject of 'mark' suggests another interpretation of the speaker's response, and further distinguishes him from Sara.

While the speaker and the clouds share the subject position for the third main infinitive, the next two verbs seem to belong exclusively to the star and the sea respectively; they are the grammatical subjects. But by analogy with the interpretation of both speaker and cloud sharing subject position syntactically, we may take the model to a metaphorical level, turn the direction of energy around, and say that the speaker is also 'shining' and 'telling'. The star 'shine[s] opposite' and the speaker shines back with his sparks of imagination, as he brightens the star with an intellectual significance in relating it to wisdom. And indeed he sees it *as serenely* brilliant, the simile being an interpretation humanizing the light. He is thus colouring the star with his own imaginings, and it consequently reflects his light. As a further analogy, the speaker also 'tells', for the sea can only metaphorically be said to tell of silence; it is the speaker who interprets the bland sounds from the sea as a 'stilly murmur' telling him of silence.

If the speaker can be understood metaphorically as yet another subject of 'shine' and 'tell', Stanza I offers a delightful topographical design, emerging from this latest point. The 'landscape' of the heavens is now mirrored by the landscape of the earth in terms of the relations amongst the predominant elements. In the heavens the star of eve is at the centre; the fading clouds are hovering round, seen against the background of a darkening sky. At the very humble ground level, the same circular imagery is evident, as the speaker becomes a metaphorical star or source of imaginative light; the 'exquisite scents' snatched from 'yon bean-field' correspond to the clouds emitting their last rays of light, and the distant sea functions in the background like the darkening sky. 'The world *so* hush'd' seems to unify both upper and lower landscapes from the perspective of a circumference, but they are also connected at a centre by the polar line flashing between the star of the heavens, shining opposite, and the imagination of the observer. The word 'opposite' may refer indirectly to the philosophic 'reconciliation of opposites', and be anticipating the reconciliation of subject–mind and object–lute, through the identification of the speaker with the subsidiary image of the star.[5]

These two circles of radiating light attached at the centre seem an apt emblem of the workings of the imagery of this first stanza. The analogy of earth and heaven suggests a further metaphorical level of interpretation: to the literal, sensual, surface level of images and meaning in the poem there is a corresponding intellectual or metaphorical realm of meaning, a realm not of things or images, but of relations, or thoughts, or relations of thoughts.[6] The analogy suggests more specifically that the figure of the circle and of radiation may play an important role in the organization of that intellectual realm of significance, by suggesting the form imaginative activity takes.

Language as Music and Silence

After constructing these corresponding fields of radiating imagery, the first stanza ends with a gentle oxymoron, 'The stilly murmur of the distant Sea/Tells us of silence', poising upon personification, a technique characteristic of the entire stanza. Both devices carry theoretical import, for the lute, the central image of the poem, emerges only after the mind has gone through the preparatory exercises of internalization, that is, through the humanizing of nature and the lulling of the busy faculties by the silence and hushed atmosphere. The stanza finally reaches its apex, through these two conditionings, in an oxymoron of discursive nonsense. Meanwhile in Stanza I there is a movement through the various sense faculties, from simple physical touch ('thy soft cheek reclined'), to sight, smell, and finally sound. When the lute and breeze take over in Stanza II the sound is explicitly musical. But we are warned in the final line that even when sound begins, it will tell us only of silence, suggesting that the words to come will not do more than 'reach into silence'.[7] This too is conceivably a theoretical gesture purporting to reorient the value and function of language, at least in poetry, toward some other end than discursive language; an end paradoxically involving silence. The substitution in Stanza II of music for words to fill this mysterious and entrancing silence may be a mode of specifying more precisely what the function of words is; that is, here they function like music, almost non-verbally, perhaps in an effort to reach back into remote and pre-linguistic intelligence and feeling, into experience, and indeed knowledge.

The speaker's relation to the lute seems then to progress: the setting of Stanza I makes possible the eventual prominence of the lute in Stanza II, where it rises into existence out of the profound hush of the world, but as '*that* . . . Lute', an object only of contemplation and pleasure. Its apparently simple *mechanical* relation to the breeze is described, but the humanization leading to eventual total identification is already taking place in the first few lines. The lute is 'by the desultory breeze *caress'd*', and the next explicit simile is exceeded in personifying power even by the metaphor describing the sound of its music: it is the sound of 'sweet up-braiding', and it calls forth the simile of the 'coy maid'. Indeed this simile seems to have additional reference to the speaker personally: but as a contrast. For Sara's upbraidings starting at line 49 are far from sweet, and far from imaginative—*she* is no character corresponding to the lute, and she does not tempt him 'to repeat the wrong', nor does she 'half-yield'.

The next few lines far exceed the achievement of the humanizing breeze 'caressing' the lyre to pour forth 'sweet upbraidings'. For the words themselves, as was warned in the end of Stanza I, leave 'wordiness', concepts, information, and imagery far behind, as their predominant genius is pure rhythm and musicality: they become music as we read:

> And now, its strings
> Boldlier swept, the long sequacious notes
> Over delicious surges sink and rise,
> Such a soft floating witchery of sound

The meanings of the words are flooded into oblivion by the power of their music. The word 'sequacious' is probably the most effective instance here, taken alone; the richness of the sound of the word is vital to the phrase. The word's semantic content, from the noun 'sequence', is nevertheless enriching: 'following with a smooth, unreasoning regularity'; the meaning itself involves a skilful synthesis of apparent opposites of order and spontaneity, logic without conscious thought, a *sequence* of notes, not a mere succession, and this distinction implicates imagination as the source. The form as adjective is rarely met with and acts both to distance the semantic content and to add a strangeness in the midst of familiarity; it also makes the sound more melodious. Both of these qualities, strangeness in the familiar, and musicality, are characteristic of products of imagination. Such complexity in the 'minute particulars' of the poem are emblems of the poem as a whole and act as symbols of the most basic sort.

Language trembles here as close to the brink of dissolution into a realm of non-verbal experience and beauty as anywhere in poetry, as is explained by the next few lines, this hovering and floating between or amongst the senses and the intelligence. These lines express what the words quoted above and dissolved into music are like for the listening mind:

> Melodies round honey-dropping flowers,
> Footless and wild, like birds of Paradise,
> Nor pause, nor perch, hovering on untam'd wing!

A variation of the lines in the poem occurs in a notebook entry (*CN* I 51):

> Light cargoes ~~waff~~ waft of modulated sound
> From viewless Hybla brought, when Melodies
> Like Birds of Paradise on wings, that aye
> Disport in wild variety of hues,
> Murmur around the honey-dropping flowers.

(According to a letter comment, Coleridge is supposed to have tried to delete the above lines from the published version; see *CL* I 331.)

These lines do not lack musicality either, but they hardly compare to the former. For their predominant mode is imagery, but imagery of a very special force and richness. Such imagery immediately transports the mind away from any crude internal representation by means of the 'mind's eye' of the creatures here referred to and toward metaphorical relations. The 'Melodies . . . nor pause, nor perch, hovering on untam'd wing!', is Coleridge's (and Keats's) favourite characterization of the faculty of imagination, as hovering between or amongst possibilities.[8] Thus the metaphorical relation between melodies and the imagination here emerges. Keats's definition of negative capability catches at a similar suspension of the excluding faculty or the understanding; his criticism of Coleridge here is amusing in its misinterpretion of Coleridge's enthusiasm for following up associations with glee:

> . . . several things dovetailed in my mind, & at once it struck me, what quality went to form a Man of Achievement especially in Literature & which Shakespeare posessed so enormously—I mean Negative Capability, that is when man is capable of being in uncertainties, Mysteries, doubts, without any irritable reaching after fact & reason—Coleridge, for instance, would let go by a fine isolated verisimilitude caught from the Penetralium of mystery, from being incapable of remaining content with half knowledge . . . with a great poet the sense of Beauty overcomes every other consideration, or rather obliterates all consideration.

> (Letter to George and Thomas Keats, 21, 27 [?] December 1817)

The simile of the melodies as 'Like birds of Paradise', 'round honey-dropping flowers,/Footless and wild . . ./hovering on untam'd wing', has another importance. For it brings the harp one further step in its progression from a mechanical object toward ultimate assimilation with the speaker. It is now, through its music, likened to the bird, the latter itself a 'living Harp of Eolus', 'abandoning itself to the Joy of its Frame' (*CN* III 3314). And of course the conventional associations of imagination with the singing bird strengthen the gradual symbolism of the harp through this bird–lute comparison. The two preceding lines do more perhaps than any to bring about explicitly or allegorically the transformation of the external landscape and the here and now of twilight and bean-fields into an internal imaginative realm, and then become a description of the composing of the poem:

> [Such a soft floating witchery of sound]
> As twilight Elfins make, when they at eve
> Voyage on gentle gales from Fairy-Land

Again, like the previous lines, these do not lack musicality, nor indeed do they lack imagery, but their predominant mode of significance is that purely self-referential technique pointing directly at imagination and its play. That is, there is no objective correlative for 'twilight Elfins' of 'Fairy Land'. Both appeal to the pure imagination and are in that way disembodied images: they elude the literal mind's effort to form pictures in the mind's eye, and they force it toward imaginative response.

The mind of the speaker, now opened emotionally by musical release, reacts in the next lines with an instance of what he has been describing in lines 16–24, that is, with one of those melodies that 'neither perches nor pauses', a 'bird of Paradise, . . . footless and wild'. The poem charts its own progress and is self-activating as a reflection of imagination's self-originating power:

> O! the one Life within us and abroad,
> Which meets all motion and becomes its soul,
> A light in sound, a sound-like power in light,
> Rhythm in all thought, and joyance every where—
> Methinks, it should have been impossible
> Not to love all things in a world so fill'd;
> Where the breeze warbles, and the mute still air
> Is Music slumbering on her instrument.

(These lines were added later to the poem, in the errata to *Sybilline Leaves* (1817); see *PW* I 101.)

The first two lines of this 'Melody', referring to the 'One Life' theme, raise the lute to the stature of life through a rather abstract, philosophical gesture more thoroughly integrated into poetry later on in the poem. It attempts to overcome the chasm between mind and nature, subject and object, life and 'dead' matter. Not only does the next line now intimately relate the senses of sound and sight (through 'light'); it also suggests that in the musical sounds of the language of the poem there is light, that is, intelligence and knowledge. The 'sound-like power in light' may further indicate that even in the parts of the poem where the imagery predominates, the musicality of the language still deepens the effects of the lines as they reach into pre-linguistic experiences and feelings. 'Rhythm in all thought' pushes the musical importance of thought and language more insistently, as do the last few lines of this passage. For the ultimate outcome of the 'One Life' theme seems to be the knowledge of 'joyance every where', and the 'love[of] all things', since all things are one life.

One cannot be reasoned to such knowledge and experience, but only stirred and wakened. Poetry can offer itself as a rival to or, more properly, a necessary supplement to discursive reasoning. For it too seeks to explore the questions of the relation of mind to nature, of subject to object, of ego to other, and of perception to knowledge. It also offers an interpretation of 'reality', and while it uses language meaningfully and conceptually, it also taps the rich resources, in language itself, of 'light and sound', and completes its conceptualizings with imaginative explorations that reach behind the linguistic surface of the mind into the depths of experience.

Love seems, in the last three lines, to be the result of the speaker's imagination filling the world with creatures of his thought, those relations amongst disparate elements and things that release immense energy. The speaker himself brings to life the music of the breeze as a warbling, as if it were a bird. His genius then interprets the 'mute still air' as nevertheless alive as well, but simply momentarily at rest, potentiality instead of absence: 'the mute still air/Is Music slumbering on her instrument'. Even emptiness is humanized, and a theoretical statement about imagination is also implied: silence and absence are only the moments before conscious awakening; they are not loss, emptiness, or vacancy, but, at the conscious level, rest. The apparent opposition between 'mute still air' and music is overcome, as at ground the metaphor shows them to be qualitatively the same. This of course is the hallmark of Coleridge's (and Blake's) philosophy, an example of the 'reconciliation of opposites' (for a definition see *The Friend (CC)* I 94*). The theme constantly recurs throughout Coleridge's writings, and is another formulation of the distinction between opposites and contraries, occurring with equal frequency (as in, for example, *Church and State (CC)* 24, and *BL* II ch. xiv 12–13). Both concepts arise in Coleridge's extensive marginalia on Kant, Boehme, Baxter, Tennemann, and others. (Blake's use of the idea is obvious in 'The Marriage of Heaven and Hell', and 'The Songs of Innocence and Experience', and in his myth of the path to regeneration generally.)

The pun on 'air' as melody allows the first few words alone to achieve a synthesis in an oxymoron: 'mute still air', meaning melody (see Keats's Nightingale Ode, Stanza IV for a similar pun on 'air'). At the same time one can see the implicit claim Coleridge was later to make explicitly about imagination, that it is at once the 'instrument and the solution' (*BL* I ch. xiii 198) of creation: here the air is both instrument and music. '*So* fill'd' suggests too that where the imagination is peopling the world, there is no empty space, no loneliness or loss, for all things, including apparent muteness and emptiness can be infused with its life: death is overcome as illusion, and the world of imagination becomes a paradise: the state of mind of love and 'joyance *every where*'. 'Kubla Khan' had also ascended to the postulation that genius is ultimately paradise, a very Blakean conception, ridiculing the notion that paradise exists in any time–space continuum, including the hereafter. The last two lines make a further statement about poetic language, that it includes both music and music slumbering. Coleridge himself explains this necessity in saying that no poem can be all poetry, all 'breeze warbling' (see for example *BL* II ch. xiv 11).

The Subject and the Object Lute

Thus far, the 'One Life' theme has been introduced somewhat abstractly, and the lute has almost been left behind as the breeze seems to take over its role. The next stanza makes an advance on a more immediately experienced, less intellectual level. As the speaker mentions the scene at *noon* on the *midway* slope, we realize that the poem continues to chart its own progress, for this is also *its* midpoint. In the reference to a midpoint in time and space (the two basic categories of perception) corresponding to the midpoint of the poem, it is notable that the description starting at line 34 is not a reminiscence of any particular previous experience (*vide* 'stretch' not 'stretched'). It is a generalized statement carrying representative force. It adds a dimension to the poem in its total contrast with the time and space grid of the rest of the verse, and seems like a leap out of the constraints of the laws of space and time, precisely to signal that imagination is reaching its height of intensity (see above p. 52 in the chapter on 'The Ancient Mariner', on time–space transcendence as a characteristic of imagination).

The leap from outside the cot with Sara at twilight to 'the midway slope/Of yonder hill . . . at noon' charges the landscape with imaginative meaning, as the speaker seems to reach the height of his experience through the ascent of these lines 34–43, by the summit of which he has identified himself explicitly with the lute. This change of scene and time seems to suggest that the cot and twilight are only the preparative conditions for a full awakening at 'noon on a hill-side', where the speaker is able then to achieve imaginative, empathic identification with the lute. He thereby overcomes the subject/object dichotomy and participates in, instead of theorizing about, the One Life. Or rather, the lines following this identification, 'this subject Lute!', are an ideal fusion of theorizing and participation. 'That simplest Lute', an external object, now referred to as 'this subject Lute', concisely illustrates the ambiguity in the latter phrase: is the 'subject' the speaker or the harp? Note too how little change in the sound and rhythm of the phrase has occurred from lute as object to lute as subject. These are, moreover, the only two occasions in the entire poem when the lute is mentioned by name.

These lines are full of indications about the imaginative experience, and lines 39–43 make some of the most explicitly theoretical gestures in the poem. Tranquillity is once again the generative condition of imaginative awakening, and the next two lines suggest the self-activating nature of imaginative thought:

> Full many a thought *uncall'd* and *undetain'd*,
> And many idle flitting phantasies,
> Traverse my indolent and passive brain,
> As wild and various as the random gales
> That swell and flutter on this subject Lute! (my italics)

Conscious volition is subdued as some mysterious mode of introducing and chasing away thoughts takes over. The brain, or reasoning, is held 'indolent and passive', as the mind is flooded with 'phantasies'. Clearly these lines by themselves might be interpreted as associationist in intent, the 'indolent and passive brain' suggesting a passive theory of mind. But within the context of Stanza II especially, as well as the poem as a whole, the more consistent interpretation seems to be the one accounting for these lines according to the paradoxical relation of the active–passive impulses on a conscious–unconscious topography. Or indeed the 'passive brain' might be understood as an explicit distinction from the faculty of producing fantasies; thus only from the point of view of reason are these fantasies 'idle' and mysterious in origin, wild and various, but exhibiting an order and logic intelligible to the imaginative eye. The problem is caused partly by the vagueness of the scope of the harp image. Is it mechanical and suggestive of a passive theory of mind, or is it simply too dualistic, so that body, the harp, is not related synthetically to mind, the breeze? Or is the breeze too simple an image for the play and variety of the power of genius? (See below for a further discussion of the harp image.)

Other elements in these lines demand consideration as theoretically rich. 'I stretch my limbs at noon' is delightfully poised to waver between activity and passivity, for one can read the speaker as stretching out his limbs in a passive, supine position, or as actively striding up the hill. The next two lines set up the active/passive contrast somewhat differently. The line 'Whilst through my half-clos'd eyelids I behold' presents a state of half sleep, but the 'behold' is exposed as inadequate as we realize that by squinting his eyes the speaker *creates* the 'dancing sunbeams', dancing and in motion only because of his flickering eyelids. (Personification is also operative in 'dancing sunbeams'.) This minor perceptual experience is also a model of the creativity of perception itself, and the active role the supposedly passive percipient can play. In the next line, the phrase 'tranquil muse' threatens at first to change into an adjective and a noun as the speaker becoming a poet 'beholds' his 'tranquil muse'.

Lines 44–9 become an example of the wild and various and random gales 'that swell and flutter on this subject Lute!' The poem, that is, constructs by increments what it describes, and has now reached its 'noon' in a fusion of musicality, imagery, philosophical reflection, and subject–object identification. For the lines are an intensely felt expression of the more abstractly conceived theme of lines 26–33. And they are intensely speculative, neither merely pantheistic nor exclusively Christian, but reachings out into the mystery of existence and the individual's relation to nature. They are more an expression of a yearning to understand or experience this unity of all things than a dogmatic statement that man's relation to nature and God is this or that. Perhaps they are indeed not just a yearning to feel unity, but an expression of the creative achievement of unity, the yearning being rather to find appropriate words for that experience. However inadequate the harp–breeze image may be as an expression of the origins of consciousness, it nevertheless demonstrates the creativity of mind, in taking an external object and turning it into a symbol of mind, thereby humanizing it, which for Coleridge (and Blake) was the hallmark of imaginative activity. The discovery of similarity in the midst of difference is also for Coleridge a way of illustrating imagination at work, relating and integrating experience. The fact of focusing in upon the harp as a symbol, and then in these lines attempting a sweeping identification with all living things, was the sort of mental event that must have forced Coleridge into a confrontation with the passive theories of mind. For they could only fail utterly to account for such self-activating analogical gestures.

The progress of the lute through the poem has been from 'simplest lute' and mechanical external object, to a comparison with a bird, then to a motion ensouled, and at the end of line 43 'this subject Lute' is both lute and speaker. But it is now carried further by becoming a symbol of all organic bodies in nature. It is never separated from its ensouling breeze, however. This suggests that the lute is not itself a symbol of imagination, as has been occasionally assumed. The function of the lute might rather be to imply that all organic bodies are potentially imaginative beings, or participate and respond to the common life as pre-eminently imaginative, joyful, and loving. For the breeze does not sweep them from *without*, but from within: it is an intellectual breeze. Only an overly literal reading of the symbolic nature of the eolian harp would make this reversal a point of resistance to the effectiveness of the harp as symbol. These lines also effectively express the part–whole relation that became such a central part of Coleridge's philosophy, and the essence of his definition of symbol,[9] in '. . . one intellectual breeze/At once the Soul of each, and God of all?' These lines might instead be criticized not for an overly passive image of the imagination; it is rather the relation between the harp as frame, or self, and the intellectual breeze, which is objectionable. For it suggests a dualism, but dualism, as an account of reality, was certainly not Coleridge's view at any time of his life.[10] Lines 20–33 deal more effectively with this apparent dualism, when they virtually leave the lute behind and replace it with its melodies, or with air, warbling or slumbering. Thus the self-originating or self-activating quality of imaginative experience is better symbolized than with the harp–breeze relation. On the other hand, the harp–breeze does more vividly portray the experience of mind–body dualism at the surface level, and is able to depict the conscious–unconscious tension. For the image to work, it only need be taken as a metaphor, with the emphasis upon intellectual breeze, not external breeze.

Some thirty years after writing this poem Coleridge returned to the image of the eolian harp, and solved some of the problems raised above. He was responding to a statement that 'corporeality in general is but a husk for the mind':

And what then *is* a Hülle[husk]? If it be the Husk of the Spirit, it is not the Spiri(t) but a Husk. And wherein does this differ from saying, that the Body is not body, but merely the Soul's Body? or our Bodies are not body because they are the Bodies of our Souls? Why not say at once, that Spirit condenses & shapes itself into an Eolian Harp, on which the unindividual-ized Spirit as the + Power plays and that the resulting *Tune* is what we call *body*, or phaenomenal existence/the living Harp being at once the Mother & the Auditress of the music?

(Marginal note to J. C. Heinroth, *Lehrbuch der Anthropologie* (1822), I i S 71. BM *MS* C 43 b 18. This note was made in approximately August 1826.)

It seems correct then that the harp and its music is not limited as a symbol of mind, but of body, its value being to assert that all nature's creatures originate in and are potentially able to participate in or respond to the intellectual breeze. Another comment about the eolian harp seems to affirm this view. Coleridge was reading Kant's *Kritik der reinen Vernunft*, and wrote the following on one of the empty pages at the end of the volume:

Doubts during a first perusal—i.e. Struggles felt, not arguments objected.
    1. How can that be called ein mannigfaltiges ὑλξ [confused manifold] which yet contains in itself the ground, why I apply one category to it rather than another? one mathematical form and not another? The mind does not resemble an Eolian Harp, nor even a barrel-organ turned by a stream of water, conceive as many tunes mechanized in it as you like— but rather, as far as Objects are concerned, a violin, or other instrument of few strings yet vast compass, played on by a musician of Genius. The Breeze that blows across the Eolian Harp, the streams that turned the handle of the Barrel-Organ, might be called ein mannigfaltiges, a mere sylva incondita, but who would call the muscles and purpose of Linley a confused Manifold?

(Marginal note to Kant, *Kritik der reinen Vernunft*, (1799), back flyleaf BM *MS* C 126 i 9. The note could have been written at almost any time after 1799.)

Even in a very late letter of 1825 when Coleridge refers to the 'Eolian Harp of my Brain', the harp still seems not to refer to unindividualized mind, so much as to the soul or self (*CL* V 414 to an anonymous cor-respondent).[11]

The Conflict between Reason and Imagination

As the speaker reaches the apex of his imaginative experience with the yearning and speculative strain of 'And what if . . .', he is jolted back to Sara, the cot, and twilight, or now perhaps night-time, by the dart-ing arrows of Sara's disapproving eye. Her extreme negativism toward these melodies is intensified by the double negative syntax of 'nor such thoughts/Dim and unhallow'd dost thou not reject'. The language of the poem suddenly loses its musicality and the wonderful exoticism that related it closely to the poems of the supernatural (composed largely within the next two years). These last lines are much more prosaic and moralizing in tone, with stock religious phrases replacing the pure originality of the preceding lines, with the single exception of lines 55–8. This framework language encloses the 'melodies . . . footless and wild', very much like the gloss of 'The Ancient Mariner', or indeed part of the preface to 'Kubla Khan', in a husk of discursive rhetoric, not wholly without its poetry, but nevertheless conventional and moralizing.[12]

An examination of the first five lines of the poem reveals a similar artificiality and conventional, stock language in disharmony with the rest of the poem. The discursive gestures in these lines function superficially like the openings of a conventional eighteenth-century lyric. The physical closeness of the two lovers is mocked by the spiritual gap revealed in lines 49–55. In these lines only the most passive verbs are used and the most generalized and basic sense of touch introduced, in contrast to the progressive development immediately taking place in line 6, as the poem begins to surge out of its prison of convention. Doubtless the imprisoning quality of the language is subtle, but reflection renders the subtle differences significant. The contrast between the 'white-flower'd Jasmin, and the broad-leav'd Myrtle,/ (Meet emblems they of Innocence and Love!)',[13], and the metaphor of the star of eve as wisdom emphasizes precisely the contrast marked here between lines 1–5 and those following. These first five lines may not be conclusive in themselves, but in conjunction with the last sixteen they build a framework with a sinister and ironic face, which stubbornly disturbs the apparent peace and orthodoxy asserted at surface level.

The framework disrupts the consistency of the poem in several ways, first and most obviously by being in stylistic contrast to the rest of the poem, as has been noticed by numerous critics. It further alienates because dogmatic rhetoric is allowed to prevail, and diminishes the splendour and magnificence of the preceding earnest speculations. The foregoing 'Melodies', the 'long sequacious notes' hardly seem to be 'dim and unhallow'd' in any pejorative sense. If they are dim it is because the subjects they treat of are high, and if they are unhallowed because not sanctioned by orthodox religion then much speculation and art could be arbitrarily rejected. But dimness and obscurity were not always condemnable to Coleridge:

What then is or can be the preventive, the remedy, the counteraction, but the habituation of the intellect to clear, distinct, and adequate conceptions concerning all things that are the possible objects of clear conception, and thus to reserve the deep feelings which belong, as by a natural right to those obscure ideas that are necessary to the moral perfection of the human being, notwithstanding, yea, even in consequence, of their obscurity—to reserve these feelings, I repeat, for objects, which their very sublimity renders indefinite, no less than their indefiniteness renders them sublime: namely, to the Ideas of Being, Form, Life, the Reason, the Law of Conscience, Freedom, Immortality, God! To connect with the objects of our senses the obscure notions and consequent vivid feelings, which are due only to immaterial and permanent things, is profanation relatively to the heart, and superstition in the understanding.

(*The Friend* (CC) I 106; cf. 186)

This explanation is almost a direct reply to the response of Sara in the poem and a proof of the inappropriateness of her attitude. The following notebook entry, written much closer to the time of the composition of 'The Eolian Harp', expresses Coleridge's defence even more relevantly:

The elder Languages fitter for Poetry because they expressed only prominent ideas with clearness, others but darkly—Therefore the French wholly unfit for Poetry; because *clear* in their Language—i.e.—Feelings created by obscure ideas associate themselves with the one *clear* idea. When no criticism is pretended to, & the Mind in its simplicity gives itself up to a Poem as to a work of nature, Poetry gives most pleasure when only generally & not perfectly understood. It was so by me with Gray's *Bard*, & Collins' odes—*The Bard* once intoxicated me, & now I read it without pleasure. From this cause it is that what *I* call metaphysical Poetry gives me so much delight.

(*CN* I 383, January—May 1799)

It might be too extreme to insist that the entire passage is spoken with forked tongue, 'Meek Daughter in the family of Christ' uttered between clenched teeth almost as a curse on the rigidity of mind displayed by our character Sara. But perhaps Coleridge is struggling with censors in his own mind as well. The irony, however, is skilfully brought into sharp focus by the beauty of the lines describing the speculative flights of the poem:

> These shapings of the unregenerate mind;
> Bubbles that glitter as they rise and break
> On vain Philosophy's aye-babbling spring.

In these lines the speaker reverts to the musicality and richness of imagery of the rest of the poem, just at the moment he is supposed to be condemning it. The beauty itself argues for their truth and for his unwillingness to acquiesce totally in the disapproval, couched as it is in stagnant, unconvincing, and stock religious phrases. Thus the words 'unregenerate' and 'vain' seem hypocritical, or ironic, or even gently mocking.

These lines themselves contain too much that Coleridge clung to throughout his life to be seriously rejected by him here. The 'shapings of the unregenerate mind' already foreshadows the theory of mind as its own shaping process,[14] articulated in the *Biographia Literaria*.[15] The spring as an image of mind as creative is one of Coleridge's dearest and most often used metaphors.[16] Philosophy was never vain to him; it was the soul of his personality from a very early age as well as of his poetry and later writings. The pun of 'I' on the Miltonic (and Biblical) phrase 'vain Philosophy's aye-babbling spring', in addition to the optimism and affirmativeness it shows in contrast to Sara's negatives and reproofs and darts, connects with the play and irony when Coleridge wrote the following (in a letter discussing the poem) as a definition of life:

> Plato says, it is Harmony—he might as well have said, a fiddle stick's end—but I love Plato—his dear *gorgeous* Nonsense! And I, tho' last not least, I do not know what to think about it—on the whole, I have rather made up my mind that I am a mere apparition—a naked Spirit!—And that Life is I myself I! which is a mighty clear account of it.
>
> (*CL* I 295, to Thelwall, 31 December 1796)

The phrase 'Life is I myself I' contains the germs of Coleridge's later sophisticated philosophy based on the will and the 'I AM'. But it also contains the Fichtean version stridently rejected as egotism (in *BL* I ch. ix 101–2; see also his marginal notes to Fichte's *Bestimmung des Menschen* and *System der Sittenlehre*). In the same letter Coleridge prefixed these remarks with the lines from the poem that called upon him Sara's reproof, lines 44–9 especially, and comments 'by the bye—that is my favorite of *my* poems—do *you* like it?' Nor is the transience of the 'bubbles that glitter as they rise and break' to be taken as a condemnation of the dynamic activity suggested in these lines, in contrast to the stagnant pools of repetitive, dogmatic rhetoric. In this letter speaking of Southey, Coleridge used again the images of bubbling for ideas:

> Dismissing mock humility, & hanging your mind as a looking-glass over my Idea-pot, so as to image on the said mind all the bubbles that boil in the said Idea-pot . . . I think that an admirable Poet might be made by amalgamating him & me. I think too much for a Poet; he too little for a great Poet. But he abjures thinking—& lays the whole stress of excellence—on feeling.—Now (as you say) they must go together.

The criticism of Sara in which the speaker seems to acquiesce is on the contrary actually rejected toward the end of the poem, when he says:

> For never guiltless may I speak of him,
> The Incomprehensible! save when with awe
> I praise him, and with Faith that inly *feels*.

The speaker here raises a defence of his previous speculations, and insists on his guiltlessness, for his feeling and awe were evident, as was his faith in 'the Incomprehensible', even if not in purely Christian terminology.

If the reader has not been stirred by any of the questionable aspects of these lines up to '*feels*', Coleridge draws him up short with a footnote astonishing both in content, ambiguity, and simply in the fact that it is there at all. Nor is it always there. Editors of anthologies frequently delete it. The original appears above, and a translation is given here:

The atheist is hardly, in my eyes, a false spirit; I can live with him just as well or better than with a devotee, for he reasons more, but he lacks a sense, and my soul is hardly able to bed itself entirely with his: he is cold to the most ravishing spectacle, and he seeks a syllogism where I find an action of grace.

Coleridge was in the habit of occasionally placing footnotes to his poems on unusual or interesting subjects, but in later years (even in later months), especially in the *Biographia Literaria*, his footnotes, advertisements, chapter descriptions, chapter headings, and his glosses and prefaces, and so forth, came to look more and more suspiciously like means of alerting the reader to underlying intentions, ironies, and peculiar observations, say about natural phenomena, that were metaphorical, delightful illustrations of some purpose he was only indirectly communicating. There is, for example, the amusing footnote to 'Lines at Shurton Bars' (line 93), about the electric flame as a natural phenomenon of marigolds. The irony of this note is far from certain, but the footnote was later deleted. 'Religious Musings' is full of notes.

In the case of this footnote to 'The Eolian Harp', it is dramatically effective that the content is rather ambiguous: it is not clear whether the elaboration is about the *dévot* or the *athée*. Which one of them is 'cold to the most ravishing spectacle', who is it that seeks for a syllogism instead of an 'action of grace'? Since the syntax is uncertain, we must admit that the placement of the dependent clause suggests that it is the *dévot*. But if it is the *dévot*, is this not also a description of Sara? The latter being the case, it would seem that the framework effect as ironic is thoroughly intentional. If there is any doubt that the *dévot* should be likened to Sara's attitude and character, it is well to consider the comment, 'car il *raisonne* davantage, mais il lui manque un sens'. Sara has been described as pensive at the beginning of the poem, and it would be wrong to make much of this epithet, but it does seem an extraordinary coincidence in the light of the footnote. The last stanza however furthers the sense that she has replaced an 'action of grace' with a 'syllogism', meaning in this case simply deductive reasoning, and this contributes greater ironic import to her pensiveness.

The contrast between Coleridge as feeling and Sara as coldly reasoning is not at all out of keeping with the history of their relationship. For at the time of Coleridge's hasty engagement to Sara Fricker, he was still 'grieving' for Mary Evans (see *CL* I 149 headnote), and was rushed into an engagement largely as a result of Southey's meddlings. He prolonged his absence from Bristol, until Southey's insistences and reminders of his duty compelled him to submit to a commitment about which he had grave misgivings; or he at least suspected that he lacked the feelings necessary for a successful marriage. He said in explanation of his decision finally to marry, that he did so only out of 'principle' and 'duty', Sara's commitment springing from strong feeling (see *CL* I 151 and see *CL* I 149: 'Wherein when roused to the recollection of my Duty have I shrunk from the performance of it?—I hold my Life & my feebler feelings as ready sacrifices to Justice'.) In a later letter to Southey he referred to his attachment to Mary, the necessity of 'bursting a Fetter' and 'that it snapt, as if it had been a Sinew of my Heart'. Here he also maintained that he first paid his addresses to Sara from 'Principle not Feeling'.

The protestations of his love for Sara which began shortly before their marriage—and which were to last such a despairingly short time: that 'domestic happiness [which] is the greatest of things sublunary' (*CL* I 159)—may have been a result of a desperate effort to make his marriage work and to help to awaken feelings in himself which were never fully to mature, at least not for Sara Fricker. But the ambivalence of his feelings is clear from the beginning, and conscious or not at the moment of writing 'The Eolian Harp', they are effectively portrayed and are all too prophetic of the strained relations shortly to follow. As early as 16 November 1795, in the same letter to Southey where he defended the performance of his duty toward Sara from principle, he referred to Mary Evans in the following way, indicating that as late as the autumn of 1795 she was still the centre of his affections (he refers to Southey's Pantisocracy Plan): 'the plan, for which I abandoned my friends, and every prospect & every certainty, and the Woman whom I loved to an excess which you in your warmest dream of fancy could never shadow out' (see also *CN* I 18 which may refer to his wife; and see *CN* I 72).

Such facts as these suggest that Coleridge's attitude toward Sara was extremely ambivalent. But both the origins of their relationship and the culmination of their marriage in final separation add some support to the interpretation of Sara's role in these lines as censoring, whether intentional and conscious or not. Coleridge was constantly complaining about Sara's lack of sympathy and warmth, and her penchant for a cold and disapproving attitude towards him; he complained for example, of the 'freezing' welcome with which she would greet him. Although of a late date, the following notebook entry aptly expresses his attitude towards this lack of feeling, while it should be noted that he never once, in writing at least, doubted her intelligence or her capacity for deductive reasoning. He speaks of the 'love-killing Effect of cold, dry, uninterested looks & Manners' (*CN* III 3316, May 1808). But by 1802 he despaired of continuing to live with Sara. Whether his meeting with Sara Hutchinson in 1799 was the beginning of more serious tension leading to the hopelessness of 1802 and the escape to Malta and Italy, the tension after the move in 1800 to Greta Hall in Keswick, to be closer to the Wordsworths (and Sara Hutchinson?), increased to an intolerable level. This is evident from the letters of this period, where Coleridge complains of Sara's coldness and hostility to his friends and her disapproval of his frequent visits to them. The July 1797 'accident' that was the occasion of 'This Lime-Tree Bower' may also constitute an all too ominous sign of marital tension (see *CL* I 571, 12 February 1800, for a temporary reconciliation but an admission that early married life had at times been miserable).

Whatever conclusions one may or may not be able to draw from such biographical details, Coleridge's attitude to atheism and unthinking faith also intensifies the ambiguity of the footnote. On 16 June 1795 he gave a 'Lecture on the Slave-Trade'. He there commented that 'Atheists (are) the most religious!' (*Lects 1795 (CC)* 249). And in later years he explained to Thomas Allsop what atheism *could* mean:

The law of God and the great principles of the Christian religion would have been the same had Christ never assumed humanity. It is for these things, and for such as these, for telling unwelcome truths, that I have been termed an atheist. It is for these opinions that William Smith assured the Archbishop of Canterbury that I was (what half the clergy are in their lives) an atheist. Little do these men know what atheism is. Not one man in a thousand has either strength of mind or goodness of heart to be an atheist. And, were I not a Christian, and that only in the sense in which I am a Christian, I should be an atheist with Spinoza; rejecting all in which I found insuperable difficulties and resting my only hope in the gradual and certain because gradual, progression of the species. This, it is true, is negative atheism; and this is, next to Christianity, the purest spirit of humanity!
(*Letters, Conversations and Recollections of S. T. Coleridge*, by T. Allsop, I 88–9)

Atheism then could mean two nearly opposite things for Coleridge, the 'negative atheism' of Spinoza, as described above, and the positive atheism of the materialist, who was not to be distinguished from the sensualist, no matter what the latter's professed creed.[17] To this positive atheism seem to apply the qualities of coldness and the inability to perceive any whole unifying the universe of little things to which the senses testify (see *Lects 1795* (CC) 92). As early as 1795, no doubt because of his early love of Spinoza, Coleridge was clearly marking the distinction. Through the tension in the meaning of the word 'atheism' the ambiguity of the footnote is substantiated, and that ambiguity supplements the uncertainty of Sara's role in the poem. Coleridge never ceased to resist the fetters that an unthinking and dogmatic, orthodox religion imposed upon thought and imagination. Sara's rejection of innocent, imaginative strivings as depicted in 'The Eolian Harp', are a model of that narrowness and intolerance of speculation deplored by Coleridge. The dogmatism characteristic of some professed Christians which for Coleridge killed its spirit, drove him to a profound respect for the so-called atheism of Spinoza, or indeed the religion of Plato. It led him to an appreciation of, if not acquiescence in, pantheism as one outcome of the metaphysical speculations of transcendentalism dear to his intellect and imagination.[18] Pantheism could be entirely free from the fanaticism that corrupted the intellectual and philosophical side of religious faith.

The footnote to 'The Eolian Harp' becomes a point of focus for the uncertainty of the role of the framework, of Sara, of the reproof, and of the defence of the speaker's imaginative (religious) musings. It is a discursive gesture in the midst of a beautiful poem, like the gloss and the preface, calling attention to complexities and uncertainties otherwise 'glossed over'. Such a gesture also functions in a way characteristic of Coleridge, and as a method of procedure for him. It 'selects' its readers, and this technique may be said to be the device *par excellence* of irony. The technique functions on several levels. There are the readers who will simply ignore the footnote, as an inessential part of the poem. This attitude is facilitated by many editions simply omitting the footnote. There are also those who read but do not absorb the footnote as important. Or there are readers who simply do not know French; this acts as another automatic, though rather arbitrary, filter. Even those who read the footnote with interest may easily miss the ambiguity, and assume that it is decidedly the atheist who is cold and unfeeling. In this case the footnote would play a much less integral part in the poem; it would be merely an appendage tacked on by Coleridge and of peripheral interest. But those who are moderately amused or confused by the ambiguity, and then learn or know already that Coleridge had two very opposing ways of using the word 'atheist', would begin to see the footnote in a more important way, as a signal of some ambiguity or complexity in the structure of the poem. The fact that the footnote is attached to the section of the framework where the speaker indirectly defends himself against Sara's disapproving and 'Urizenic' dart of reproof and rejection strengthens its role as a signal of another level of meaning operating in the poem.[19]

The framework, then, may act to depict Coleridge's troubled relations with his wife;[20] it may also show his strong opposition to dogmatic and unthinking belief. But from the perspective of art and the reader, these biographical factors are primarily important in so far as they give further reason for thinking that the framework acts ironically in an aesthetic context. In this latter context the framework is important as a dramatization of the struggle between a tyrannizing and incredulous reason (in Blake–Shelley terminology), or deductive faculty, and a striving and questioning imagination committed to the truth in beauty and the wholeness of wisdom, or thought enlivened and testified to by feeling.[21] The contrast is between the imagination, which takes seriously its beautiful creations as a source of knowledge, and a reason which sees them as amusing and pleasing, but as only 'idle fantasies' without any import for truth or philosophical reflection.

Sara, as a character in the poem, may act as a personification of this 'censoring' faculty, or Blake's Urizen. Indeed, the description of her response in lines 49–51 corresponds closely to Blake's characterization of 'your reason'. The structure of the poem then becomes a unity of a struggle between this repressive, incredulous faculty and the self-affirming faculty of inspired vision. It operates for example to depict Coleridge's own reason, and his fears and doubts about his poetic visions, doubts that assail every mind, since after the inspiration the reflective faculty goes to work on material requiring a different comprehension. This faculty sees gaps that it cannot fill, and therefore denies the worth or reasonableness of the truths affirmed by the imagination. For only the imagination perceives the connections amongst those linking elements; memory may help partially to preserve these insights, but alone it can never recreate them.

Sara serves to depict the reader in his relation to the poem, and it is through identifying with her that the reader is able to overcome the limited perspective she represents. Like the gloss and the preface, the framework is an opportunity for the reader to catch his reason in the act of hindering his imaginative response to the complexity of the poem. The awareness of this caricature is the moment of release from it, and the rest of the poem can then open up as the skilful and delicate fusion of sensuous language and theoretical implications about the nature of art and imagination. Once again the poem can be seen as a work of art enriched by its own account of what art is, how it operates, and why it is worthwhile. Perhaps its most important theoretical statement is, paradoxically, that art demonstrates practically what theory explains; the poem then demonstrates this practical experience by making it occur for the reader, who has been helped along by all the 'devices' in the poem.

The framework becomes a mirror of the initial reading situation (or a mirror of Coleridge's later uncertainties about his vision, thus operating effectively for both reader and poet), and it functions as the device whereby the reader is helped to overcome such initial blindness and move on into a full and rich appreciation of the poem. The appreciation of beauty may indeed come to some extent without an awareness of the role of the framework. But the framework is essential for depicting the struggle between the reason and the awakening imagination as rival authorities of truth; more importantly it depicts the almost inevitable doubt and anxiety about the truths seen by the imagination after its demise. But it also explains why those doubts occur. The framework helps to mitigate their effect and to prolong the faith in imagination until it is revived to testify for itself. Thus the poem contains a level of reflection not only about the nature of imagination but also about its relation to the reason and consciousness, and to truth.

'The Eolian Harp' seems to be a poem which rests upon a fundamental contradiction; it demands silence and celebrates music.[22] And yet this paradox illuminates the way poetry reaches beyond the words, images, and symbols constituting its surface; it explores a depth of the mind vitally connected to and perhaps even partly dependent upon language for its awakening and experiencing. But this depth is nevertheless beyond words and unexhausted by them. Poetry is frequently associated with music, for they both are sources of knowledge about an otherwise inaccessible region of the mind.[23]

4

'Frost at Midnight':
a Study of Identity in Difference

The Text

Frost at Midnight

The Frost performs its secret ministry,
Unhelped by any wind. The owlet's cry
Came loud—and hark, again! loud as before.
The inmates of my cottage, all at rest,
Have left me to that solitude, which suits   5
Abstruser musings: save that at my side
My cradled infant slumbers peacefully.
'Tis calm indeed! so calm, that it disturbs
And vexes meditation with its strange
And extreme silentness. Sea, hill, and wood,   10
This populous village! Sea, and hill, and wood,
With all the numberless goings-on of life,
Inaudible as dreams! the thin blue flame
Lies on my low-burnt fire, and quivers not;
Only that film,* which fluttered on the grate,   15
Still flutters there, the sole unquiet thing.
Methinks, its motion in this hush of nature
Gives it dim sympathies with me who live,
Making it a companionable form,
Whose puny flaps and freaks the idling Spirit   20
By its own moods interprets, every where
Echo or mirror seeking of itself,
And makes a toy of Thought.

*In all parts of the kingdom these films are called *strangers* and supposed to portend the arrival of some absent friend.

But O! how oft,
How oft, at school, with most believing mind,
Presageful, have I gazed upon the bars,   25
To watch that fluttering *stranger!* and as oft
With unclosed lids, already had I dreamt
Of my sweet birth-place, and the old church-tower,
Whose bells, the poor man's only music, rang
From morn to evening, all the hot Fair-day,   30
So sweetly, that they stirred and haunted me
With a wild pleasure, falling on mine ear
Most like articulate sounds of things to come!
So gazed I, till the soothing things, I dreamt,
Lulled me to sleep, and sleep prolonged my dreams!   35
And so I brooded all the following morn,
Awed by the stern preceptor's face, mine eye
Fixed with mock study on my swimming book:
Save if the door half opened, and I snatched
A hasty glance, and still my heart leaped up,   40
For still I hoped to see the stranger's face.
Townsman, or aunt, or sister more beloved,
My play-mate when we both were clothed alike!

Dear Babe, that sleepest cradled by my side,
Whose gentle breathings, heard in this deep calm,   45
Fill up the interspersed vacancies
And momentary pauses of the thought!
My babe so beautiful! it thrills my heart
With tender gladness, thus to look at thee,
And think that thou shalt learn far other lore,   50
And in far other scenes! For I was reared
In the great city, pent 'mid cloisters dim,
And saw nought lovely but the sky and stars.
But *thou*, my babe! shalt wander like a breeze
By lakes and sandy shores, beneath the crags   55
Of ancient mountain, and beneath the clouds,
Which image in their bulk both lakes and shores
And mountain crags: so shalt thou see and hear
The lovely shapes and sounds intelligible
Of that eternal language, which thy God   60
Utters, who from eternity doth teach
Himself in all, and all things in himself.
Great universal Teacher! he shall mould
Thy spirit, and by giving make it ask.

Therefore all seasons shall be sweet to thee,   65
Whether the summer clothe the general earth
With greenness, or the redbreast sit and sing
Betwixt the tufts of snow on the bare branch

Of mossy apple-tree, while the nigh thatch
Smokes in the sun-thaw; whether the eave-drops fall   70
Heard only in the trances of the blast,
Or if the secret ministry of frost
Shall hang them up in silent icicles,
Quietly shining to the quiet Moon.

February 1798

'Frost at Midnight'[1] was composed in February 1798 shortly after the supernatural poems must have been finished (as well as *Osorio*, completed in October 1797, just after 'Kubla Khan'), and it seems to mark a turning away from the exotic imagery of its predecessors. It reverts to the naturalism[2] characteristic both of the poems to follow ('The Nightingale', 'Fears in Solitude', 'France: An Ode'; 'Lewti' seems to be an exception, or at least a peculiar mixture of the exotic and the natural), and of the poems preceding the supernatural poems of autumn 1797 (such as 'The Eolian Harp', 'Reflections on having left a Place of Retirement', 'Religious Musings', and the mature version of 'Monody on the Death of Chatterton' of 1795; 'Ode to the Departing Year' of 1796; and 'This Lime-Tree Bower' of July 1797).

While it illustrates the three techniques of internalization common to these poems, namely, landscape, characterization, and dream, vision, or fantasy states, it seems to lack the framework or highlighting of the communicative act that the three poems discussed earlier exhibit in some form. In the techniques of internalization the metaphoric level permits theoretical gestures about the essential creativity of mind, the nature of imagination, and its relation to the reason, the ego, and nature. At one level of discourse these gestures seem to be made primarily from the point of view of the poet as a perspective on his act of creative production. It has been frequently suggested above that there is also often an active level of theorizing by the poet from the reader's perspective, accomplished by means of a framework parodying skilfully the communicative act or the reading situation. An obtuse observer may be dramatized, and his faulty or inadequate responses charted as a model of the errors common to aesthetic 'non-responsiveness', errors which arise from an (unconscious) attitude toward the mind as essentially passive in its basic perceptual processes. This mirroring effect makes conscious the normally unconscious filtering of perception which interferes with an appreciation of the richness of the work. And it asserts the essential similarity of the process of reading with composition: both are active, creative roles; however different they may be from each other or from passive, habitual response, they are both creative and active. In order to emphasize this similarity of author and reader roles, reversals of roles are often designed in poetry, so that authors act as spectators and perceivers, while readers become meta-phorically authors and makers. Such reversals and identifications are not meant to erase the obvious differences in author and reader activities, but rather to emphasize the difference of both from ordinary, fossilized perception.

In 'Frost at Midnight' this active level or mirror seems to be absent, so that the reader does not overtly constitute a dramatic element in the poem.[3] The model for reading is not offered by caricature or parody, but rather by direct analogy with the poet's process of objectification and simultaneous internalization. One might distinguish these two structural models for reading in terms of polarity and analogy. The framework method uses the polarity technique—it sets up an opposition between reader and poet, or between inappropriate and appropriate response. Analogy on the other hand requires not a perception of the difference, but of the similarity. The poetic mind isolates objects or persons in the environment, imbues them with the aesthetic values of symbols, and thereby internalizes them or makes them a part of its imaginative experience. The reader follows this example, isolating elements in the environment of the poem, and then discovers the possible symbolic import conveyed by their relations. In the case of this poem the analogy is aptly designed because the speaker is specifically engaged in a 'self-watching' of his mind in the beginning of the first stanza.[4] The immediacy of the analysis of perception as it intensifies into imaginative response to the surroundings itself high-lights the effect of immediate analysis by the reader of his own similar perceptions. The speaker is trying to report what is happening to him right now, and thereby to provide the reader with a model of 'nowness'. Not only are external objects observed, assimilated, and made actively present and valuable to the mind; the process of assimilation itself becomes an object of observation. This latter act is the point of trans-formation in the poem from consciousness to self-consciousness, from mediation of the feelings and observations of another to the immediacy of feeling and observing for oneself: the mind moves from 'attention' to 'thought' in Coleridgean terms, or to the representation in one's own mind of the things described.[5]

The Landscape of the Mind

Both the trance-like silence and the solitude which often seem to be the generative conditions of imaginative awakening are explicitly introduced in the first few lines. They are emphasized by contrast:

the owlet's cry loudly pierces the stillness, somewhat as the music of the eolian harp and the song of the nightingale pierce the stillness in those poems: 'All is still/. . . And hark! the Nightingale begins its song.' (lines 6 and 12) In 'Frost at Midnight', the time of night and the lack of wind further contribute materially to the silence, and the gentle, slow, and regular rhythm adds stylistically to the effect.

The frost is a problematic image in the poem. The 'secret ministry of frost' both introduces and ends the poem, and on both occasions it is vividly contrasted with another season or state. The cold, frozen whiteness of the frost is surrounding the little cottage with its 'thin blue flame' and 'low burnt fire'; nevertheless the outside world of frost and cold is not lifeless, for the owlet's cry pierces the dead of night, and has some (limited) correspondence with the speaker, who is, like the owl, 'the sole unquiet thing'. In the last stanza, the icicles hung up by the frost, and the lack of wind—the silence—is contrasted with the 'eave-drops fall' and the 'trances of the blast'. The frost seems to have both threatening and friendly connotations. In the latter case, it almost seems an image of imagination at work, colouring the land-scape with its own 'light'. The phrase 'unhelped by any wind' encourages the equation and the metaphor of mental landscape as it implies freedom from any intention or accident, but guidance by a self-activating power. And the word 'secret' places the source of energy beyond the confines of the consciousness and the will. The strivings of frost toward the organic in the shapes that often appear on the panes of windows after a heavy frost indirectly create an association with the 'One Life' theme which is more fully developed in Stanza III, and link the frost again with imagination. But its cold, frozen whiteness and the antithesis with wind, often an image of imagination (as is the breeze in 'The Eolian Harp'), disturbs the simplicity of the association of imagination with the frost. The implications of this uncertain image will be further discussed below.

If the image of frost subtly suggests the conflicting claims of imagi-nation and a repressive reason which freezes up perception, the contrast is still more evident in the following lines. Internalization continues, as 'the inmates of *my* cottage, all at rest', plays upon 'my' and allegorizes the senses and other faculties of mind, such as judgment and reason, as inmates of the cottage, mind, that are 'at rest'. The 'abstruser musings' and 'meditation' guided by these faculties are 'vexed and disturbed'. The immediacy of the speaker's experience, his concern with the 'now' is clear as his original intention to muse abstrusely is deflected by 'idling phantasies' about the surroundings.

Exactly what interrupts his meditation is effectively left without a referent, as 'it' and 'its' dangle in the syntax of lines 8–10. The im-personal construction allows much space for reflection, and the 'it' can indeed be left as impersonal as the phrase 'it rains', as in "'Tis calm indeed!' But it can also be related to the content of these lines. For the image of the sleeping infant interrupts the *poem* after the words 'abstruser musings'. The infant is the only inmate who has not left the speaker 'to that solitude, which suits/Abstruser musings'. The infant is sleeping, it is peaceful; and, appropriately upon this pronouncement, the words "'Tis calm indeed' immediately follow. Thus the ambiguous referent of 'it' causes the mind to rest upon the infant, and foreshadows the importance of the child–infant motif in the rest of the poem. It also foreshadows the significance of that motif as an image of imaginativeness, in the opposition that its occurrence immediately following 'abstruser musings' has as an interruptive device: the infant, like imagination, somehow vexes and disturbs the reasoning faculty. These 'abstruser musings' which are interrupted may be specifiable as speculations about the doctrine of pre-existence, inspired as well as interrupted by the infant and his 'proximity' to the other world, as suggested in Wordsworth's Immortality Ode (see further discussion below). The babe, like the harp and the nightingale, then becomes the focal image of the poem; as such it also acts as a part representative of the whole, and for the reader becomes an emblem of the whole poem. By analogy then, not only 'it', and the infant, but also for the reader the poem 'disturbs and vexes meditation with its strange and extreme silentness'.

This immediate experience of the speaker is further charted as Stanza I continues to depict the intensification of imaginative response. Lines 10–13 show the external world gradually becoming unreal for the mind as the speaker's attention centres more and more upon the symbolic associations of the immediate surroundings. This retreat into the mind is described in a notebook entry of 1796 as of great importance to intellectual experiencing:

> In the paradisiacal World Sleep was voluntary & holy—a spiritual before God, in which the mind elevated by contemplation retired into pure intellect suspending all commerce with sensible objects & perceiving the present deity—
>
> (*CN* I 191)

Thus the filtering and rejection of external objects is just as integral a part of symbol-making as is attending to some one object, and is necessary to the eventual internalization of one or two chosen or valued elements. These two very different movements of filtering and then isolating elements might in Coleridgean terminology be distinguished as attention and thought. While being passive or active relative to each other, both are active in relation to non-focused, ordinary consciousness (see for example *The Friend (CC)* I 16–17, and see the related notebook entry *CN* III 3670).

This filtering and exclusion is directly contrasted with the act of mind depicted in the next line, which seems to be the result of filtering: the mind focuses again on an object closer to it and then proceeds to imbue it with metaphorical value: 'the thin blue flame/Lies on my low-burnt fire'. 'My' is once again used to encourage the metaphor of consciousness as the 'low-burnt fire', as 'my cottage' was used before. The introduction of the fluttering film on the grate of the fire seems, as the speaker says, to express the relation between the superficial consciousness of the ego and a deeper consciousness. The explicitness with which, in the final lines of Stanza I, the speaker makes theoretical statements about the acts of the mind characteristic of imaginative response is astonishing, for the essence of poetical quality is preserved nevertheless.

Notable is the intrusion of overly discursive speculation in the rejected lines, in which the poetic character is not as well preserved, nor kept as the predominant quality (between lines 19–25):

> . . . With which I can hold commune. Idle thought!
> But still the living spirit in our frame,
> That loves not to behold a lifeless thing,
> Transfuses into all its own delights,
> Its own volition, sometimes with deep faith
> And sometimes with fantastic playfulness.

(See also the second variant lines in *PW* I 241 n, which give a similarly incongruous effect.)

The following analysis of his own poetry in a letter of Coleridge's to John Thelwall, 17 December 1796, clarifies the necessary relation between philosophy and poetry:

'Poetry to have it's highest relish must be *impassioned!*' true! but first, Poetry ought not always to have it's *highest* relish, & secondly, judging of the cause from it's effect, Poetry, though treating on lofty & abstract truths, ought to be deemed *impassioned* by him, who reads it with impassioned feelings . . . I feel strongly, and I think strongly; but I seldom feel without thinking, or think without feeling. Hence tho' my poetry has in general a *hue* of tenderness, or Passion over it, yet it seldom exhibits unmixed & simple tenderness or Passion. My philosophical opinions are blended with, or deduced from, my feelings: & this, I think, peculiarizes my style of Writing. And like every thing, else, it is sometimes a beauty, and sometimes a fault. But do not let us introduce an act of Uniformity against Poets—I have room enough in my brain to admire, aye & almost equally, the *head* and fancy of Akenside, and the *heart* and fancy of Bowles, the solemn Lordliness of Milton, & the divine Chit chat of Cowper: and whatever a man's excellence is, that will be likewise his fault.

(*CL* I 279)

Empathetic identification is then expressly referred to in lines 16–17 by the references to 'dim sympathies' and 'companionable form'. The occurrence of 'Idling Spirit' is no careless use of epithets, for 'idling' suggests that freedom from volition and conscious intention expressed in 'The Eolian Harp' as 'idle flitting phantasies'. The phrase 'by its own moods interprets' states that this idle, imaginative spirit acts to 'interpret' or imbue objects with symbolic meaning accord- ing to its own laws and nature. In 'seeking an echo or mirror of itself' it posits itself as object to itself, by humanizing the apparently lifeless things around it. That is, it everywhere finds metaphors of itself, and fills up the chasm between subject and object with these relations, or 'toys of Thought' (see *CL* I 267). 'Toy of thought' aptly illustrates the double layer of discourse constant throughout the poem: there are the thoughts occupying the mind of the speaker for their intrinsic value. But the speaker is not wholly occupied with them in this way: he is also watching *them*, or 'thinking about thinking'. He is toying with them as thoughts revealing the workings of the mind, as the constant use of metaphors throughout Stanza I indicates.

The Bard, Who Present, Past, and Future Sees

Stanza II illustrates this double level of discourse as the past is used to depict the present: the memory is a 'toy of Thought' as well as a memory. That is, the movement into Stanza II is at one level a step into the past, but the description of this past which follows is metaphorically applicable to the present response of the speaker as an elaboration of his mental acts of Stanza I. Thus 'nowness' continues to be the concern of the speaker, and the remembered past event is significant for its connection with the present experience. Coleridge seems to try to point to deep and complex connections of Stanzas I and II with his footnote to 'only that film'. The film of Stanza I becomes the 'stranger' of Stanza II, and this expectancy shows that the mind is now at that threshold experience (see above on 'The Ancient Mariner') of waiting for something to happen, for some relation to emerge, and for some unknown to be transformed into a known.

One of the most important aspects of Stanza II is the illustration of memory as itself a kind environment that can provide the imagination with a treasure-house of objects to internalize. Thus where in Stanza I the speaker interprets his surroundings imaginatively and focuses upon specific objects as central vehicles of metaphor, in Stanza II he continues with the same sort of mental act of seeking a mirror or echo, but this time memory provides the surroundings and the objects to be made toys of thought. The relation of memory and imagination is depicted in this stanza in its positive integration: memory is working *for* imagination, not repressing it as it can do when it operates too much at the call of the conscious volition. But here we see the memory aroused by the association of feeling and by the metaphorical connection of the film and the stranger.[6] Coleridge emphasized the importance of feeling in recalling ideas when he wrote to Southey, 'I almost think, that Ideas *never* recall Ideas, as far as they are Ideas—any more than Leaves in a forest create each other's motion—The Breeze it is that runs thro' them/ it is the Soul, the state of Feeling' (*CL* II 961, 1803). The view is also hinted at in the first stanza of 'This Lime-Tree Bower My Prison'.

The memory described in the poem mirrors the present situation, and contributes to the double level of discourse in Stanza II. Hence Coleridge's often felt sense of the present receding into a dream as the past becomes real (*CL* I 246 and 261). It is a memory of the experience of remembering, and it is the result of that musing upon the music of the church bells, a state of intense expectancy:

> they stirred and haunted me
> With a wild pleasure, falling on mine ear
> Most like articulate sounds of things to come!

Thus the schoolchild sitting in front of the fire musing upon the fluttering film is quickened to a state of intense expectancy and (imaginative) apprehensiveness by the memory of music that once 'stirred and haunted me/With a wild pleasure'. The adult speaker has thus made himself, as child, an object of thought, and this partial identification of personality helps to carry over the presentness of Stanza I into the past of Stanza II. For the speaker too is sitting in front of the fire, remembering, and this exactly mirrors and 'echoes' the child's situation. The connection is then complete as the speaker's memory moves out of the child's past, 'dreaming' of origins ('my sweet birth-place, and the old church-tower'), into the child's present situation, and the connection is once again this sense of expectancy, this threshold experience of alertly awaiting a happening. The dreaming of origins may be another echo of the pre-existence theory (see below), thus further identifying the present 'abstruser musings' of the adult with the past dreamings of the schoolchild, though the musings on origins take on a more sophisticated form for the adult. The 'stranger' then becomes a metaphor also for the self in its pre-existence. This confluence of present and past more exactly mirrors the speaker's situation as the film on the grate stimulates the mood. The child's mind has actively taken up the superstition that the film portends a stranger, and has transformed it into a symbol of his deep longing for a 'companionable form' in the midst of the alien school, 'Townsman, or aunt, or sister more beloved,/My playmate when we both were clothed alike!' A notebook entry points to the psychological source of this this longing: 'Dreams sometimes useful by ~~making~~ giving to the well-grounded *fears & hopes* of the understanding the *feelings* of vivid sense' (*CN* I 188).

The analogy between present and past is intensified when it is recalled that the speaker was in a sense also at school: he was intent on 'abstruser musings' and 'meditation', when, as with the child, the 'idling Spirit' vexed and disturbed his meditation, and the struggle between imagination and reason began, as the mind fixed upon the fire and was stirred by the metaphor of the film and the stranger. Lines 34–6 so exactly describe the situation of Stanza I that the identity of the past 'I' and the present speaker[7] is further assured, as line 37 reminds us with a jolt that this is, at least at the literal level, actually the past that is being described. The infantile fantasy remembered here is perhaps well interpreted as a metaphor for the craving for certainty that the adult 'still' hopes to see. Stanza I presents the resignation of the adult mind that this 'stranger', this unknown element of experience, the origin of things, will never be established as an external certainty.

The question of origins is at the centre of all religion and metaphysics; and Coleridge referred frequently to the mystery and *necessary* 'Incomprehensibility' of the first cause or origin of all things (see e.g. *CL* I 192–3, to John Edwards, 20 March 1796). Throughout his writings Coleridge constantly admonished his reader not to seek for external certainty, but to battle against this 'prejudice of outness' (*BL* I ch. xii 175–6). The aesthetic counterpart for the reader would be that the origins of the poem remain uncertain; thus the significance of the poem can never be fully established, and the poem remains an indeterminate fragment. The speaker thus compares himself to the film, the stranger, affirming that ultimately he is always thrown back upon himself and upon subjectivity, and that this is all the certainty he can ever expect. The myth of a reality and certainty is overthrown, but the fantasy and wish for it is never overcome, as the reliving of the childhood desire suggests. That is, at some level even the adult 'still' hopes to see the stranger, the unknown, turn into a recognition. Perhaps the visitations of imagination keep alive this hope that the certainty and freedom from doubt glimpsed and felt in those experiences could somehow be made more permanent.

The speaker then moves out of the past back into the immediate present and projects his desire for permanence of this experience of hopeful expectancy onto his babe. The present immediately becomes swamped by the future, by hopes, and by expectations, a feeling well expressed by the following lines:

> For dimly on my thoughtful spirit burst
> All I had been, and all my Babe might be!

                                                    (*PW* I 153)

The babe becomes an image of the speaker's ideal self,[8] the self that is or might have been 'certain' because it has been taught from infancy by that 'Great Universal Teacher'. And now in the image of the babe the speaker recognizes the stranger, who has thus become a known 'relation'.

The babe, 'like a breeze', bears the metaphor of imagination, as the speaker transcends his own limitations, his lost childhood and innocence, that is, and by emerging from the 'mundane shell' of his own lost chances gains imaginative vision of this certainty of imagination through his love and hope for his child. Indeed, the myth of childhood as a permanent state of imaginative play works for the adult as a metaphor only. He can never literally return to childhood, but the myth becomes valuable as a metaphor for rejecting and overcoming preconditioned response, habit, and the prejudices of adulthood that spread a film over spontaneous perception. Blake frequently used the myth of lost children as a metaphor for adulthood (see for example the *Songs* for the lost and found boy and girl, and their variants from 'Songs of Innocence' to 'Songs of Experience'). The myth of innocence versus experience is also used as a metaphor for genius versus stagnation, but only as a metaphor. The yearning to be literally a child again would be for an adult a neurosis; his aim must be 'Higher Innocence', or the transcendence of experience, not a rejection of it (as Thel wrongly thinks; see 'The Book of Thel', Keynes, op. cit., 127–30).

Stanza III thus becomes a specification of what in Stanza II were the unknown 'sounds of things to come', the explanation of what is hoped for and expected. They are expressed at one level in terms of the child's future, and the oneness he will feel with nature, or the permanent sense of his participation in the 'One Life', which shall not be marred by unseasonable doubts and loss of a sense of certainty: 'All seasons shall be sweet to thee'. But lines 55–64 indicate the second metaphorical level of discourse, where the childhood projected for the infant is a description of imaginative activity, idealized as permanent and lasting. For the way the child shall see nature is a description of metaphor-making, and at two levels. First, nature makes metaphors of itself: 'the clouds . . . image in their bulk both lakes and shores/And mountain crags'. Then, '*So* shalt thou see and hear'. The shapes and sounds of nature are then lifted to a higher plane of metaphor, as things 'intelligible', indeed as language (lines 59–60). Once again landscape is functioning as a device for internalization, or in this case, as a model for internalizing acts.

Nature here is not only contrasted with the city as more pleasing to the *eye*. The following letter extract indicates how profoundly Coleridge believed that surroundings could affect the observer:

It is melancholy to think, that the best of us are liable to be shaped & coloured by surrounding Objects—and a demonstrative proof, that Man was not made to live in Great Cities! Almost all the physical Evil in the World depends on the existence of moral Evil—and the long-continued contemplation of the latter does not tend to meliorate the human heart.—The pleasures, which we receive from rural beauties, are of little Consequence compared with the Moral Effect of these pleasures—beholding constantly the Best possible we at last become ourselves the best possible. In the country, all around us smile Good and Beauty—and the Images of this divine καλοκάγαθόν are miniatured on the mind of the beholder, as a Landscape on a Convex Mirror.

(*CL* I 154, 1795 to Poole; cf. *CL* I 240)

Such poems as 'Frost at Midnight' and 'The Nightingale', or even 'The Eolian Harp', seem to testify to this claim, as their inspiration seems in part to derive from the surroundings. The supernatural poems may certainly owe something of their colour and individuality or exoticism to the astonishing beauty of the moors in Somerset, with their purples, oranges, and reds, and the changes of light and haunting mists playing over the steep hills and deep valleys of this uneven terrain, with its strange and various vegetation. Coleridge foresaw this effect upon him when he wrote to Thomas Poole a few days after his marriage, from Clevedon: 'The prospect around us is perhaps more *various* than any in the kingdom—Mine Eye gluttonizes—The Sea—the distant Islands!—the opposite Coasts!—I shall assuredly write Rhymes —let the nine Muses prevent it, if they can' (*CL* I 160, 1795).

The description of landscape in poetry is not the only response that the beauty of landscape can inspire. The internalization of landscape is a different response, and the eye cannot accomplish this alone in passive receptivity and perception, but only in conjunction with the imagination. Coleridge's criticism of Erasmus Darwin in a notebook entry draws attention to the unintegrated use of landscape in poetry; it lacks the 'unifying passion' to help internalize, and can actually inhibit the appropriate response: 'Dr Darwin's Poetry, a succession of Landscapes or Paintings—it arrests the attention too often, and so prevents the rapidity necessary to pathos.—it makes the great little' (*CN* I 132, 1795–6). A year later Coleridge was longing for a perception of 'something one & indivisible' which allows all things to 'counterfeit infinity' (*CL* I 348–9 to Thelwall, October 1797). The 'One Life' theme which recurs in the poetry of this period in various disguises is also an expression of this yearning. As nature acts upon the mind to make us 'the best possible', so can art affect the observer, not by describing beautiful landscapes or unusual scenes which the mind's eye is meant simply to recreate internally. Landscape description is rather an inspiration to the mind's imagination; using it as its surroundings the imagination can then choose predominant elements for vehicles of symbols or metaphors of value to the mind. The distinction being made is one between idea and image (as in *CN* I 634, 902, 1842, or III 4047). Thus the speaker's progression through Stanza I of 'Frost at Midnight' is an instance of the imaginative use of his surroundings and is a model for the reader.

Stanza IV seems to transcend the present, past or future of the preceding stanzas. It uses landscape description effectually to mirror the different seasons of the human soul, and it applies not only to moods of creativity and productivity: it also seems to speak of the cycle of life itself, man's journey from youth to age; imaginative living shall make the cycle 'sweet to thee'. Compare the light-hearted lines from the very late poem 'Youth and Age':

> Life is but thought: so think I will
> That Youth and I are house-mates still.

(PW I 439)

Keats had suggested the same transcendence of the cyclic process in 'To Autumn', an exhortation not to try to deny any one of the seasons, but rather to learn to see the beauty in all of them, making them all spring, but *metaphorically* speaking. That is, genius transforms every season into a productive time, a spring-time, by projecting its own creative energies out into what appears to be winter and cold lifelessness: 'the living spirit in our frame,/That loves not to behold a lifeless thing,/Transfuses into all its own delights' (variation of lines 19–25; see *PW* I 240–1). The timelessness of Stanza IV, and its generalized reference to seasons and scenes suggests the freedom from specific time and space designation characteristic of the creative mind, but it also suggests that the speaker is being what he hopes his child will become, responsive to nature, both human nature and external nature. For responsiveness to nature is, as Blake said, imagination itself. The character of the babe–child is thus assimilated into the speaker, another mark of imaginative experience, and the child, like the nightingale, the harp, and the friend, is further internalized as an image of imagination as this identification is achieved.

Conversion of objects into subjects, the general formula for the internalization of landscape (as discussed in *CN* I 189, 1796, or *BL* II, 'On Poesy or Art', 259), is accomplished in the last two lines of the poem in a most skilful and compact reversal of relations. The icicles 'quietly shining *to* the quiet Moon' seem to have become the source of light, reflecting their light to the moon. Here the frost seems, as the agent producing the icicles, to be once again a metaphor of imagination, the moon changed into a quiet observer, 'dreaming on things to come' (*CN* I 215, 1796–7). Or, as the speaker muses imaginatively on the church bells: 'Most like articulate sounds of things to come! So gazed I, till the soothing things, I dreamt,/Lulled me to sleep, and sleep prolonged my dreams!' (lines 33–5), another case of reversal. In the former case, the falling eave-drops have been frozen by the frost into something relatively more lasting, more firmly shaped, and apparently capable of seeming to emit light toward that from which the light is actually borrowed.

The Image of Frost

But the falling eave-drops and the 'trances of the blast' suggest tears and sorrow, and 'blast' suggests a withering, blighting effect. The 'tears' are frozen by the frost, and the beauty is the sort described regretfully by Coleridge in 'Dejection: An Ode':

> And those thin clouds above, in flakes and bars,
> That give away their motion to the stars;
> Those stars, that glide behind them or between,
> Now sparkling, now bedimmed, but always seen:
> Yon crescent Moon, as fixed as if it grew
> In its own cloudless, starless lake of blue;
> I see them all so excellently fair,
> I see, not feel, how beautiful they are!
>
> (*PW* I 364, lines 31–8)

Indeed the moon frequently occurs in contrast to the sun as a source of light without heat, or thought without feeling. In notebook entries shortly before the composing of this poem, Coleridge writes of the cold in association with hope, inspired by images of the moon. He writes, for example:

> And one or two poor melancholy Joys
> Pass by on flimsy wing in Hope's cold gleam,
> Moths in the Moonlight.—

> 'Twas sweet to know it only possible—
> Some *wishes* cross'd my mind & dimly cheer'd it—
> And one or two poor melancholy Pleasures

In these, the ~~cold~~ pale unwarming ~~gleams~~ light of Hope
Silvring their flimsy wing flew silent by,
Moths in the Moonlight—

(*CN* I 214, 1796–7)

Even in the passage in the notebooks most closely associated with 'Kubla Khan' the association of ice and moon seems to have interesting relevance for 'Frost at Midnight', for it raises the question of a mysterious causal relation between the moon and ice. This relation is part of the strangeness of the connection of the icicles and moon in these two final lines of the poem. The passage runs as follows:

Hymns Moon
In a cave in the mountains of Cashmere an Image of Ice, which makes its appearance thus . . . two days before the new *moon* there appears a bubble of Ice which increases in size every day till the 15th day, at which it is an ell or more in height: then as the moon decreases, the Image does also till it vanishes.

(*CN* I 240, 1796–7)[9]

If, in such a passage as this, one follows up the associations, a closer relation seems to be called for between the frost and the moon too, the icicles being a kind of intermediary between them. The 'secret ministry' of the frost and the fact that it is 'unhelped by any wind' may draw attention to its self-activating power as imagination. But in the alternative interpretation of the frost as threatening, that is, as freezing over perception through inactivity, or at least in its cold and frozen lifelessness as antithetical to feeling and warmth, its relation to the moon seems to fit more closely: the moon is itself the symbol of light without warmth, one of Coleridge's most central and recurrent distinctions, a fusion of light and warmth being essential for wisdom and faith, and also for any genuinely effective moral base. The sun was the symbol of light and warmth synthesized, and thought and feeling unified, or head combined with heart (see for example *CN* III 3379). Coleridge had stated this union succinctly in a notebook entry of 1799: 'Socinianism Moonlight—Methodism &c a Stove! O for some Sun that shall unite Light & Warmth' (*CN* I 467; cf. *CN* I 1233). His comments on Unitarianism are also relevant to this image in the poem:

God becomes a mere power in darkness, even as Gravitation, and instead of a moral Religion of practical Influence we shall have only a physical Theory to gratify ideal curiosity—no Sun, no Light with vivifying Warmth, but a cold and dull moonshine, or rather star-light, which shews itself but shews nothing else.

(*CL* II 1196)

One might then closely associate the frost with the moon, the latter being the secret minister and the helper, instead of the wind. The wind would thereby retain its imaginative associations, as the breeze of Stanza III. The frost performs, then, without feeling, but with the cold light of the moon, and the icicles are the form in which water ceases to flow: not tears dried up from relief of happiness, but tears frozen by cold (as in 'Dejection: An Ode'; but compare *CN* I 219, later used in 'The Nightingale' for a more positive connection of tears and moonlight). This is the unrelieved grief bemoaned in the poem 'Dejection'. There the symbol of the moon had also been used, in the epitaph from the 'Ballad of Sir Patrick Spence' (note in the lines following these the mention too of the new moon and the 'blast').

> Late, late yestreen I saw the new Moon,
> With the old Moon in her arms;
> And I fear, I fear, My Master dear!
> We shall have a deadly storm.
>
> (*PW* I 362, lines 9–14)

The frozenness and unhealthiness of the grief implied in Stanza IV and in the image of the frost as a 'Urizenic' figure is encouraged by other lines in 'Dejection', aptly characterizing the dangers of un-expressed pain:

> A grief without a pang, void, dark, and drear,
> A stifled, drowsy, unimpassioned grief,
> Which finds no natural outlet, no relief,
> In word, or sigh, or tear—   (lines 21–4)

Throughout 'Dejection' images of flowing water, of showers, rains, and tears, are suggestions of the necessity for a fountain-like action of the heart to express not only its joys but its sorrows. In the final Stanza IV of 'Frost at Midnight' water images keep coming up: there is the snow in line 68 and the 'sun-thaw' of line 70, then the 'eave-drops' of line 70, and these all seem to move toward a flowing state, from frozen, motion-less water-forms; but then in line 72 the frost, also a water image, is called forth, and the hardest, most frozen and cold form yet mentioned in the poem occurs as the icicles are described in lines 73 and 74.

The importance of water images for Coleridge in the few months preceding the writing of the poem is clear from the notebooks; they record entries in Greek from Ralph Cudworth, where water is said to be the origin of all generation. Once again, the 'abstruser musings' seem to be about origins, now in the cosmic sense, with the water cycle as the predominant image. The water image does of course have its strong Biblical associations, to which Coleridge often referred in his theological musings. Furthermore, the father of all gods is said to be the ocean, and in one entry 'Wind & rain & stars' are associated (see *CN* I 244–9, 1797).

But perhaps the most important aspect of water imagery for Coleridge which tends to give some credibility to the notion that the frost may work also as a negative, threatening image in the poem, an image of stagnation and frozen passivity as contrasted with the vital warmth of the active, imaginative mind, is the relation of fountains and flowing streams to truth. Fountain and spring imagery abound throughout Coleridge's writings. One of the most characteristic passages occurs in an early notebook entry: 'Truth is compared in scripture to a streaming fountain; if her waters flow not in perpetual progression, they stagnate into a muddy pool of conformity & tradition. Milton.' (*CN* I 119, 1795–6). The following passage consolidates water, spring, snow, river, and season:

In fine, Truth considered in itself and in the effects natural to it, may be conceived as a gentle spring or water-source, warm from the genial earth, and breathing up into the snow drift that is piled over and around its outlet. It turns the obstacle into its own form and character, and as it makes its way increases its stream. And should it be arrested in its course by a chilling season, it suffers delay, not loss, and waits only for a change in the wind to awaken and again roll onwards.

(*The Friend (CC)* I 65)

(See also 'Religious Musings', lines 403–4, and 412–19 for the spring or fountain image, *PW* I 124–5; for the source of the passage from *The Friend*, see *CN* III 3578.)

Perhaps a passage more interesting still in view of the fire in the first stanza of this poem is the entry often associated with 'Kubla Khan'; it seems to bear upon this poem as well:

> There is not a new or strange opinion—
> Truth returned from banishment—
> a river run under ground—
> fire beneath embers—
> (*CN* I 179; *CN* III 3578 is related to the fire imagery.)

These fire and water images reveal the connections of this very domestic poem with the exotic primitivism of Coleridge's more popular poetry. The very next entry in the notebooks suggests that this association of the exotic with 'Frost at Midnight' is not as tentative as it might at first appear: 'Men anxious for this world—Owls that wake all night to catch mice' (*CN* I 178; on the owl, see discussion below.)

In a letter passage relating closely to 'Frost at Midnight', Coleridge mentions the sleep of Vishnu, and then quotes these lines from *Osorio*; they substantiate the connection between the domestic and exotic:

> The many clouds, the Sea, the Rock, the Sands,
> Lay in the silent moonshine—and the Owl,
> (Strange, very strange!) the Scritch-owl only wak'd,
> Sole Voice, sole Eye of all that world of Beauty!
>
> (*CL* I 350–1)

The imagery here is startlingly like that in 'Frost at Midnight', and the phrase 'strange, very strange!' enhances the connections.

An entry from a notebook closely following the one above reinforces the imagery associations as well as the threatening aspect of frost and ice: 'Smooth, shining, & deceitful as thin Ice' (*CN* I 179).[10] Much later, between December 1798 and May 1799 (the next winter after the poem was written), a strange entry occurs: '~~Infants~~—Severity of the Winter— the King's-Fisher, its slow short flight permitting you to observe all its colours, almost as if it had been a flower' (*CN* I 381). Written as this entry is in the midst of notes apparently taken while in Germany, one cannot help wondering whether this is not actually a compression of two entries, the first part dating perhaps from an earlier period, say the winter before (but see *CN* I 381n for the reasons for the dating). Other entries during this period immediately following the composition of the poem also seem to relate to it, and may suggest that the dating of the entry is too late in the year. It may however be more likely that Coleridge was reworking old themes and images (for see *CN* I 335 f3, where he compares the clouds and moonlight in Germany with Stowey and the contrast of silence and the ocean). But the entry here seems to express one of the most pressing themes of 'Frost at Midnight' as well as some of its imagery, and was also written in December 1798:

> The silence of a City—How awful at midnight—
> ~~As silent as a sleeping Hermit's cell,~~
> ~~Mute as the cell of a sleeping anchoret,~~
> ~~As silent~~
> Mute as the battlements & crags & towers
> That fancy makes in the clouds—yea as mute
> As the moonlight that sleeps on the steady Vanes,—
> The cell of a departed Anchoret,
> His skeleton & flitting ghost are there,
> Sole tenants—
> And ~~the huge~~ all the City, silent as the moon
> That steeps in quiet light ~~her~~ the steady Vanes
> Of her huge temples—
>
> (*CN* I 348)

The silence, muteness (line 6), and quietness (line 12), the 'silent moon' (line 11), the lack of wind suggested by the 'steady vanes, the phrase, 'fancy makes in the clouds', the time—midnight—and the solitude of the hermit, compared to something sleeping; all of these similarities suggest origins (or continuations) of 'Frost at Midnight' and substantiate the negative connotations of the imagery offered as an opposing aspect of frost as a symbol of imagination.

That the frost can be an image both of imagination and of the force which may freeze up or inactivate imaginative activity, that is, an image of mind as creative or as repressively mechanical, is an example itself of imagination at work fashioning a paradoxical image with apparently contradictory implications. The 'identity in difference'[11] suggested by this image makes it a richer metaphor because of the integrity of the relation of frost to imagination and of frost to a repressive, censoring faculty. The simultaneous use of contradictory meanings for one image itself is a compression characteristic of imaginative activity. Coleridge exhorted Southey to 'study compression!' (CL I 351, to Thelwall). And Coleridge achieves in this doubly connotative image a truer characterization of the nature of imaginative experience and its inherent conflict with the passive and the degenerate. For along with the joy of vision comes inevitably the chilling sensation of falling back into unenlivened ordinary perception. The dual nature of imaginative experience is thus captured in this complex image of frost, expressing the conflict between the mind as essentially creative or passive.

The multivalence of the image of frost sets the tone for the poem and both begins and ends it. It can also be taken as a gesture at a theory of language. Shelley best expresses this character of language as exhibiting a cold and frosty side when he discusses the concept of the 'dead metaphor'. But Coleridge may be the origin of the form in which Shelley clothes the concept of language as degenerative. For Coleridge repeatedly admonishes his readers that words lose the power of truth by becoming too familiar to excite the mind to a perception of the vital and integral relations represented, especially by metaphor (see *The Friend* *(CC)* I 110, and *LS (CC)* 25). In one notebook entry Coleridge explicitly states that 'language degenerates', and that 'words slide into common use, generally much alloyed by the carelessness of common Life . . .' (*CN* I 1835, January 1804; the entire entry is of interest).

In addition to this aspect of language generally as 'degenerate', a more relevant formulation to this analysis is that *metaphor* degenerates especially easily into literal meaning; it can be interpreted literally so as to fail to communicate what it was intended to achieve. Shelley's theory of metaphor seems to apply exactly to this aspect. But Coleridge was frequently warning his readers about the tyranny of the literal over the metaphorical (as in *CN* II 2711 and 2723–4, autumn 1805), though he often used the word symbol as one would now use metaphor. By metaphorical language one might actually communicate the opposite of what one intended. And Coleridge felt a deep obligation to communicate truth, not merely to write it in a form intelligible to himself (see *The Friend (CC)* I Essay v, especially pages 39–41, and Essays vi–xii, for an expression of this commitment). But since all language is probably ultimately metaphorical, and poetry only an activating and highlighting, or an environment for regenerating or creating new metaphors, metaphor could hardly be avoided. It is not merely a luxury, as some eighteenth-century theorists of language insisted.[12] In order to avoid the likelihood that the metaphor should be interpreted literally, tension can be built up as it is in the frost image, in order to keep the mind actively apprehending the complexity of the image in the poem. Or, as we have seen in other poems, a framework gently mocking the literal response to language may be incorporated. The image of the frost may be correctly interpreted as a very subtle and well-integrated kind of framework for this poem, since its complexity ultimately functions as a reflection upon the nature of imaginative response as active or passive. The subject/object reversal at the end of the poem, with the change in source of light (or authority?), seems to encourage such an interpretation, as the reader as subject is encouraged to contemplate his relation to the poem as object. The end of the poem takes him back to its beginnings, or origins, as it fails to give a satisfactory, clear-cut equation in the struggle to interpret meaning and value.

This uncertainty about language, its positive encouragements to thought and imaginativeness, and its negative side as actually inhibiting insight by misleading with respect to the object of signification, may also be one way of enriching the constant associations of imaginative activity with silence and quietness. Coleridge wrote numerous entries in his notebooks about this dual aspect of language (for example, *CN* III 3954, 3973, 4247, and 4265 f27). Some of these entries are the basis for passages in the *Biographia*, *Aids to Reflection*, and other published works. The notion of language as the 'market coin of intercourse', subject to bankruptcy, is of course Plato's metaphor, in the *Meno*.

In the last two lines of the poem adjectives or adverbs about silence and quietness occur three times within a total of thirteen words. The apparent contradiction of using language while advocating silence is somewhat ameliorated when it is realized that language can be a vitally important means, but to another end than is expected. Its purpose may be the evocation of rhythm, music, and the general effect that language can convey. This effect helps the mind to move into a state of greater awareness about the meaning of the world around it, and the mind's relation to it. Music was for Coleridge particularly evocative of the trance-like states that encourage imaginative response; he wrote in a notebook entry:

> Love is the Spirit of Life, and Music the Life of the Spirit.—
>
> ---
>
> What is MUSIC?—Poetry in its grand sense?
> Answer.
> Passion and order aton'd! Imperative Power in Obedience!
> What is the first and divinest Strain of Music?
> In the Intellect
>
> (*CN* II 3231, and see III 4319)

In Stanza II of 'Frost at Midnight' it is the music of the church bells which stirs the child to recollection. Both music and silence encourage imaginativeness, and while seeming somehow to be contrary to language, are also part of it. This apparent contradiction in language mirrors the contradictory meanings inherent in the image of frost, and inherent in imagination too.

Finally, Coleridge sums up his frustration with winter just a few days before he is supposed to have composed 'Frost at Midnight', in a comment testifying to the unfriendly connotations of cold:

> I long to be at home with you . . . My Joy is only in the bud here—I am like that Tree, which fronts me—The Sun shines bright & warm, as if it were summer—but it is not summer & so it shines on leafless boughs. The beings who know how to sympathize with me are my foliage.
> (*CL* I 381; the tree image is characteristic; see for example *CN* I 926, and
> *The Friend (CC)* I 458.)

At the same time, this passage illustrates Coleridge's use of seasonal imagery to express his own mood and attitude toward his home and friends—an example of internalization, discussed further below.

The Metaphor of Pre-Existence

A number of notebook entries made during the few months previous to the writing of 'Frost at Midnight' express Coleridge's preoccupation with the formulation and thematics of this last stanza, with its cycle of seasons, of water, and its contrast between the snow outside and the 'nigh thatch [which]/Smokes in the sun thaw'. The latter contrast is mirrored in the first stanza of the poem in the image of the frost outside compared with the cottage and fire within. But the seasonal metaphor also seems to have its analogy in the poem, so that the final stanza is not bringing up wholly new themes but reformulating less obvious ones obscured by the more immediate concerns of the poem. For the previous stanzas give intimations of the cycle of life from birth and infancy to the stage of adolescence and finally adulthood. Death is not explicitly represented by any character in the poem, but is more intimately suggested by the cold and silent winter surrounding the 'Life' and the cottage, on all sides, as if the outside were a metaphor generally for the unknown. This cycle is another dimension of the seasonal cycle discussed in Stanza IV, the cycle of life.

The notebooks suggest, along with corresponding letters, that another cycle of birth, death, and rebirth in addition to the life-cycle may enrich the seasonal metaphor still further. For in the years preceding the writing of this poem the birth of Coleridge's first child seems to have aroused in his mind speculations about the possibility of pre-existence, thoughts no doubt encouraged by his reading of Plato during this period. Wordsworth was to take up this theme in 1802 with his 'My heart leaps up' and the Immortality Ode, and while Coleridge insists that he never adopted the belief literally, it is clear that it fascinated him as a speculation and as a poetic metaphor. He wrote in December 1796:

> Now that the thinking part of Man, i.e. the Soul, existed previously to it's appearance in it's present body, may be very wild philosophy; but it is very intelligible poetry, inasmuch as Soul is an orthodox word in all our poets; they meaning by 'Soul' a being inhabiting our body, & playing upon it, like a Musician inclosed in an Organ whose keys were placed inwards.— Now this opinion I do not hold.

But he went on to say, 'I, who do not believe in this descending, & incarcerated Soul, yet said, if my Baby had died before I had seen him, I should have *struggled* to believe it.' (*CL* I 278 to Thelwall; note the metaphor of the musical instrument.)

The metaphor of pre-existence seems to operate as an attempt to account for experiences inexplicable as results of sensations and perceptions, as a passive theory of mind would explain all experience. Rather it is a metaphor for a creative theory of mind, and explains such experiences as intimations of the mind itself, that is as acts expressive of its structure. Thus Plato can be understood as using the myth of anamnesis and pre-existence to elucidate the insights and intuitions of the creative faculty, imagination, which constitute genuine knowledge, and which advance beyond the mere assimilation and generalization of sense experience. The truth of the myth of pre-existence and anamnesis, like the childhood myth, lies in its rejection of the notion that ordinary sense experience is all that the mind experiences. In both, present adult experience is a degeneration and a shadow of the more substantial experience postulated by the theory that another sort of existence is possible to the mind. This connection in the function of the two myths of pre-existence and childhood may explain why the sleeping babe often arouses in Coleridge's mind thoughts about pre-existence. It may however be an accident of his reading Plato at the time of the birth of his first child.

In the following letter passage, Coleridge seeks to establish the link between sleeping infants and speculations about origins and first causes such as pre-existence, and the validity of the cycle metaphor of nature's seasons, stages of life, and cycles of rebirth; all of these are concerns lurking within the dimensions of 'Frost at Midnight':

> Now as the very idea of consciousness implies a recollection of the Last Links, and the growth of it an extension of that retrospect, Immortality— or a recollection after the Sleep and Change (probably and by strict analogy the growth) of Death (for growth of body and the conditional causes of intellectual growth are found all to take place during Sleep, and Sleep is the Term repeatedly and as it were fondly used by the inspired Writers as the Exponent of Death, and without it the aweful and undoubtedly taught, Doctrine of the Resurrection has no possible meaning)—the very idea of such a consciousness, permit me to repeat, implies a recollection after the Sleep of Death of all material circumstances that were at least immediately previous to it. A spacious field here opens itself for moral reflection . . . when we consider the growth of consciousness . . . as the end of our earthly Being . . . how habits of Vice of all Kinds tend to retard this growth, and how all our sufferings tend to extend & open it out . . .
>
> (*CL* II 1197–8)

'A spacious field here opens itself for . . . reflection' of all sorts, especially upon the implications revealed by this passage as hidden in the innocent sleep of the babe, the recollection in Stanza II, and the 'One Life' theme suggested in lines 60–64, explicated in the passage of this letter preceding the quoted one. It may also illustrate that 'compression' (see *CL* I 351), one of the methods of poetry along with internalization, lends the sleep of the babe its richness and inexhaustible associations. This quality of compression makes it difficult to determine the 'legitimate' boundaries of meaning of a poem. This latter passage is also noteworthy for its similarities in theme with Keats's letter on 'soul-making' and the world as a school for the human heart (see the letter to George and Georgiana, 1819, in the section under 21 April). Interestingly enough, Keats's letter was written only about two weeks after his encounter with Coleridge in a park near Highgate. The detailed similarities between the thoughts of the two men and their expressions are extraordinary.

But a passage from a letter to Thelwall, 14 October 1797, further establishes the symbolical value of sleep. It suggests the sorts of 'heretical' speculations Coleridge was concerned with at a time prior to composing the poem:

It is but seldom that I raise & spiritualize my intellect to this height—& at other times I adopt the Brahman Creed, & say—It is better to sit than to stand, it is better to lie than to sit, it is better to sleep than to wake—but Death is the best of all!—I should much wish, like the Indian Vishna, to float about along an infinite ocean cradled in the flower of the Lotus, & wake once in a million years for a few minutes—just to know that I was going to sleep a million years more . . .

(*CL* I 350)

The associations aroused by sleep, and specifically the sleeping infant, are enriched by the dream element. Coleridge was fascinated by dreams, as is clear from many notes scattered profusely throughout all of the notebooks. These musings upon sleep may also contribute to an understanding of the preface to 'Kubla Khan' and the symbolical value of the claim that the poem was composed in a 'profound sleep, at least of the external senses'.

Thus the image of an infant seems frequently to arouse in Coleridge's mind thoughts about pre-existence not explicit in 'Frost at Midnight', but which nevertheless seem to inform it at the level of sources (and indirectly at the level of the seasonal metaphor relating to the cycle of life). For whenever Coleridge talks about pre-existence, a comment about an infant is not far distant, and on many occasions when he discusses infancy, pre-existence is hovering over the discussion. For instance, in a notebook entry mixed in with entries associated with 'Kubla Khan'—entries also, however, connected with this poem— Coleridge quoted from Plato's *Phaedo* on pre-existence, mentioned Synesius (who also held to that doctrine), gave a related quote from Plotinus in the next entry (*CN* I 200 and see n), and then suddenly followed these philosophic speculations with the entry, 'Discontent mild as an Infant low-plaining in its sleep' (*CN* I 202). The connection taken alone is admittedly vague, but seems relevant to the first stanza of the poem with its image of the sleeping babe and mild discontent. In searching for sources of 'Frost at Midnight' this entry turns out, however, to be in the midst of other vaguely associable but no less relevant entries. The frequency of these (in themselves) vague associations suggests more substantial links. For throughout this section of the notebooks Coleridge is contemplating the implications of dreams, sleep, infancy, pre-existence, children growing up outside cities and close to nature, seasons; and interspersed are passages which are apparently variations of Stanza IV.

Coleridge's first recorded thoughts of pre-existence occur in a letter to Poole including the manuscript of the sonnet inspired by the birth of Coleridge's first child. But the feeling he describes has certain affinities with the movement in Stanza I of 'Frost at Midnight', into the past of Stanza II; the feeling then becomes a living present through imaginative memory. This feeling is associated with pre-existence, but not dependent entirely upon it. Most relevant to this analysis, pre-existence seems almost always sparked off by the sight of the sleeping infant. The entire sonnet is related to the poem:

> Oft of some unknown Past such Fancies roll
> Swift o'er my brain, as make the Present seem,
> For a brief moment, like a most strange dream
> When, not unconscious that she dreamt, the Soul
> Questions herself in sleep! and Some have said   5
> We liv'd ere yet this fleshly robe we wore.
> O my sweet Baby! when I reach my door,
> If heavy Looks should tell me, thou wert dead,
> (As sometimes, thro' excess of Hope, I fear)
> I think, that I should struggle to believe,   10
> Thou wert a Spirit to this nether sphere
> Sentenc'd, for some more venial crime to grieve—
> Didst scream, then spring to meet Heaven's quick Reprieve,
> While we wept idly o'er thy little Bier!

Coleridge then explained:

Almost all the followers of Fenelon believe that *men* are degraded intelligences, who had once all existed, at one time & together, in a paradisiacal or perhaps heavenly state.—The first four lines express a feeling which I have often had. The present has appeared like a vivid dream or exact similitude of some past circumstances.

(*CL* I 246 to Poole, November 1796)

This last line seems to suggest the peculiar relationship of the memory of Stanza II and the present of Stanza I, and their close resemblance of feeling. The reality of the present in Stanza I has faded, and the past takes over with the memory of such a similar occasion, that the present experience of the fire and grate seems almost a mystical reliving of the past occasion.

The connection of this sonnet with the poem is strengthened by an examination of the sonnet which immediately follows it in the letter version; part of the sonnet gives a rather precise account of Stanza III of 'Frost at Midnight':

Charles! my slow Heart was only *sad*, when first
I scann'd that face of feeble Infancy:
For dimly on my thoughtful spirit burst
All I had been, and all my Babe might be!
But when I watch'd it on it's Mother's arm   5
And hanging at her bosom (she the while
Bent o'er it's features with a tearful smile)
Then I was thrill'd & melted, and most warm
Imprest a Father's kiss! And all beguil'd
Of dark Remembrance and presageful Fear   10
I seem'd to see an Angel's form appear—
'Twas even thine, beloved Woman mild!
So for the Mother's sake the Child was dear,
And dearer was the Mother for the Child!

(*CL* I 247)

Lines 3–4 and 9–11 are the ones most interesting for Coleridge's later use in the poem. A letter three weeks afterwards gives a variant of the feeling Coleridge seemed fascinated by, and seems to reproduce in Stanza II:

Oft o'er my brain mysterious Fancies roll
That make the Present seem (the while they last)
A dreamy Semblance of some Unknown Past
Mix'd with such feelings, as distress the [Soul]
Half-reas'ning in her sleep
(*CL* I 261 to Thelwall, November 1796)

A return to the notebooks reveals yet another association of infants and pre-existence besides the apparently accidental one noted above. This entry is dated somewhat later than the ones discussed above, and it is explicitly related to 'Frost at Midnight'. It is a long list on 'Infancy & Infants—'; only a few sections are reproduced here. The section most immediately interesting for the present purpose is the line which reads, '11. The Souls of Infants, a vision—(vide Sweden-borg—)'. Coleridge then wrote several descriptions reading like a programme for 'Frost at Midnight': '2. Asleep . . .', '4. Seen asleep . . .', '5. Sports of infants—their incessant activity, the *means* being the end.— Nature how lovely a school-mistress—A blank-verse, moral poem . . .', '10. . . . The infants of the very poor, especially in cities', '14. The wisdom & graciousness of God in the infancy of the human species— its beauty, long continuance &c. &c. Children in the wind—hair floating, tossing, a miniature of the agitated Trees, below which they play'd . . .' (*CN* I 330, 1797–8).
The next entry needs no justification for the association with the

poem; it precedes the entry quoted above: 'The reed-roof'd Village, still bepatch'd with snow/Smok'd in the sun-thaw' (*CN* I 329, 1797–8). Compare an entry of a (probably) slightly earlier date: 'From the snow-drop even till the rich Grape-cluster was heavy—' (*CN* I 269), a possible variation on lines in Stanza IV.

The first entry above provides the clue to relating previous entries in the notebook to 'Frost at Midnight' that went unnoticed as variants of this section of Stanza IV. They suggest that Coleridge was thinking for a long time about the poem as all the speculative elements discussed above were gradually grouping themselves. These elements may finally have crystallized after a year of eddying in the mind. Other entries, apparently variants of the above line in Stanza IV or other parts of the stanza, are as follows: 'The Sun-shine lies on the cottage-wall/Ashining thro' the snow' (*CN* I 229). This entry occurs twice removed from another entry on an infant: 'The Infant playing with its mother's Shadow—/Rocking its little sister's cradle & singing to her with inarticulate voice.' (*CN* I 226). But the entry immediately pre-ceding is even more relevant to the poem, both thematically and with regard to imagery, though it is not actually a variant of lines as the other entries are: 'The Life of the Siminole playful from infancy to Death compared to the Snow, which in a calm day falling scarce seems to fall & plays & dances in & out, to the very moment that it reaches the ground' (*CN* I 228, apparently from *Bartram's Travels*.) Here suggestions of the cycle of life are evident in the connections with the snow, though in this case the metaphor is more direct and dispenses with the water-cycle. The next entry but two (*CN* I 231) is a draft of seven lines from 'The Nightingale', composed a few months after 'Frost at Midnight', a fact substantiating the connections being drawn here between these surrounding entries and the latter poem, connections which are clearly tentative and uncertain when taken alone, rather than for their cumulative effect.

Other variants for this section of Stanza IV occur only slightly earlier than these, indeed on the preceding pages. One reads: 'The subtle snow in every breeze rose curling from the Grove, like pillars of cottage smoke (*CN* I 217). Immediately preceding this entry are the entries quoted above on the moon and its relation to the coldness of the frost, and then occurs a vaguely associated entry:

> . . .
> Sabbeth day—from the
> Miller's mossy wheel
> the waterdrops dripp'd
> leisurely—
>
> . . .
> Broad-breasted Pollards with broad-branching head.
> (*CN* I 213; note the snow–fire connections in foregoing entries.)

In an entry on the next page but one the seasonal metaphor is used for a lengthy description of the ceaseless blossoming of a species of tree (*CN* I 222). Interspersed between the entries relating to the composition of 'Frost at Midnight' are unmistakable sources of 'The Nightingale', written a few months afterwards. Indeed, the entry on Hartley ceasing to cry when he is carried outside and catches the light of the moon in his eyes (*CN* I 219), directly incorporated into 'The Nightingale', has certain obvious connections with the moon and its relation to the 'eave-drops' as tears and the cycle of water, as was discussed above.

Once these entries have been noticed, their proximity to the entries on pre-existence tends to support the connections suggested above; the pre-existence entries occur on the preceding page to these variants of Stanza IV. Other entries, (*CN* I 177, 178, 179) have already been noted for their connection with the poem, and it is not surprising that the entries on pre-existence falling between these two groups should also elucidate the poem. The exquisite phrase, 'makes a toy of Thought' also has sources in the complaint of another notebook jotting (repeated in a letter of December 1796): 'Our quaint metaphysical opinions in an hour of anguish like playthings by the bedside of a child deadly sick' (*CN* I 182). This variation on Jeremy Taylor, who used the image of baubles, is an example of Coleridge's genius for 'compression' and metaphor-making. And compare the following extract from a letter to Benjamin Flower: 'My philosophical refinements, & metaphysical Theories lay by me in the hour of anguish, as toys by the bedside of a Child deadly-sick.' (*CL* I 267, 1796) This extract, with 'toy' instead of 'bauble' or 'plaything', displays the development toward 'toy of Thought' in the poem.

Another notebook jotting of this period suggests a source for the occurrence of the child's fervent hopes in Stanza II: 'Dreams sometimes useful by giving to the well-grounded *fears & hopes* of the understanding the *feelings* of vivid sense.' (*CN* I 188) The next entry but two on sleep, as 'voluntary & holy—a spiritual before God . . .' (*CN* I 191), has already been related to the poem's gradual derealization of the present as imagination takes over. Finally two entries on love seem to act as a commentary on Stanza I and on the sleeping babe as profoundly affecting the speaker's mind, stilling it from its 'abstrusest musings' and 'meditations' to awaken it to imaginative activity. First: 'Made my heart tender thro' the power of Love—/My mind preserved watchful & *inward*' (*CN* I 193). Compare the omitted lines: 'subtle toys of the self-watching mind' (*PW* I 241). The second entry on love is also related to the way in which imaginative activity involves the surroundings: 'Love transforms the souls into a conformity with the object loved' (*CN* I 189; cf. *BL* I ch. xii 173, 184, and 188.) For both entries indirectly describe the process of internalization going on throughout the poem, and the final metaphorical reversal and assimilation of subject and object. But these two entries explain that love can be the source of the ability or the stimulus for imaginative assimilation. Love is an expression of imagination when the ego transcends its narrow limits and sees another as itself in the identification of object with subject. Love thus becomes a metaphor for imaginative acts and aesthetic response (see *CN* III 4244 for Coleridge's own development of this metaphor).

The sources of 'Frost at Midnight' have been obscured in the literature partly because entries in the notebooks and letters have been quickly perceived to relate to 'Kubla Khan', 'The Ancient Mariner', 'The Nightingale', or 'Ode to the Departing Year'; all these poems were written during the months surrounding 'Frost at Midnight'. While the more explicit connections with 'Frost at Midnight' had been noted already, the more subtle and complex associations can be easily missed. For one entry often refers to more than one poem, or refers to mixed images or related images which were later transformed into slightly different constituents in the poetry.

These sources help to elucidate the poetry by suggesting connotations and meanings not easily noticed, such as the ambivalence of the frost image or the metaphor of childhood as related to pre-existence. But sources also help to chart the process of assimilation of elements which finally crystallize into a work of art. How that crystallization of the discovered sources and elements takes place, and what stimulates it, must, according to the Romantic aesthetic, remain causally unanalysable by the conscious, rational mind, at least. For the process seems to involve faculties or areas far below the consciousness. Imagination is a law unto itself, it seems, and while it is an expression of the mind's nature, it remains unanalysable, at least by the reason. But it is not therefore necessary to brand the imagination a mystical faculty; it may rather be necessary to broaden the concept of what constitutes knowledge.

Domesticity and Exoticism in 'This Lime-Tree Bower My Prison'

The Text: Published Version

This Lime-Tree Bower My Prison
(Addressed to Charles Lamb, of the India House, London)

In the June of 1797 some long-expected friends paid a visit to the author's cottage; and on the morning of their arrival, he met with an accident, which disabled him from walking during the whole time of their stay. One evening, when they had left him for a few hours, he composed the following lines in the garden-bower.

> Well, they are gone, and here must I remain,
> This lime-tree bower my prison! I have lost
> Beauties and feelings, such as would have been
> Most sweet to my remembrance even when age
> Had dimm'd mine eyes to blindness! They, meanwhile,   5
> Friends, whom I never more may meet again,
> On springy heath, along the hill-top edge,
> Wander in gladness, and wind down, perchance,
> To that still roaring dell, of which I told;
> The roaring dell, o'erwooded, narrow, deep,   10
> And only speckled by the mid-day sun;
> Where its slim trunk the ash from rock to rock
> Flings arching like a bridge;—that branchless ash,
> Unsunn'd and damp, whose few poor yellow leaves
> Ne'er tremble in the gale, yet tremble still,   15
> Fann'd by the water-fall! and there my friends

Behold the dark green file of long lank weeds,*
That all at once (a most fantastic sight!)
Still nod and drip beneath the dripping edge
Of the blue clay-stone.   20

               Now, my friends emerge
Beneath the wide wide Heaven—and view again
The many-steepled tract magnificent
Of hilly fields and meadows, and the sea,
With some fair bark, perhaps, whose sails light up
The slip of smooth clear blue betwixt two Isles   25
Of purple shadow! Yes! they wander on
In gladness all; but thou, methinks, most glad,
My gentle-hearted Charles! for thou hast pined
And hunger'd after Nature, many a year,
In the great City pent, winning thy way   30
With sad yet patient soul, through evil and pain
And strange calamity! Ah! slowly sink
Behind the western ridge, thou glorious Sun!
Shine in the slant beams of the sinking orb,
Ye purple heath-flowers! richlier burn, ye clouds!   35
Live in the yellow light, ye distant groves!
And kindle, thou blue Ocean! So my friend
Struck with deep joy may stand, as I have stood,
Silent with swimming sense; yea, gazing round
On the wide landscape, gaze till all doth seem   40
Less gross than bodily; and of such hues
As veil the Almighty Spirit, when yet he makes
Spirits perceive his presence.

               A delight
Comes sudden on my heart, and I am glad
As I myself were there! Nor in this bower,   45
This little lime-tree bower, have I not mark'd
Much that has sooth'd me. Pale beneath the blaze
Hung the transparent foliage; and I watch'd
Some broad and sunny leaf, and lov'd to see
The shadow of the leaf and stem above   50
Dappling its sunshine! And that walnut-tree
Was richly ting'd, and a deep radiance lay
Full on the ancient ivy, which usurps
Those fronting elms, and now, with blackest mass
Makes their dark branches gleam a lighter hue   55

---

*The *Asplenium Scolopendrium*, called in some countries the Adder's Tongue, in others the Hart's Tongue, but Withering gives the Adder's Tongue as the trivial name of the *Ophioglossum* only.

Through the late twilight: and though now the bat
Wheels silent by, and not a swallow twitters,
Yet still the solitary humble-bee
Sings in the bean-flower! Henceforth I shall know
That Nature ne'er deserts the wise and pure;   60
No plot so narrow, be but Nature there,
No waste so vacant, but may well employ
Each faculty of sense, and keep the heart
Awake to Love and Beauty! and sometimes
'Tis well to be bereft of promis'd good,   65
That we may lift the soul, and contemplate
With lively joy the joys we cannot share.
My gentle-hearted Charles! when the last rook
Beat its straight path along the dusky air
Homewards, I blest it! deeming its black wing   70
(Now a dim speck, now vanishing in light)
Had cross'd the mighty Orb's dilated glory,
While thou stood'st gazing; or, when all was still,
Flew creeking o'er thy head, and had a charm*
For thee, my gentle-hearted Charles, to whom   75
No sound is dissonant which tells of Life.

*Some months after I had written this line, it gave me pleasure to find that Bartram had observed the same circumstance of the Savanna Crane, 'When these Birds move their wings in flight, their strokes are slow, moderate and regular; and even when at a considerable distance or high above us, we plainly hear the quill-feathers: their shafts and webs upon one another creek as the joints or working of a vessel in a tempestuous sea.'

The Text: Version from Letter to Robert Southey, 17 July 1797

Charles Lamb has been with me for a week—he left me Friday morning.—/ The second day after Wordsworth came to me, dear Sara accidently emptied a skillet of boiling milk on my foot, which confined me during the whole time of C. Lamb's stay & still prevents me from all *walks* longer than a furlong.— While Wordsworth, his Sister, & C. Lamb were out one evening;/sitting in the arbour of T. Poole's garden, which communicates with mine, I wrote these lines, with which I am pleased—

Well—they are gone: and here must I remain,
Lam'd by the scathe of fire, lonely & faint,
This lime-tree bower my prison. They, meantime
My friends, whom I may never meet again,
On springy* heath, along the hill-top edge,   5
Wander delighted, and look down, perchance,

elastic, I mean. (S.T.C.)

On that same rifted Dell, where many an Ash[1]
Twists it's wild limbs beside the ferny rock,
Whose plumy ferns* for ever nod and drip
Spray'd by the waterfall. But chiefly Thou,   10
My gentle-hearted CHARLES! thou, who hast pin'd
And hunger'd after Nature many a year
In the great City pent, winning thy way,
With sad yet bowed soul, thro' evil & pain
And strange calamity.—Ah slowly sink   15
Behind the western ridge; thou glorious Sun!
Shine in the slant beams of the sinking orb,
Ye purple Heath-flowers! Richlier burn, ye Clouds!
Live in the yellow Light, ye distant Groves!
And kindle, thou blue Ocean! So my friend   20
Struck with joy's deepest calm, and gazing round
On the wide view,** may gaze till all doth seem
Less gross than bodily, a living Thing
That acts upon the mind, and with such hues
As cloathe the Almighty Spirit, when he makes   25
Spirits perceive His presence!

A Delight

Comes sudden on my heart, and I am glad
As I myself were there! Nor in this bower
Want I sweet sounds or pleasing shapes. I watch'd
The sunshine of each broad transparent Leaf   30
Broke by the shadows of the Leaf or Stem,
Which hung above it: and that Wall-nut Tree
Was richly ting'd: and a deep radiance lay
Full on the ancient ivy which usurps
Those fronting elms, and now with blackest mass   35
Makes their dark foliage gleam a lighter hue
Thro' the last twilight.—And tho' the rapid bat
Wheels silent by and not a swallow twitters,
Yet still the solitary humble-bee
Sings in the bean flower. Henceforth I shall know   40
That nature ne'er deserts the wise & pure,
No scene so narrow, but may well employ
Each faculty of sense, and keep the heart
Awake to Love & Beauty: and sometimes
'Tis well to be bereav'd of promis'd good   45
That we may lift the soul, & contemplate
With lively joy the joys, we cannot share.

[1]Wandering well-pleas'd, look down on grange or dell
Or deep fantastic [originally that deep gloomy] Rift, where many an Ash [Cancelled version
of lines 6 and 7] (E.L.G.)
*The ferns that grow in moist places, grow five or six together & form a complete 'Prince of
Wales's Feather'—i.e. plumy. (S.T.C.)
**You remember, I am a *Berkleian*. (S.T.C.)

My sister & my Friends! when the last Rook
Beat it's straight path along the dusky air
Homewards, I bless'd it; deeming, it's black wing   50
Cross'd, like a speck, the blaze of setting day,[2]
While ye stood gazing; or when all was still,
Flew creaking o'er your heads, & had a charm
For you, my Sister & my Friends! to whom
No sound is dissonant, which tells of Life!   55

2. Had cross'd the flood [originally orb] & blaze of setting day. [Cancelled version of line above]
(E.L.G.)

'This Lime-Tree Bower My Prison'[1] stands chronologically at the
head of the astonishing output of poetry of the year 1797-8, including
in addition 'Kubla Khan', 'The Ancient Mariner', 'Christabel' Part I,
'Frost at Midnight', and 'The Nightingale: A Conversation Poem'.
Osorio was also being composed during the summer of 1797 when
Coleridge wrote 'This Lime-Tree Bower'. The poem invites investigation from several perspectives: for example, a manuscript version of
the poem exists (*CL* I 334-6), substantially different from the published
version. Indeed, two manuscript versions are known, though only one
is known to survive, namely that occurring in a letter to Robert Southey.
The misplaced manuscript version, in a letter to Charles Lloyd, does
not vary significantly from the Southey manuscript.[2] A comparison
of these two versions with the published version (the poem was first
published in the *Annual Anthology* of 1800) is revealing in a number of
ways, but particularly of the structure of the poem as a whole; some
twenty lines were added to make up Stanzas I and II of the final
version, altering the shape of the poem considerably.

The poem is interesting too for its 'mini-preface'; the preface explains
briefly the circumstances surrounding the composition of the poem.
This passage also has its own manuscript version in the letter manuscripts, and it differs noticeably from the polished version accompanying
the published poem. This 'preface' invites comparison with the preface
to 'Kubla Khan' in spite of the apparently qualitative difference between the two. As will be suggested below, such a comparison (which
may at first seem far-fetched) does reveal some interesting details
about the function of the 'This Lime-Tree Bower' preface, and suggests
that this brief prose passage may have a more important role than is
usually ascribed to it.

Coleridge was fond of giving details about the dates and circum-
stances of his poems. In addition to the prefaces to 'Kubla Khan' and
'Christabel', there is a fascinating 'Prefatory Note' to the fragment of
'The Wanderings of Cain' (*PW* I 285f), first published in 1828,

giving the origins of 'The Ancient Mariner'. 'The Three Graves' (1797–1809) also has a long, explanatory preface (*PW* I 261), and there is also the witty 'introductory letter' to 'The Raven' (1797) that accompanied its first appearance in the *Morning Post* (*PW* I 169). Both 'France: An Ode' (February 1798) and 'Ode to the Departing Year' (1796) contain arguments (*PW* I 243 and 160). In addition, a large number of poems prior to 'This Lime-Tree Bower' have a very brief phrase or two describing the dates and circumstances of the composition, usually printed rather as a sub-title to the poems. And a number of these poems are footnoted with explanatory material of an historical, scientific, or philosophical character.

The 'preface' to 'This Lime-Tree Bower' falls somewhere in between some of the early briefer gestures at introductory remarks and the high development of the prefaces to 'Christabel', 'Kubla Khan', etc. These latter cases show Coleridge at his best in taking conventional extra-poetical devices and imbuing them with an aesthetic function.

'This Lime-Tree Bower' and the Poetry of the Supernatural

However unpromising the connection between 'Kubla Khan' and 'This Lime-Tree Bower' may appear initially, other connections have been noticed which substantiate the comparison. For instance, E. L. Griggs long ago pointed out that a cancelled version of the description of the dell is very like the 'deep romantic chasm' of 'Kubla Khan'. The version is as follows:

> Wand'ring well-pleas'd, look down on grange or dell
> Or deep fantastic [originally that deep gloomy] Rift,
> where many an Ash [cancelled version of lines 6 and 7].
>
> (*CL* 335 n 1)

Indeed the final version with the 'roaring dell, o'erwooded, narrow, deep . . .', with its waterfall, suggests not only the caverns but the fountain of 'Kubla Khan' as well.

Another connection with 'Kubla Khan' occurs through a letter to John Thelwall of 14 October 1797, a few months after 'This Lime-Tree Bower' was composed. This letter contains a number of apparent references to 'Kubla Khan', and in the midst of these specific and general references, lines from 'This Lime-Tree Bower' are quoted (variation of lines 21–6 of the letter version), in illustration of the following well-known passage of Coleridge's:

I can *at times* feel strongly the beauties, you describe, in themselves, & for themselves—but more frequently *all things* appear little—all the knowledge, that can be acquired, child's play—the universe itself—what but an immense heap of *little* things?—I can contemplate nothing but parts, & parts are all *little*—!—My mind feels as if it ached to behold & know something *great*—something *one & indivisible*—and it is only in the faith of this that rocks or waterfalls, mountains or caverns give me the sense of sublimity or majesty!—But in this faith *all things* counterfeit infinity!— 'Struck with the deepest calm of Joy' I stand

> Silent, with swimming sense; and gazing round
> On the wide Landscape gaze till all doth seem
> Less gross than bodily, a living Thing
> Which acts upon the mind, & with such Hues
> As cloath th' Almighty Spirit, when he makes
> Spirits perceive his presence![3]

It is but seldom that I raise & spiritualize my intellect to this height . . .

(*CL* I   349–50)

This letter passage seems to describe the highly spiritualized ending of 'This Lime-Tree Bower' with its appeal to harmony and 'Life', to friendship and community of spirit, though it also may refer to 'Kubla Khan', especially by virtue of the landscape imagery.

It has often been noted that the landscape imagery of 'Kubla Khan' offers two opposing types, the garden of the Khan contrasted with the wild, natural scene of Stanza II. The metaphorical implications of this contrast have been discussed in the literature (and see above Chapter One). A similar contrast is notable in 'This Lime-Tree Bower', with the garden-bower (or prison transformed into paradise) set like the Khan's garden against the natural scene which the friends enjoy on their walk. A similar contrast is evident in 'Frost at Midnight' and 'The Eolian Harp', with the domestic cottage scene surrounded by an expansive nature at times alluring and at times threatening. The contrast of these two types of imagery becomes complex as it is realized that in both poems the opposing natural scene seems itself to contain another closed space, the 'romantic chasm' in one case, the 'roaring dell' in the other, which corresponds as an enclosure with the bower and garden images of the domestic landscape. Thus the wild, natural scene seems within itself to exhibit another instance of the contrast between closed and open space which is reflected also in the more general opposition between the closed space of the domestic scene, whether it be cot, bower, or garden of the Khan, and the openness and spaciousness or expansion of the natural scene. The closed space contained in nature is not however a prison, nor in any way inhibiting of imaginativeness. It seems almost to be the opposite, as the source of 'vaulting fragments', 'dancing rocks', or 'plumy ferns', that is, of productivity and creativity. Nature taken alone thus seems to offer a model of interrelating the closed with the open, and indeed the progress of both poems is towards transformation of the domestic closures into a synthesis of the closed and the open: the bower, in spite of its partial closure, becomes a paradise opening on to a sky above it which discloses the rook and blazing orb; and the dome similarly is transformed into a 'dome in air', the ambiguity of 'in' enhancing the synthetic image: a dome placed in air or a dome built of air. Either image will do as a synthesis. That such 'reconciliation of opposites' is an image of imagination is suggested by this description of intelligence as expansion (openness) and contraction (closure), both of which are necessarily co-operative in the mind: 'a nature having two contrary forces, the one of which tends to expand infinitely, while the other strives to apprehend or *find* itself in this infinity' (*BL* I ch. xiii 196).

The interpenetration of a force of closure and one of openness, represented in the imagery of the two poems, is further explained as intelligence in the following passage, intelligence in the sense of intuitive, imaginative intellectuality:

Bearing then this in mind, that intelligence is a self-development, not a quality supervening to a substance, we may abstract from all *degree*, and for the purpose of philosophic construction reduce it to *kind*, under the idea of an indestructible power with two opposite and counteracting forces, which by a metaphor borrowed from astronomy, we may call the centrifugal and centripetal forces. The intelligence in the one tends to *objectize* itself, and in the other to know itself in the object.

(*BL* I ch. xii 188)

In terminology appropriate to this analysis, the opposite forces and their necessary interaction are described as follows:

Most of my readers will have observed a small water-insect on the surface of rivulets, which throws a cinque-spotted shadow fringed with prismatic colours on the sunny bottom of the brook; and will have noticed, how the little animal *wins* its way up against the stream, by alternate pulses of active and passive motion, now resisting the current, and now yielding to it in order to gather strength and a momentary *fulcrum* for a further propulsion. This is no unapt emblem of the mind's self-experience in the act of thinking. There are evidently two powers at work, which relatively to each other are active and passive; and this is not possible without an intermediate faculty, which is at once both active and passive. (In philosophical language, we must denominate this intermediate faculty in all its degrees and determinations, the Imagination. But, in common language, and especially on the subject of poetry, we appropriate the name to a superior degree of the faculty, joined to a superior voluntary controul over it.)

(*BL* I ch. vii 86)

These passages indicate the metaphorical significance of the complex imagery of closure, openness, and the relation of the two in the poems, at least in terms of a theory of aesthetics, for in the latter quotation the 'intermediate faculty' is said to be the imagination.

At the same time, the non-reconciled, contrasting images of openness and closure, that is, the bower/nature relation on the one hand and the garden of the Khan/nature relation on the other, express the dichotomy between a force of expansion, such as the imagination, and a force of contraction, the fancy, or other active/passive faculty distinctions. For 'relative to each other', the faculties are active or passive. Thus we say that the imagination relative to the fancy (and indeed the reason relative to the understanding) is active, but that the imagination is 'an intermediate faculty, which is at once both active and passive'. The complex imagery of 'Kubla Khan' and 'This Lime-Tree Bower' manages to express this dual relation, that is, it expresses both the *opposition* between the expansive force of imagination and the restrictive force of fancy, and it expresses also the *synthesis* of expansion and contraction which constitutes imaginative activity in 'philosophical terminology'.

Turning from the imagery to formal properties of the poem, one discovers that the only other major poem of this period which has anything remotely like the preface of 'This Lime-Tree Bower' is, surprisingly, 'The Ancient Mariner' with its argument (the gloss, as well as the prefaces to 'Kubla Khan' and 'Christabel', was added later). The comparison is indeed a remote one, for the argument and preface are very different entities. Nevertheless they share the function of a prose passage commenting on some aspect of the poem to which they are affixed. This function will be further discussed below. But, like 'Kubla Khan', 'The Ancient Mariner' can be shown to have something in common with 'This Lime-Tree Bower', in respect of both language and imagery. While Stanza I seems to show connections with 'Kubla Khan', it is Stanzas II and III which exhibit similar imagery to that of 'The Ancient Mariner', especially Stanza III. In Stanza II it is the exotic richness and vividness of the coloration, and the intensity of the blazing beauty of the sunset over the ocean which in a general way paints an atmosphere akin to the scenes in 'The Ancient Mariner' on the ocean: Charles wanders

> With sad yet patient soul, through evil and pain
> And strange calamity! Ah! slowly sink
> Behind the western ridge, thou glorious Sun!
> Shine in the slant beams of the sinking orb,
> Ye purple heath-flowers! richlier burn, ye clouds!
> Live in the yellow light, ye distant groves!
> And kindle, thou blue Ocean!

Compare a variation of these lines from a notebook:

> The Sun (for now his Orb
> Gan slowly sink),
> Shot half his rays aslant the heath, whose flowers
> Purpled the mountain's broad & level top,
> Rich was his bed of Clouds: & wide beneath
> Expecting Ocean smiled with dimpled face.

(*CN* I 157)

It may be the case that this similarity in atmosphere and coloration is too general to be convincing of any genuine connection with 'The Ancient Mariner', though nowhere in Coleridge's poetry does there seem to be an intensity and richness of colour equal to these lines except in 'The Ancient Mariner', as for example in the scene with the water snakes at the end of Part IV.[4] A similar response to the beauty of the scene characterizes both the Mariner and the speaker of this poem: both are released from their self-imprisonment and alienation into a communion with the life around them. The Mariner might correctly be said to be 'Struck with deep joy . . . [and] silent with swimming sense', as he himself intimates:

> O happy living things! no tongue
> Their beauty might declare:
> A spring of love gushed from my heart.
> And I blessed them unaware

(lines 282–5)

Similarly the 'albatross' of self-pity which has hung about the neck of the speaker in 'This Lime-Tree Bower' falls to the ground as he gazes on the beautiful scene: 'A delight/Comes sudden on my heart, and I am glad/As I myself were there!' (lines 43–5).

The empathic identification which characterizes both of these liberating responses is even more pronounced in Stanza III, for the vehicle of liberation from imprisonment becomes a black rook, which is an image comparable to the black and green water snakes. More importantly, the speaker explicitly blesses it as does the Mariner the water snakes:

> when the last rook
> Beats its straight path along the dusky air
> Homewards, I blest it!   (lines 68–70)

This blessing is the sign of a communion with the 'One Life', and it is toward this sense of unity which the speaker had yearned (see *CL* I 349), just as the Ancient Mariner had been shut out from the blessings of communion until he transcended the narrow limits of his ego.

Stanza III contains the most explicit references to 'The Ancient Mariner' in terms of imagery as well. The alteration of the manuscript lines (lines 50–51) to the published version (lines 70–72), with the additional line, draws attention to the striking similarity of these lines with a passage in the ballad poem. The manuscript lines run as follows; the speaker describes the 'last rook':

> Homewards I bless'd it; deeming, it's black wing
> Cross'd, like a speck, the blaze of setting day

The final version reads:

> Homewards, I blest it! deeming its black wing
> (Now a dim speck, now vanishing in light)
> Had cross'd the mighty Orb's dilated glory

These lines compare with the opening of Part III of 'The Ancient Mariner', when the Mariner sees 'a something in the sky', which at first seems a speck, a mist, a shape; note especially the similarity of the following stanza with the added line of 'This Lime-Tree Bower', 'Now a dim speck, now vanishing in light':

> At first it seemed a little speck,
> And then it seemed a mist;   150
> It moved and moved, and took at last
> A certain shape, I wist.
>
> A speck, a mist, a shape, I wist!
> And still it neared and neared:

Then the sunset is described, and the ship-like shape 'crosses the Orb's dilated glory':

> The western wave was all a-flame.
> The day was well nigh done!
> Almost upon the western wave
> Rested the broad bright Sun;
> When that strange shape drove suddenly   175
> Betwixt us and the Sun.
>
> And straight the Sun was flecked with bars,

The blazing sun, the twilight, the sail of the ship like a wing of the bird, the ship crossing the sun, all of these echo the imagery of the last stanza of 'This Lime-Tree Bower'. In both poems the stillness of the evening is interrupted by a 'something' moving across the sky under its own power, and this 'something' is, in an annotation to 'The Ancient Mariner', compared with a living thing, a 'Being of the Sea', which relates it more closely to the rook:

> This Ship it was a plankless thing,
> —A bare Anatomy!
> A plankless spectre—and it mov'd
> Like a Being of the Sea!
>
> (*PW* I 194)

    The footnote in the final version to the 'creeking rook' seems to suggest a consciousness and intention with regard to the connections between these two poems. The footnote refers to 'some months after I had written this line', which was about the time when 'The Ancient Mariner' was being written; but more importantly the reference to William Bartram draws attention to a work which has long been noticed to be a source of much of the imagery of 'The Ancient Mariner'. By means of the footnote Coleridge indicates that the same work has proved to be a source for this other poem as well. Moreover, the quotation chosen from Bartram explicitly draws the connection between the rook and a ship. It is possible that Coleridge quoted the lines from Bartram for the sake of this comparison, which would have been lost had he only referred to Bartram's work. That the comparison of rook and ship seems a coincidence when put into the mouth of Bartram renders the footnote somewhat ironic.

    The fusion of these exotic elements with the domestic or commonplace in 'This Lime-Tree Bower' is one of the great achievements of the poem and a mark of its originality. This fusion is operative at the level of imagery, style, and conception. For a Christian conception of brotherly love and empathy is joined with a sweeping, pantheistic conception of the 'One Life'. (Indeed, a comparison of the ending of 'This Lime-Tree Bower' and 'The Eolian Harp' with its 'One Life' theme might further suggest that the end of the latter exudes a heavily ironic undertone.) 'Divine and wild' natural scenes are joined to a domestic garden bower. A common black rook is made the vehicle of an extraordinarily exotic and vivid image, as its wing is imagined (not seen) to cross the orb of the blazing sun at twilight. A comparison of the poem with the supernatural poems makes the exotic character of 'This Lime-Tree Bower' more evident. By drawing out these similarities between 'This Lime-Tree Bower' with 'Kubla Khan', and 'The Ancient Mariner', it is not intended that the differences should be minimized: they are great, and hence do not need emphasis. But some differences may be instructive. For instance, the rook in 'This Lime-Tree Bower' seems to combine several images in 'The Ancient Mariner': the black (and green) water snakes, the ship-like shape, and the albatross. Such a fusion of these separate images may be confusion, or it may suggest that these images act potentially in a single way in relation to the Mariner, as the single image of the rook acts in 'This Lime-Tree Bower', as a source of communion and fellowship with all life. In 'The Ancient Mariner', a breakdown of this communion having occurred, the three separate images chart the stages of the breakdown and eventual reawakening of communion: in 'This Lime-Tree Bower' the reawakening of fellowship is emphasized in the single comprehensive image of the rook.

The fusion of the exotic and the domestic draws attention too to the philosophical conceptions about the nature of truth and beauty which Coleridge was anxious to clarify. The domestic could be understood to represent habit, custom, and the familiar. The exotic represents the new, inspiring and unfamiliar. Imagination must 'strip away the veil of familiarity' which renders objects and language powerless to inspire. Or as Coleridge says,

To carry on the feelings of childhood into the powers of manhood. to combine the child's sense of wonder and novelty with the appearances which every day for perhaps forty years had rendered familiar,

>With Sun and Moon and Stars throughout the year,
>And Man and Woman—

this is the character and privilege of genius, and one of the marks which distinguish genius from talents. And so to represent familiar objects as to awaken the minds of others to a like freshness of sensation concerning them . . . this is the prime merit of genius, and its most unequivocal mode of manifestation. Who has not, a thousand times, seen it snow upon water? Who has not seen it with a new feeling, since he has read Burns's comparison of sensual pleasure,

>To snow that falls upon a river,
>A moment white—then gone forever!

In philosophy equally, as in poetry, genius produces the strongest impressions of novelty, while it rescues the stalest and most admitted truths from the impotence caused by the very circumstance of their universal admission. Extremes meet—a proverb, by the bye, to collect and explain all the instances and exemplifications of which, would constitute and exhaust all philosophy. Truths, of all others the most awful and mysterious, yet being at the same time of universal interest, are too often considered as so true that they lose all the powers of truth, and lie bed-ridden in the dormitory of the soul, side by side with the most despised and exploded errors.

(*The Friend (CC)* I 110)

The transformation of the bower as prison into the bower as paradise through its identification with nature is an instance both of 'extremes meeting' and of 'rescuing the stalest . . . truths' from impotence. 'Dead metaphors' are revitalized, habitual feelings are made fresh and novel, but only by creative acts of perception which transform the ordinary, passive perceptions of the familiar into new objects of contemplation.

The contrast between the domestic and the exotic has its important counterpart in Coleridge's aesthetic theory as well. It is reasserted in new terminology in the distinction between primary and secondary imagination: ordinary (primary) perception is *essentially* the same as creative (secondary) perception. The former is originally creative perception made familiar and customary. The imaginative, that is, the exotic, is the ordinary overspread by a 'figured curtain', or, to quote Shelley again, it is 'life's dark veil withdrawn from before the scene of things'.[5] While 'Frost at Midnight' and 'The Eolian Harp' also have their exotic elements, 'This Lime-Tree Bower' seems most effectively to illustrate this particular mode of expressing the duality of experience and its oppositions, which are overcome by an inherent unity of the apparent contraries. 'Exoticism and domesticity' thus becomes another designation for the concept of the reconciliation of opposites, accompanied in this poem by closure and openness, self-pity and empathic identification, and so on. But let us now turn to a more precise examination of the structure and action of the poem.

Landscape as Structure: A Comparison of the Manuscript and Published Versions of 'This Lime-Tree Bower'

A comparison of the two versions given in full at the beginning of this chapter reveals that the published version of the poem exceeds the letter version by some twenty lines. Almost all of the expansion occurs in Stanzas I and II, while Stanza III of the published version is almost unchanged from the letter. A careful perusal of the exact nature of these changes suggests some important facts about the structure of the poem and the role of certain elements within the structure.

The first change in the manuscript version is simply to delete the second line, 'Lam'd by the scathe of fire, lonely & faint', perhaps because it seemed too personally accusing, or showed too much resentment and petty disappointment. Lines 3–5 of the published version take over the role of this deleted line but express the disappointment and loss without blame or resentment. They further add to the poem by introducing the element of memory as a source of beauty and pleasure (as in Wordsworth's Daffodils poem). These lines hint at the more general problem of the role of memory in imaginative activity, as did the poems discussed above. Memory occurs as an important element in Stanza II of 'Frost at Midnight', Stanza II of 'The Eolian Harp', the preface to 'Kubla Khan' and Stanza IV, and it is a structural element of 'The Ancient Mariner', for the Mariner relates past happenings as he remembers them. Lines 3–5 foreshadow the eventual importance of memory in liberating the speaker from his prison, achieved by his imagining, as present to his friends, those beauties which are for him only remembered. The peculiar fusion of past memories and present imaginings is quite different from simply remembering a walk which the speaker might have himself taken some time previous to this occasion. The irony of lines 3–5 is clear once we realize that while the speaker seems to see only the disadvantages of his present lost beauties, these lines at the same time are a programme for action; the speaker unconsciously acts immediately according to the programme, of drawing on remembered beauties to stimulate his imagination in his apparently disadvantaged state. For though he is not blinded by old age, he is lamed by fire; thus his situation at present is analogous to that imagined future state of deprivation.

The first significant expansion of the manuscript version occurs between lines 10–20 of the published version: four lines in the letter manuscript (7–10) have become eleven lines in the final copy. The dell description is more detailed, in such a way as to intensify the connection with the 'deep romantic chasm' in 'Kubla Khan': 'that same rifted Dell . . .' becomes 'the roaring dell, o'erwooded, narrow, deep . . .' The description of the ash is also amplified significantly, and in that amplification its contrast with the 'long lank weeds' is marked: the latter are thriving in the 'unsunn'd and damp' atmosphere of the dell, while the leaves of the ash are few and yellow, and it is wholly without branches. This contrast is not emphasized in the manuscript letter version at all, but is intense in the published alterations: the weeds are green and fresh and full of life; the yellow leaves are barely alive. Even in this contrast one might glimpse the dichotomy between the exotic and the commonplace. The footnote on the 'ferns', turned into a 'dark green file of long lank weeds . . . (a most fantastic sight!)' tends to heighten the exotic character of these plants, called the *Asplenium Scolopendrium*. Indeed the altered footnote is also far more exotic than the original, even if the change from 'ferns' to 'weeds' seems the opposite.

The yellow leaves and the dark green ferns (or weeds) may then be functioning within the context of the dell as metaphors for poetic language and tropes, rather like the 'vaulting fragments' or 'dancing rocks' of the chasm's fountain in 'Kubla Khan'. As in Shelley's 'Ode to the West Wind', the near dead leaves may be dead thoughts and dead metaphors, while new metaphors and fresh techniques are referred to ironically as 'weeds' to the eyes of those still steeped in traditional modes, but undeniably green and vital. A most striking connection with these expanded lines is Shakespeare's Sonnet 73, in which the metaphor of a failing power of imagination is clearly constructed, and out of similar materials, of twilight, yellow leaves, and so on.

The alteration in the footnote to these lines is interesting from more than one point of view. For while it adds to the exotic quality of these weeds, 'a most fantastic sight', by giving them their splendid-sounding scientific name, and their common name of Adder's Tongue (once again lightly touching upon the exotic/domestic contrast), it calls attention to the effect of naming. The footnote also creates another connection with 'The Ancient Mariner', as did the footnote on the following image of the rook. Here these long, lank, dark green weeds in their watery element are called 'Adder's Tongues', and the connection with the green watersnakes in 'The Ancient Mariner' again emerges: for in all cases imaginative fulfilment comes from a change in the speaker's appreciation of these images. Mere weeds become a 'most fantastic sight'; a common black rook is transformed into the carrier of a stunning image as it flies across the sun, or creaks in the stillness of the night, its sounds musical instead of dissonant; water snakes which previously repelled now are seen as inexpressibly beautiful. All of these examples might be seen as instances both of a change from 'single' to 'two-fold vision', as ordinary passive perception becomes active or imaginative; and they might also be seen as metaphors for poetic forms, and of the necessity both of transforming and revitalizing old forms which have become too familiar, and of creating new forms which will at first be rejected as ugly and unacceptable, as were the water snakes. Thus, metaphors seem to be offered as models of transformation at the perceptual and aesthetic level, at the individual moral level, and at a cosmic religious level. It is likely that these latter two are dependent for their full effect of immediacy upon the first, where the reader is confronted most directly. These specific images as metaphors at a level of poetic self-commentary operate within a larger field where, as will be discussed below, the landscape itself acts in a similar way, as bowers, dells, and open landscapes become emblems of poetic devices or aesthetic activities. The importance of the expansion of Stanza I will be further discussed below.

Lines 20–27 of the published version are a completely new addition to the poem, not just an alteration or variation of manuscript lines. In these lines, which mark the beginning of Stanza II, an entirely new emphasis is added to the landscape unknown in the manuscript version, which prepares more adequately for the 'wide landscape' at the end of the stanza, and which contrasts vividly with the dell, which was at the centre of the speaker's imaginings in the manuscript version. From the closure of the dell the friends emerge

> Beneath the wide wide Heaven—and view again
> The many-steepled tract magnificent
> Of hilly fields and meadows, and the sea,
> With some fair bark, perhaps . . .
>
> (lines 21–4)

The addition of these few lines to the poem intensifies the landscape contrast of dell and open, spacious nature which was hardly evident in the original, or which certainly was not emphasized, as in 'hill-top edge' (line 7) or later in 'wide landscape' (line 40). The 'roaring dell' as closure and the wide landscape as openness complicate the natural imagery, as we see that nature now exhibits both types of space, just as it did in 'Kubla Khan'. Thus there is no simple single analogy between closure/openness and domestic (cot, garden bower, city, culture) and wild nature, since nature exhibits both forces of closure and openness.

The rest of the stanza is largely unaltered, but two minor alterations do tend to draw attention to an important event in the poem. In lines 26–7, 'Yes! they wander on/In gladness all; but thou, methinks, most glad', these words help to single out Charles from the group of friends, and emphasize that one of the friends holds a special relationship to the speaker. This relationship is further developed in the second alteration, line 38, as the words 'as I have stood' are added to heighten the identification between the speaker and Charles, which is to take place consciously in the beginning of Stanza III. The speaker thus anticipates the empathic identification which acts as the turning point of the poem in lines 43–59. The gradual progression toward this focal point of release from self-imprisonment in Stanza III is more adequately prepared for by these minor changes: the reader can see it gradually stealing upon the speaker while he seems unaware of it. In the letter manuscript it seems to spring suddenly upon reader and speaker alike. The final addition, 'Silent with swimming sense', characterizes the empathic experience as intensely imaginative, for silence and the overpowering of the senses are familiar descriptions of this state.

The increasing importance of singling out Charles from the group of friends is evident from the alteration in this stanza, from the sub-title of the published version, and from the alterations in Stanza III. Clearly the speaker only achieves complete freedom after focusing upon Charles. The logic of this selection and emphasis on Charles is discernible in lines 29–30. For the speaker actually first identifies with Charles here, in commiserating with him: Charles has been trapped in the city, hungering and pining after nature, as the speaker is trapped in the bower. It is the necessity of finding empathy in his present state that seems to stimulate the speaker to single out Charles. The leap from his own unhappiness to the good fortune of his group of friends out on the heath is probably too far to make. But the middle point, of moving out of his present egoism by means of sympathy with Charles's prior suffering, allows the initial escape. Once that leap is made the speaker then easily moves into Charles's present happiness, delights in that for his sake, and thereby achieves his own transformation: the progression is from self-pity, through pity for Charles, to happiness in Charles's good fortune, and finally the speaker's own joy. In the manuscript version, this development is not as clear, for the speaker seems to identify both with Charles and with the group of friends indiscriminately. The final version is thus more expressive of the psychological truth of the difficulty of empathic identification and of the path which it is most likely to take.

The language and imagery of Stanza II express correspondingly the effect of singling out Charles. As long as the speaker is lost in meditation about the friends generally, his imagination and empathy are unable really to take flight. The contrast between the description of nature in the first half of the stanza with that in the second half registers this difference. Lines 21–6 are tame, conventional, and unimpressive compared with lines 32–7, though in themselves they are not without charm and expressiveness. But by the time the speaker has uttered the words 'strange calamity', the analogy with his own accident is so moving that he is carried out of himself in his identification with Charles, and his exhortation to nature to reveal to Charles its most splendid brilliance is perfectly mirrored in his splendid imagery and language. The analogy is clear: while external nature revives Charles, the poet's nature (imagination) revives him as well, by revealing itself in the most brilliant language of the poem. From the domesticity of the first half of the stanza, the wild, exotic beauty reaches its heights in the second half. As nature becomes a medium for the perception of spirit, so the language of the poem becomes the medium for the perception of imagination.

This analogy between nature and imagination (the poet's or, indeed, human nature) is extended in Stanza III, in the following lines, where the meaning of 'nature' oscillates between external nature and the imagination, and illustrates Blake's claim that 'To the Eyes of the Man of Imagination, Nature is Imagination itself' (William Blake, *Complete Writings*, ed. Geoffrey Keynes, 793):

> Henceforth I shall know
> That Nature ne'er deserts the wise and pure:
> No plot so narrow, be but Nature there,
> No waste so vacant, but may well employ
> Each faculty of sense, and keep the heart
> Awake to Love and Beauty!

(lines 59–64)

The implicit analogy between nature and imagination sets up the problematic relation between the two, or between mind and nature, in more philosophically familiar terms. This relation has been treated at various levels in most of the other poems discussed here with respect both to perception and aesthetic response, that is, to primary and secondary imagination. It is treated also in lines 40–43, in the 'Berkeleian avowal' at the end of Stanza II:

> . . . gaze till all doth seem
> Less gross than bodily; and of such hues
> As veil the Almighty Spirit, when yet he makes
> Spirits perceive his presence.

Nature is here the veil of the 'Almighty Spirit', thus at ground it is of the same substance as the spirit which perceives its presence. It is not essentially other than the perceiving mind.

While these two passages most explicitly deal with the relation between mind and nature, the poem as a whole clearly grapples with precisely the same problem; as it seeks to chart the interaction between the two, it raises the more interesting question of the mind as passive or active in its perception of nature. Charles's appreciation of nature expresses the interaction at the more basic level of perception, while the speaker's involvement with nature and his eventual liberation through nature delineates the alternating passive and active impulses which characterize that response. That is, at some points the speaker seems acted upon, at others he seems to act upon nature. The development of the poem as a whole leads it to a firm commitment to the essentially creative, active nature of mind, as the external world, the bower, is transformed by the awakening of the mind 'to Love and Beauty'. And of course the transformation involves a change of values, which is at the root of any mental liberation. What seemed bad, ugly, or imprisoning, becomes good, beautiful, and releasing, not because the nature of the thing changes, but because the perception of it or the perceiver's perspective upon it changes.

The analogy between nature as external world or landscape and nature as human nature, or imagination, helps to make clear the more general way in which the alterations of the manuscript version into the published version enrich the poem. For the expansion of Stanzas I and II creates a balance with Stanza III and a mirroring effect which is lacking in the manuscript poem. The first two stanzas develop external nature, and Stanza III develops the nature of imagination, but on a similar pattern. The speaker's situation in his bower in Stanza III is made to correspond almost point by point with Charles's and and the friends' situation out on the heath, and the speaker's leap from a preoccupation with the 'other' to an application to himself is the source of his transcendence to delight. This is tantamount to a move from nature as external nature to nature as imagination, as internal.

The mirroring effect between Stanzas I and II and Stanza III is developed in detail at the level of landscape. The dell of external nature is related to the bower, the ash to the walnut tree.[6] The description of the foliage in Stanza III corresponds to the yellow leaves in lines 14–16, even though the metaphorical implications are different. The 'dark green file of long lank weeds' seems to have a counterpart in the 'blackest mass' of dark branches of the elms. And analogously as the speaker imagines his friends emerging beneath the 'wide Heaven' he turns his own eyes upwards to the sky, and sees a bat 'wheel silent by', the bat against the sky like the bark on the ocean. These detailed correspondences operate only at the level of imagery: their significance is apparent, that is, only at the level of a general effect of mirroring one situation with another, and the importance of moving from one frame of reference to another. Thus there is no inherent connection between ash and walnut, bat and bark, etc.: the significance is functional only.

The mirroring effect continues at line 68 as the lines up to the end of the poem seem to be a repetition of the second stanza, from line 27, in several respects. The empathic identification with Charles occurs again, the exotic imagery is repeated and intensified, and the last line is a gesture of universalizing similar to the Berkeleian avowal at the end of Stanza II. The 'One Life' theme is gently hinted at in this final line just as it is at the end of Stanza II. All of this repetition is occurring from a new perspective, however, of heightened consciousness, for the turning point of the speaker's awareness has already occurred by the beginning of Stanza III. This increased intensity and activity is skilfully depicted in the contrast between the end of Stanza II and that of Stanza III. For in the latter, the creative mind seems explicitly to act upon nature, while in Stanza II the mind is more acted upon, relatively speaking.

This acting upon nature indicates a heightened imaginative power, as the common rook, for example, is turned into an extraordinarily exotic image by means of imaginative perception. The explicit manner in which the speaker infuses the image of the rook with imaginative force is an instance of the more general transformation of the bower which has been going on.

Here the imagination has taken the familiar and commonplace and acted upon it to render it the vehicle of inspiration. Neither the sight nor sound of the rook has any such force in itself. In Stanza II this difference is not as clear, for nature seems in itself beautiful, however mistaken this conception may be; thus Charles seems more acted upon than acting, unlike the speaker in the final stanza. Perhaps it is more correct to interpret this difference as one between primary and secondary imagination, Charles exhibiting the former, naturally at an unconscious level of activity, while the speaker illustrates the latter, which is more obviously active at a conscious level from certain perspectives. In another line (line 46), even observation of the bower is made active, as the speaker '*mark'd*/Much that has soothed me' (my italics). The entire poem could also be seen in these terms, Stanza III mirroring at the level of secondary imagination or self-consciousness the activity of the primary imagination in the first two stanzas.

The landscape imagery of the poem seems to illustrate two aspects of the nature of imagination, which we may describe firstly as the perception of 'identity in difference' (metaphor-making), and secondly as defamiliarization. In so doing the poem becomes a 'self-reflecting' artifact, mirroring at a metaphorical level its own nature through its imagery, and the mirroring of Stanzas I and II in Stanza III becomes a model of this further mirroring of internal by external. The perception of 'identify in difference' is expressed through the opposition in imagery between bower and nature (or city and nature, domestic and wild, etc.). The speaker's imagination is fired when he finally realizes that the bower is a kind of nature, and can delight him as much as the natural landscape which he is deprived of seeing. This identification of bower with nature is made explicit in the following lines:

> No plot so narrow, be but Nature there,
> No waste so vacant, but may well employ
> Each faculty of sense, . . .

> (lines 61–3)

Defamiliarization is merely another aspect of this process, and is illustrated when the bower as familiar, domestic, and imprisoning, is newly perceived as a place of exotic beauty and freshness, with the aid of imaginative perception. Thus the opposition of bower and nature is superseded by the opposition of bower as prison and bower as paradise: identification of sameness in difference is achieved through defamiliarization.

This escape from domesticity has no doubt its personal ramifications in Coleridge's ambivalence toward his family, and later toward his wife. But because it is through imagination that he escapes from the bower, the imprisonment becomes not only personal or physical but intellectual in its application. It engages the reader both at the emotional level of release from self-pity and egotism, and at the aesthetic and epistemological levels, as analogies are perceived between the images or metaphors of the poem and language or poetry generally. That is, the transformation of the familiar and customary bower into a paradise is a formulation of how imagination operates. In all of the conversation poems discussed, cot, cottage, and bower take on the sinister aspect of unimaginative, ordinary perception, as language is used conventionally and familiarly, the result being dead metaphors. However, these images of the domestic, the ordinary, and the familiar are not rejected, for in all of the poems the speakers return to some form of the domestic. But the domestic is now a transformed scene, a scene revitalized by imaginative appreciation of the beauties and truths once forgotten because too familiar. In such a way poetic images and metaphors become the vehicles of philosophical statements about art, perception, and thought generally. But because these 'statements' are not made discursively, but through illustration, they are often unrecognized, in spite of the fact that they are more powerful vehicles of their truth when they illustrate instead of only discussing.

Characterization and the Reading Analogy

One of the most important changes from the manuscript letter version of 'This Lime-Tree Bower' for characterization in the poem is the singling out of Charles Lamb from the group of friends, including Wordsworth and his sister. This is done in the final version first by addressing the poem to Lamb, and secondly by changing all occurrences of 'my Sister & my Friends' (or 'My Sara and my Friends', manuscript letter to Lloyd) in Stanza III to 'My gentle-hearted Charles'. The relationship between the speaker and Charles which is established in the second stanza is now maintained throughout the rest of the poem, whereas in the manuscript version it becomes diffused and almost forgotten, replaced by the more general references to the group of friends. The singling out of one special friend from the group has the effect of making the relation of friendship more significant. The special relationship between Charles and the speaker is intensified too as we realize that after line 26 the group of friends is never referred to again;

as the speaker's imagination awakens it firmly focuses upon Charles and does not again deviate from him throughout the rest of the poem, as it does in the letter version.

It was earlier noted that the speaker's escape from his bower–prison was probably aided by his being able to empathize first with Charles's own imprisonment in the city, because it was so like his own situation in the bower. The general group of friends provided no such midpoint of identification. But this focus upon Charles is already evident in the manuscript version. By strengthening the role of Charles, the friend, in the poem, Coleridge strengthens a relationship which becomes a distinct model for the reader. In later years Coleridge was explicitly to refer in *The Friend* to the work of art and the author as a friend to the reader, not only because of the general notion of help and succour between friends; he also named the reader/author relation a friendship because both friendship and aesthetic response are characterized by the special experience of empathic identification and self-transcendence. This experience becomes in the poem the crucial point at which the speaker frees himself completely of his unhappiness, and its repetition at the end of the poem at a universal plane marks the highpoint of imaginative activity.[7]

Through empathic identification of the speaker with Charles, this relationship becomes a model for the reader or a recipe for reading: the reader's empathic identification with the speaker involves the recognition that the reading situation is at first a kind of prison too. The poem and language are bower–prisons which must be transformed into sources of imaginative delight. The reader is imprisoned as long as he imagines that his role is primarily passive, and that he is cut off from the imaginative, poetic beauties which the poet (like Charles) sees at first hand. The speaker's drama delineates with some degree of preciseness the necessary role of the reader if he is to realize the imaginative potential of the poem–bower. For while the speaker's attention is directed outward toward nature and the imagined sights which the friends see, he is a model for the reader's attitude to the poem as an external object whose profoundest secrets are hidden from him. The poet, engaged in the creative activity of composition, is as far away from the reader as the group of friends enjoying the heath is from the speaker. But the speaker's imprisonment in the bower offers the reader the same sort of midpoint for identification and sympathy which Charles's entrapment in the city offered the speaker. Once the leap from seeing the speaker as 'other' to seeing him as similar in situation is made, the reader can go on to become aware of his reading situation just as the speaker suddenly becomes aware of his 'bower situation'. This self-conscious awareness of the speaker, who finally looks at his bower and his immediate situation as his proper objects of contemplation, exactly mirrors the necessary change of the reader's attention. His proper object of contemplation is also his immediate situation, that is, it is his reading, perception, and interpretation of the poem which he must contemplate, not the poem as some external nature. The richness of the poem as a mirror of mind, of imaginative activity, full of insights into the nature of perception, reflection, reality, and art becomes evident only then.

The reading analogy might be further explained by saying that the reader, like the speaker, imagines himself to be cut off from the beauties which the poet, like Charles, is experiencing in his visions and imaginative experiences. The speaker rouses himself, however, and tries to participate in these beauties, even if imperfectly and from a distance, and this distance is for the reader the distance imposed by the poem and communication. Thus the poem is the reader's bower, and as long as he attends to the poem as a repository of descriptions by the author about nature and friendship, he sees the poem unselfconsciously, that is, as external to himself, just as the speaker in Stanza II attends to Charles's imagined objects of perception. This may be a necessary stage of response to the poem and it involves some imaginativeness itself, but its incompleteness is demonstrated if we imagine how much less rich, artistic, and complete the poem would have been if it had ended at line 43. Like the speaker, the reader must go further if he is to complete the response which the poem offers, and that further step involves the sudden awakening to self-consciousness about the value and importance of his own situation. What the mirror structure of the poem seems to suggest (with Stanza III mirroring the details of Stanzas I and II), is that the bower is constructed like the external natural world, and offers the same possibilities for delight and imagination as does nature. The reader may draw the analogy that the surface and content of the poem, illustrated by Stanzas I and II, are mirrored by his reading and interpretive activity at a self-conscious level, as Stanza III illustrates. But he is forced back by the poem to the fact that his primary experience is of that very interpretive activity, as the speaker's primary experience is of the bower: the rest is imaginings of someone else's experiences. It is not the latter then, which dictates structure to the former: it is the primary experience which authorizes the structure and nature of the 'other'.

The journey of the perceiving mind from unconscious acts of perception, to the objects of perception, and finally back to a consciousness of those acts as themselves the source of the objects' natures, is a long one. The poem charts this journey and registers its difficulties when it indicates the complicated and various levels of metaphor. On one level the bower is a metaphor of the poem. Thus the deleted line in the letter manuscript (lines 28–9) seems to refer metaphorically to the poet or reader and the poem as bower: 'Nor in this bower/Want I sweet sounds or pleasing shapes.' On another level it is a metaphor of mind. At one time the poem and language are represented as imprisoning; at another they are a means of freeing the mind from convention. From one perspective the poem is bower, from another it is like the landscape which the friends see. The speaker is a model both for reader and poet; metaphors of reading and composition work side by side. Charles may be seen as a model for either reader or poet. These many combinations of analogies exist partly because of the changing roles which are demanded by the different stages of experience: one moment the reader is like a poet, at another he is not; the poet both writes and observes his writing; a poem is both about experiences and about reflection on experience.

The 'Mini-Preface'

The Romantic poets probably more than many others reflected about poetry and the nature of composition, imaginative experience, its relation to ordinary experience, and the difference between the intuitive and the discursive. Probably more than other Romantic poets, Coleridge thought about poetry, and it is not surprising that this reflection about aesthetic experience should penetrate his poetic compositions and often become the primary level of metaphor.[8] Self-conscious reflection was so thoroughly fused with spontaneity in his best poetry that that poetry itself became an impressive account of his philosophy, and his philosophic writings can become a commentary on his poetry. The achievement of these poems is the best evidence for the truth of the philosophy of a creative theory of mind which they seem to express, and which the prose elucidates. Such reflection about the nature of imaginative experience and its relation to ordinary experience was not an incidental part of Coleridge's poetry. As in the poem, self-consciousness was often the organizing principle of his compositions, and thus constituted not only the unity of the works, but their integral level of metaphor.

Self-consciousness and critical reflection were to Coleridge the only sure means of guarding the mind from the crippling effects of custom, prejudice, and understanding unenlivened by reason. Hence they play a central role in all of his writings, and a variety of techniques are engaged to induce the reader into a reflective state of mind. The little preface to 'This Lime-Tree Bower' seems to be an example of one such occasion.

Like the preface to 'Kubla Khan', this short prose passage has its corresponding manuscript version which differs considerably from the published one. This preface is much briefer and less obviously fictional than that of 'Kubla Khan', and does not make extensive theoretical gestures about the nature of composition. But like the latter, a comparison with the manuscript version shows the polishing and fictionalizing which went into the final version and which distinguishes it from the dry, factual letter passage. Numerous discrepancies are obvious between the two versions. The month must have been July, not June, if Charles Lamb was visiting. And there were two separate sets of friends who arrived at different times, the Wordsworth set and Lamb, the former coming for a visit, having just settled in Alfoxden, the latter coming for a week's stay from London. The accident is described in the letter version as having happened upon the second day of the Wordsworths' arrival, three days before Lamb came. The accident is described explicitly; Sara had 'accidently emptied a skillet of boiling milk on my foot'. The arbour is in Tom Poole's garden, not in Coleridge's own. These facts have been changed, indeed romanticized, in order to make the tale more poignant, as for example the accident's happening on the *first* day of the arrival of 'long-expected' friends. And the spontaneity of the poem's *conception* is emphasized to imply that the actual *composition* was equally spontaneous, though the revisions show that over a third of the poem was altered for the published version. Finally, a third person narrative is substituted for the first person, as in the preface to 'Kubla Khan', which has the effect of distancing the author and making him the object of discussion rather than the subject–narrator. This is in sharp contrast to the first person narrative of the poem itself. Thus the author of the preface and of the poem seem to be different, a difference which may be meant metaphorically to emphasize the different states of composition, or the different selves of the visionary poet and the reading or revising author.

One must wonder what the importance or function might be of Coleridge's specification of these semi-factual, semi-fictional occasions of the writing of his poems in such prose passages. The polishing of facts to improve the story and make it more elegant suggests that the narration of circumstances may have an aesthetic, in addition to or rather than, an informative function. The most fundamental function of the preface is to establish some relation between the poem as art and the world of reality. It reminds the reader that the work of art does not occur in a vacuum, and it confronts him with the question of the nature of this relation between art and reality: for example, are these alleged circumstances causal or occasional? What is the relation between the immediate surroundings of the poet and his poetic experience? In what sense is the poem a mirror of reality, that is, an accurate account of the poet's experiences, and to what extent is it imagined?

We may clarify the importance of such questions by noting the difference between the conversation and supernatural poems. These two sets of poems seem to have very different relations to 'reality', the former being much more obviously dependent upon their occasions for existence than the latter, though the preface to 'Kubla Khan' seeks to overcome this gap between the poem's content and the circumstances surrounding its genesis. Such considerations go to the heart of the function of art in experience, because they not only ask about the nature of art, but in questioning the relation of art to reality, they raise questions about the nature of reality as well. The preface is not important in so far as it tells the reader that the poem was written in some month of some year in some particular place and under certain circumstances: all of these elements have been slightly altered to render their relation to the 'facts' problematic. The preface is important in so far as it makes the reader aware of the extraordinary mystery surrounding the relation of creative experience to ordinary experience. Indeed, the fictionalizing of the historical data surrounding the poem's composition acts as a model for what happens in the poem as well: in neither is it clear what is fact and what is fiction. Both express this uncertain relation between perception of reality and creation of fiction, and in so doing both may well function to demonstrate that the boundary between fact and fiction, art and reality, is far from certain.[9]

The problematic relation between art and reality which itself raises the question as to how far reality is reality and not fiction (and vice versa), also forces a consideration of the role of ordinary perception in creative activity. Is it true that there is nothing in the mind that was not first in the senses? (Compare *AR*, aphorism CVI, part eleven.) Or is there not another level of mental activity which has for its objects the acts of mind itself? And is ordinary perception essentially different or essentially the same as creative perception? Blake's terminology of single versus two-fold vision also suggests that ordinary perception is only a degenerate or 'contracted' form of imaginative activity, and not altogether 'other' (see the letter to Thomas Butts, 22 November 1802, William Blake, *Complete Writings*, ed. G. Keynes, 816).

The preface seems to help to suggest to the reader that not only in the poetry but also in the prose preface—that is, in ordinary perception —the relation between fact or reality and fiction is uncertain. The preface also emphasizes the importance to the reader of considering the poem's relation to reality. Is the experience described in the poem a mirror of what happened to the poet while his friends were out, or is it a fiction of his, of what he *might* have or should have felt? The poem itself poses this problem in all the stanzas, for they are full of speculations as to what the friends *might* have seen, not what they saw.

We may wonder about the details of the poem once the basic historical facts are questioned, as they are in the preface as well. For instance, was there really a rook, or did the poet invent it? If there was a rook, did it really fly across the sun and did it really creak, or did the poet not admit that he only imagined these things? The footnote on the rook seems now to serve a similar purpose to the preface: it strives to establish the creaking of the rook as a real phenomenon, and thus alerts the reader to the relation between art and reality. Such questions are important for understanding how imagination works, not because one should really worry about whether there was a rook or not: that is, the reader must wonder at what point perception of real events ends and imagination begins.

These points seem to suggest that it is difficult to determine in what sense art mirrors reality: we do not know if the basic experience of the poem actually is a report of the author's, or an idealization and imagining; many of the details of the poem are equally uncertain. We know that they are already at one remove from reality, because they are only imaginings and memories, and not the actual sights and sounds heard by the friends. But are they spontaneous imaginings or 'imagined imaginings': is the speaker a persona of the poet, or is the poet reporting his experience? Through the use of the third person in the preface, the reader is given a sense of two distinct personalities, the experiencing poet *qua* poet, and the man reflecting afterwards upon his composition. (See Chapter One above on the importance of persona distinctions.) Can even the poet determine to what extent the poem is fiction and to what extent it is reality? If not, the speaker is only a persona, even if unintentionally so.

The value of the poem can hardly lie in whether it is historically true or not, since this truth seems indeterminable. The preface points out that the purposes of the poem are other than this, when it reminds the reader of this uncertain relation between the narrative and the truth of the experience narrated. And it points the reader's attention in the new direction of wondering exactly how the poem, and art generally, is valuable. It is hardly an answer to say that beauty, not truth, is the value of art, for the concept of beauty is not clear: is beauty a correspondence with the reality of some object, or an expression of its essence? Beauty and truth seem intuitively to be related in some way, but it is not always clear how.

If the author's relation to the poem as a mirror of reality of some sort is problematic, this is repeated from the reader's perspective in several ways. The preface acts as a model for the reader to reflect not only about the poem's content, that is, its landscape descriptions, friendship, and the 'One Life' theme, but also about the composition of the poem, and correspondingly about the reading of it. It is impossible for the reader to determine precisely the boundaries between the poem as object, and the poem which results when he reads and interprets. The preface points up this mythical real poem in a delightful way, for it alludes to the poem as coming into being all at once and of a whole, spontaneously. Yet we know that much alteration went into the poem after the initial conception. But what relation do these alterations bear to the 'original'? The reader similarly alters the poem on successive readings of it. Indeed, whether there is a real, stable poem is a legitimate question to pose.

The preface acts as a model for the reader in a further way because it broadens the boundaries of the poem. Experience, expression of that experience (composition), and reflection about composition indicate three levels of discourse which may be distinguished even if they cannot be clearly divided. The reader is far too likely to concentrate on the first level of external experience only, as if the poem contains some core or fixed experience which is to be determined. Reflection upon composition shows not only how the language of the poem functions, but how expression to some extent determines the experience expressed. The myth of a core experience is exploded, and the reader's efforts to pin down some poetically static reality are thwarted. He is forced by insoluble uncertainties to give up the task of determining what the author experienced and to attend to his own experiences. Once he does this, the breakdown of the elusive (or illusory?) boundary between art and reality is ensured, as the art of the poem becomes the reality of the reading of it, and the reading reality is not perception of poetic facts but creation of fictions.

Conclusion

A Project of Thought

The foregoing chapters have been an effort to demonstrate that many of the predominant elements in some of Coleridge's most appreciated poetry are expressive of a creative theory of mind. This theory of mind has application both to the realms of art and imagination, and to that of reality and perception. A theory of aesthetics and a theory of knowledge are expressed which are said to be integrally related to each other: that is, art and reality are supposed to be essentially alike, and not easily distinguished even though on the surface they appear to be contraries. The present analysis has functioned on several levels relating these two poles: it has explored Coleridge's aesthetics as the poems illustrate the general elements of a theory of art; the epistemological implications of such a theory have been broadly sketched; and finally the consequences of the special relation of art to reality for the reading situation have been discussed.

Certain techniques in Coleridge's poetry demonstrate that aesthetic activity (both for the spectator and the artist) is an intensification of ordinary experience and perception. This point is turned to time and again throughout Coleridge's prose. It is the root of the distinction between primary and secondary imagination made in Chapter Thirteen of the *Biographia Literaria*. The constant linking of poetry and philosophy is another gesture to show the relation of perception to aesthetic acts, as is the effort to show the essential identity of truth and beauty. And the often quoted exhortation to unify thought with feeling is an example of the insistence that divisions between art and reality, poetry and philosophy, beauty and truth, and thought and feeling must be overcome, however useful and necessary such distinctions may be, if we are to gain an understanding of the nature of experience. As Coleridge insists,

> The office of philosophical *disquisition* consists in just distinction; while it is the privilege of the philosopher to preserve himself constantly aware, that distinction is not division. In order to obtain adequate notions of any truth, we must intellectually separate its distinguishable parts; and this is the technical *process* of philosophy. But having so done, we must then restore them in our conceptions to the unity, in which they actually co-exist; and this is the *result* of philosophy.
>
> (*BL* II ch. xiv 8)

The distinction between art and reality, fact and fiction, or illusion and truth is no exception to this rule. One might say that art is not so much opposed to reality as that it is a highly compressed experience and account of it. Art, then, like philosophy, is a source of knowledge and a mode of reflection about reality.

According to Coleridge, one of the primary truths art gives us about reality is that the mind is, or at least at some times is, essentially creative in its perception of the world. The notion that the mind is primarily a receptor for an already independently organized externality, and that its activity is constrained to manipulating these fixed and determinate elements is rejected as wholly inadequate to account for experience. Ordinary perception may degenerate to this level of passivity and receptivity or may engage in such receptive postures at times, but only as a result of a familiarity with materials and objects. Nevertheless, these objects must have been previously engaged with actively and imaginatively. In *The Friend* Coleridge grapples with this problem of renewing what has become stale through familiarity:

> But to find no contradiction in the union of old and new, to contemplate the ANCIENT OF DAYS with feelings as fresh, as if they sprang forth at his own fiat, this characterizes the minds that feel the riddle of the world, and may help to unravel it! To carry on the feelings of childhood into the powers of manhood, to combine the child's sense of wonder and novelty with the appearances which every day for perhaps forty years had rendered familiar . . . this is the character and privilege of genius . . . And so to represent familiar objects as to awaken the minds of others to a like freshness of sensation concerning them . . . this is the prime merit of genius, and its most unequivocal mode of manifestation . . .
>
> In philosophy equally, as in poetry, genius produces the strongest impressions of novelty, while it rescues the stalest and most admitted truths from the impotence caused by the very circumstance of their universal

admission . . . Truths, of all others the most awful and mysterious, yet being
at the same time of universal interest, are too often considered as so true that
they lose all the powers of truth, and lie bed-ridden in the dormitory of the
soul, side by side with the most despised and exploded errors.
                    (*The Friend (CC)* I 109–10; see also *LS (CC)* 25.)

Art seeks to overcome such paralysing familiarity and infuse the
familiar with a freshness that arouses attention and contemplation.
But art is no less subject to degeneration than language, metaphor,
and truth. All such acts of mind become, through repetition, objects
of familiarity instead of active thoughts. Thus Coleridge reminds his
reader that it is not in the nature of any of these 'objects' to be stimulating or not; it is rather a quality of mind to make them so: 'Poetry,
though treating on lofty & abstract truths, ought to be deemed *impassioned* by him, who reads it with impassioned feelings' (*CL* I 279 to
Thelwall, 17 December 1796). But Coleridge also wants us to be on
our guard constantly against the various disguises of lazy-mindedness,
and against the stagnation that familiarity breeds, as 'words slide into
common use, generally much alloyed by the carelessness of common
Life, . . . & Language degenerates . . .' (*CN* I 1835 f 66). In other words,
we mistake means for ends: linguistic formulations, metaphors,
images, pictures, etc., meant to stimulate ideas, are forms mistaken for
the idea or relation itself. The mind attending too tenaciously to the
image or form is never raised to a contemplation of the idea:

> . . . we become in a sort Idolators—for the means, we are obliged to use to
> excite notions of Truth in the minds of others or our own, we by witchcraft
> of slothful association, impose on ourselves for the Truths themselves—Our
> intellectual Bank stops payment—& we pass an act by acclamation that
> hereafter the Paper-Promises shall be the Gold and Silver itself—and ridicule
> a man for a dreamer, and reviver of antiquated Dreams, who believes that
> Gold & Silver exist—. This may do as well in the market—but O! for the
> universal, for the man himself, the difference is woful.
>   (*CN* III 3973 f 27)

If art leads us to the view that in perception the mind is equally
creative when confronted with the unfamiliar (at least), we are faced
with the view that although the reader is not an artist in the same way
that the artist is, he is nevertheless, as a perceiver of the unfamiliar
(the poem), required to respond actively and imaginatively, with an
'impassioned eye'. The reader's role might be described in the following
quotation in the *Biographia* from Plotinus's *Enneads*:

> ". . . For in order to direct the view aright, it behoves that the beholder
> should have made himself congenerous and similar to the object beheld.

Never could the eye have beheld the sun, had not its own essence been soliform," (i.e. pre-configured to light by a similarity of essence with that of light) "neither can a soul not beautiful attain to an intuition of beauty."

(*BL* I ch. vi 80)

Throughout Coleridge's prose writings he refers to his reader as a 'fellow-labourer' and a 'friend' who must rouse himself not only to attention but also to thought if he is to participate fully in the reading experience offered. This point is particularly applicable to poetry, with its compression of metaphor and symbol, two modes most rigorously demanding equal labour from the reader for comprehension. Thus the following exhortation to thought applies particularly to the labour involved in reading the poetry:

Themes like these not even the genius of a Plato or a Bacon could render intelligible, without demanding from the Reader THOUGHT sometimes, and ATTENTION generally. By THOUGHT I here mean the voluntary production in our own minds of those states of consciousness, to which, as to his fundamental facts, the Writer has referred us: while ATTENTION has for its object the order and connection of Thoughts and Images, each of which is in itself already and familiarly known. Thus the elements of Geometry require attention only; but the analysis of our primary faculties, and the investigation of all the absolute grounds of Religion and Morals, are impossible without energies of Thought in addition to the effort of Attention . . . both Attention and Thought are Efforts, and the latter a most difficult and laborious Effort . . .

(*The Friend (CC)* I 16–17)

In a notebook entry which must be a response to the poor reception which *The Friend* was accorded, Coleridge complained: 'Thought and attention very different Things—I never expected the former (viz—selbstthätige Erzeugung dessen, wovon meine Rede war) from the Readers of the Friend—I did expect the latter, and was disappointed.—3 January 1810' (*CN* III 3670).

The reader's project is a much more radical one than it is often supposed to be, and herein lies the substance of Coleridge's argument for the 'voluntary production in our own minds of those states of consciousness, to which, as to his fundamental facts, the Writer has referred us'. It involves quite literally an application of a sophisticated idealism to art. That is, art objects stand in a similarly dependent relation to the perceiving mind of the spectator as ordinary objects of perception have stood to the mind of the observer. Idealism leads us to the conclusion that the characteristics ascribed to the object are more properly understood as results of the perceiving mind, or, in Coleridge's terms borrowed from Schelling, 'the spirit in all the objects which it views, views only itself' (*BL* I ch. xii 184). Reality becomes then a projection or externalization of the mind according to its own structure and principles of objectification, or 'thingifying':

> Our Senses in no way acquaint us with Things, as they are in and of themselves: . . . the properties, which we attribute to Things without us, yea, . . . this very *Outness*, are not strictly properties of the things themselves, but either constituents or modifications of our own minds . . . Impressions which we call *Things*, are truly only Ideas, or Representations, which change with the changes of the representative Faculties in the subject . . . therefore all our Knowledge is confined to Appearances, our philosophy a philosophy of Phaenomena . . .
>
> (*CN* III 3605 f 121)

On this point many philosophers agree, as Coleridge indicates in his preamble to this passage. They differ in the accounts which they give of the powers of knowledge, and the extent and nature of the creativity of the faculties of mind.

The most obvious projections of the human mind are its modes of organizing by time, space, causality, likeness, contrast, and value. For these elements are not properly understood, according to the idealist, as inherent in reality; they are laws of mind for organizing sensations into experience. Space and time are singled out as 'forms of sensuous intuition', or as Coleridge says, speaking first of space:

> . . . tho' not a perception of anything, it is still not a *Conception*/for it is inter simplicia simplicissimum, and possesses no common merkmahl or class mark—it is not a generative, nor a representative Image, nor an intellectual notion, nor a perception of any thing—what then is it? Why, clearly a form of all perception—an intuitive process—It and Time, the Intuitus puri et omnis perceptionis formae universales—.
>
> (*CN* III 3973, autumn 1810)

Much earlier, in 1797–8, Coleridge had groped tentatively toward the subjectivity of space and time in this passage from a notebook, awakened to the problem no doubt partly by Berkeley: 'All our notions husked in the phantasms of Place & Time, that still escape the finest sieve & most searching Winnow of our Reason and Abstraction' (*CN* I 334). The subjectivity of these two aspects of experience is the foundation for the idealist's insistence that an independent reality, supposed to correspond somehow to the external world, is a 'prejudice of outness' . . . 'unconsciously involved in . . . [and] not only coherent but identical, and one and the same thing with our own immediate self-consciousness' (*BL* I ch. xii 178). The other categories of organization, such as causality, value, etc., were more obviously subjective and dependent upon culture or individual prejudice.

Art may function at two levels to represent this subjectivity. It may exhibit a 'marvellous independence from time and space'; it may reorder or challenge ordinary causal connections or value judgments and thereby show alternative ways of organizing a reality, a world. Or art may offer another level where it also considers its own status as object, both from the point of view of poet and from that of spectator. This level might be termed a metaphorical or self-referring level of discourse, or a level of irony. For the spectator or reader is reminded at this ironic level that the first level has explicit application to the immediate experience of perception, namely, reading. The application involves the realization, and here the irony, that the reader's notion of meaning and text, at the most basic levels, is a product of his perceptions and not a quality supervening to the poem. As a product of his perceptions, the reading of the poem is subject to constant revision. Such a conclusion forces upon the reader an active project of continuing re-evaluation and repetition of his responses to a work of art, and an admission that the work of art constantly demands revision of determined meanings and demands reinterpretation. Coleridge often ironizes the reader who thinks he has established the fixed and permanent meaning of a work of art, as in the gloss to 'The Ancient Mariner'. By ironizing such a reader, Coleridge also reminds us that neither the object nor the subject provides a stable reference point. He never asserts a naive subjective idealism where some illusory certainty can be postulated in the subjective responses: his negative models of reading testify to this view.

Stated in other terms, because the boundary between subject and object is no longer stable, verification for notions about the 'real' poem or the literal text becomes difficult. There is no stable, objective reality discoverable to which one might appeal. The line between description and interpretation is blurred. Coleridge seems to play upon this difficulty when he introduces his prose commentaries to his poems in the form of prefaces, footnotes, glosses, and circumstantial accounts of the genesis of the poems. Initially, these prose elements seem to be the language of reality as contrasted with the verse language of art and illusion. But on examination these prose passages often seem to expose the difficulty of determining both what reality is and its relation to art. For they themselves turn out to be full of fictional elements, and their 'authors' turn out to be characters of highly limited perspectives, so that they end up denying indirectly what as prose passages they seem on the surface to assert. For the surface level assures a clear distinction between reality and illusion, while a critical reflection upon the mode of articulation of that distinction leads to a doubting of it.

For the reader, the consequences of Coleridge's introducing such prose elements into his art as techniques consists in a constant pressure from these devices to reassess or criticize initial or even second level responses and assumptions, until the reader is thoroughly engaged in a conscious reflection about not only the poem and its content, but especially about his own acts of finding meaning, describing, and interpreting. These acts will be found to be analogous to those of some of the characters in the prose or verse 'frameworks', and contrary to those of others. For Coleridge offers in his devices both models of active, participatory reading and models of passive, reductionist readings. Both models liberate the reader from over-determined attitudes about the poem, and stimulate him to further response and radiating networks of significance. For the negative model can act by a recognition or mirroring effect to help the reader to see whatever is imprisoning and limiting his response, and the positive model (as the Wedding Guest in 'The Ancient Mariner') can give alternatives to these inhibiting and limiting forms of response. The preface to 'Kubla Khan' is an example of the superimposition of a positive upon a negative model by means of metaphor (see above pp. 38–40), while the speaker in 'This Lime-Tree Bower' seems to enact the entire drama, starting from a limited, restricted response, to an all-embracing imaginative experience. Sara, in 'The Eolian Harp', seems to illustrate not only the incredulous, disapproving reader, but the tendency in mind generally to reject imaginative, speculative flights in favour of the familiar and conventionally approved formulas. Indeed, one might assert that the reading analogy ascribed to these poems has its integrity precisely in this level of the conflict between reason and imagination. In one case the conflict is seen in terms of faculties within the mind, while in the other the faculties are split off into characters and the conflict dramatized more externally, as between reader and author.

This conflict between reason and imagination and between reader as active or passive (or even between poet versus conventional passive reader) is yet another illustration of the concept that all objects, including language, images, metaphors, and art objects generally, tend to imprison thought by attracting its attention outward and by fixing it there. The degenerative tendency in thought creates the chasm between subject and object, and can only be avoided by acts of the mind continuously restoring the presentness and vividness of the relations expressed by this linguistic 'currency'. Objects themselves are not stimulating or deadening; the mind's interaction with them is the decisive factor. Landscape most often illustrates the importance of the mind's role in determining the value of an object. Such is the focus of 'This Lime-Tree Bower'; the bower is transformed from a prison to a paradise by the imaginative response of the speaker. The contradictory nature of the image of the frost in 'Frost at Midnight' as threatening and deadening, at the same time that it is a symbol of imagination, makes the same point. The Khan's gardens may similarly be understood as examples either of the mechanical fancy producing artificial works, or the gardens may be imaginative products. For it may be said that works of true imagination look like mere fancy to the unimaginative eye. More generally, the contrast in these poems between the domestic and the exotic, between nature and the dell, for example, expresses the active/passive duality of experience and the overcoming of it.

This assimilation of landscape and the internalization of the external suggests another aspect of the duality between art and reality—that is, the more general issue of the artist's transformation of materials and externals into aesthetic products. For example, the 'processing' of landscape by the speaker in a poem can be related both to the poet's processing of his surroundings as they are supposed to be the stimulants and inspirations for his poem, and to the reader's processing of his own surroundings: the poem itself. The prefaces to 'This Lime-Tree Bower' and 'Kubla Khan' explicitly emphasize this relation of real sources to the poems. The harp, babe, and friend (as well as the nightingale) act as external objects which seem to be the focus, at least, if not the cause, of imaginative activity. But all of these objects are empathically identified by the speaker with himself, and the distance between the subject and object is thereby overcome as likeness is discovered in the midst of difference, while delight wells up from this establishing of relation. In the case of all of these subject–object assimilations, nature is the immediate context, and is seen as imagination itself when the assimilation occurs, as in Stanza III of 'This Lime-Tree Bower', or as in the first stanza of 'The Eolian Harp'.

The problematic relation between imagination, its products, and the external materials which go into those products can be expressed in several ways. For example, are the harp and the nightingale *causes* of the inspiration which informs the poem? Is the circumstance of the friends' walk the cause of the writing of 'This Lime-Tree Bower'? Are these elements causal in determining the imagery and content, as *Purchas his Pilgrimage* allegedly is in 'Kubla Khan', or are they causal in some other sense? And are the poems reports of the poet's experience *really* or only *imaginatively*? If there is no difference, in what sense is art different from reality? Thus the very genre of the conversation poem seems to question the relation of art to reality and the role of the mind in creating some reality. And while on the literal level the real, biographical circumstances of composition, or at least of inspiration, seem to exclude the reader from any identification with the speaker, at a metaphorical level they act to include him, by analogy, as they describe a perceiver in a specific situation confronting a world to which he proceeds to respond imaginatively.

The preface and gloss to those two supernatural poems seem to function similarly to the genre of the conversation poem, establishing a context of narration or composition as a model of negative response. The genre of the supernatural poem is different from the conversation poem; it actually denies any connection with a 'real' experience. It makes claim to the purely imaginative, while the other genre explicitly seeks to establish its genesis and meaning in a real situation. But it is clear that in both cases the relation of art to reality becomes an issue, nevertheless. For while the issue in the latter case may be in terms of what is fact and what is fiction, in the former we must ask what the meaning of the fiction is, that is, has it any reality at any level of experience, psychological, moral, aesthetic, or whatever? But the method of making meaning of the poems by drawing analogies with these other realms of experience is the same for both genres, whether their materials arise from the storehouses of fancy, memory, nature, or culture.

This question of the relation of the mind to its materials and the transformation of those materials of reality into art, is rephrased in the constant appeal throughout Coleridge's poetry to the quieting of the senses, silence, and solitude, or reference to extraordinary states of trance, swoon, dream, and vision. In these states of suspended sense-perceptions, the mind seems to be trying to defend itself from the distracting attention to external impressions in order to be able to act and to create new objects, or in order to be acted upon by forces from within itself impressing their character upon these externals, and transforming them into aesthetic objects. While Coleridge seeks explanations to many aspects of the relation of art to reality, he suffers as much as any poet from the mystery surrounding the moment of inspiration and its demise. Indeed, this transience of imagination also reaffirms in another way the dualism of experience at one level: imagination can liberate but then imprison the artist in his memory and longing for its return (as, for example, Keats's 'La Belle Dame Sans Merci' illustrates).

The relation of memory and imagination is also one of the most pervasive themes throughout Coleridge's poetry. Memory seems to play an important role in keeping the mind alive to its more inspired, imaginative moments. For while memory is not imagination, it may prevent the mind from mistaking its unimaginative states and its purely discursive experiences as the only sorts of organizing possible. Yet the relation between imagination and memory is itself riddled with obscurities, and all the poems discussed seem to be preoccupied with this relation at some point. Certainly they all stress the crucial difference between merely remembering and truly reviving an experience. Both the visionary and the preface persona in 'Kubla Khan', for example, emphasize the necessity for some imaginative revival of a previous experience as opposed to a merely passive or mechanical remembering that it occurred, or a vague memory of its outlines. Memory plays a central role in 'Frost at Midnight', where it acts in place of the external world to supply the speaker with materials for reflection and imaginative reworking. Yet even here the memory seems to be functioning imaginatively, as the speaker is reawakened to an experience in childhood similar in important ways to the present experience. Even the relation of the present to the past (and indeed to the future in Stanza III) becomes related to the question of imagination and memory. It may be correct to surmise that imagination works through several modes, such as memory, fancy, and the understanding, as a power of intelligence relating these various elements of memory, fancy, or the understanding.

By suggesting that Coleridge's poetry is informed by a creative theory of mind, and thereby awakens the reader to a sense of immediacy and expectancy about his own perception as involved in reading, it is hoped that the reader will be able to balance himself more expertly on the threshold where art and reality intermingle, and where the mind is poised between the active and passive, or the conscious and unconscious. The extra-poetic elements of prefaces, glosses, and footnotes can then take their place with the techniques of landscaping, imagery, and characterization, as literary devices for bringing the reader into a closer and richer association with the poetry, by showing how to transform the perceptual process of reading into an imaginative experience.

Afterword

The creative theory of mind implicit in the poetry of 1795–8 seems to be in conflict with Coleridge's avowed Associationism. Moreover, Coleridge's shift away from Hartley, or at least an ambivalence toward him, may have occurred much earlier than is generally supposed, affected perhaps by his intense poetic experiences at the time. The conversation poems may seem more directly involved in this conflict with Hartleianism, since the gloss to 'The Ancient Mariner' and the preface to 'Kubla Khan' were probably composed much later, and were not published until 1816. A version of 'The Ancient Mariner' had appeared of course in 1798 in a very different form, and 'Kubla Khan' had remained unpublished altogether until 1816. Thus the techniques of gloss and preface cannot be said to belong entirely to the 1795–8 period, even though the gloss seems to have important relations to the 1798 'Argument', and the preface to an early manuscript note. These techniques must belong to the later period characterized by more conspicuous ironies and artifices designed to engage the reader, such as unfinished chapters, anonymous letters, non-existent essays on the supernatural, all occuring in the *Biographia Literaria* and originating in the same spirit that inspired the gloss and preface.

These two techniques of gloss and preface are more overtly self-conscious in asserting the essential creativity of the mind, in so far as they impinge upon the reader more directly by virtue of their independence and position of commentary in the poem. But they nevertheless have much in common with the techniques of the earlier poems.

The latter keep their levels of self-consciousness about the nature of aesthetic engagement integrated into the content of the poetry, and never allow these metaphoric levels to break away from the poetry to become independent elements, as they do in the supernatural poems and in the *Biographia*. But such aesthetically sophisticated breakings-away of levels of self-awareness previously built into the fabric of the poems do seem to be foreshadowed in materials like the 'Argument', the prose accompaniment to 'This Lime-Tree Bower' and, for example, the various footnotes to these poems.

These gestures toward romantic irony never achieve the full-grown systematization of, say, Blake's writings or those of the German Romanticists, at least not until the 1815–16 productions. They remain at the level of occasional posturings, while self-consciousness is largely confined to, though nevertheless achieved in, the inner structure of the poetry, as in 'This Lime-Tree Bower'. The speaker in this poem transforms his bower from prison to paradise by an imaginative act, while levels of analogies for the poet and reader are echoed in the situation of the speaker and his relation to his friend and to nature. But these analogies remain within the fabric of the poem's basic poetic structure, except for the relatively casual gesture of the footnotes or the introductory statements to this poem which set up the reality/art tension. The third stanza of 'The Eolian Harp' with its ambiguous tone between piety and irony is another example of aesthetic consciousness built into the basic inherent poetic structure and unity of the work of art. Even here the reader's attention to this irony is ensured by a footnote almost flagrant in its inconsistency with the tone of the poem as a whole. Only in 'Frost at Midnight' do we find a poem almost entirely free of these 'extra-poetic gestures'; but it too is stratified with irony in the ambivalence of the primary, framing image of the frost and in the metaphorical search for origins and pre-existence.

Poems such as 'Kubla Khan' and 'The Ancient Mariner', which do allow for an independent level of commentary separate from the body of the poem, do not thereby sacrifice their metaphoric levels of aesthetic self-awareness as inherent in the poetry. These elements act as additional and supplementary, and not as substitutions for the more internal structural techniques. Thus the narrative in 'The Ancient Mariner', of the Mariner telling his story to the Wedding Guest and the interminable repetition of the story is such a structural technique. 'Kubla Khan' on the other hand offers its most impressive structural technique in the relation of the final eighteen lines to the rest of the poem. The preface might be said only to emphasize what is achieved artistically by these lines within the strict confines of the poem as a whole, namely a 'vision' of art as it functions both in composition and in audience response. These germinal glimpses of a theory of art are taken up more explicitly by the preface, though the latter is itself far from being merely a discursive, theoretical account. (The *Biographia Literaria* also has its inherent ironic structure, as its unconventional mixed genre testifies; its extended metaphoric situations, patchwork borrowings and constant reference of art to perception are its more inherent modes of romantic irony.) The fine subtlety required to capture the aesthetic distance ('freedom from sentimentality') necessary for self-consciousness and an awareness of the essential creativity of mind is well expressed by Coleridge in his criticism of the German playwright Heinrich von Kleist:

> I have just looked into Kleist's first play—it seemed to me harsh and branny, and the freedom from sentimentality, for which our friend Tieck gives him so much credit, too evidently a matter of purpose, and fore-thought—industrious omission not absence by nature and consequence of the some thing instead.

> (*CL* V 190–1, to J. H. Green, December 1821)

In the same letter Coleridge jabs gently at a Dr Gooch who took his 'anonymous' letter in the *Biographia*, Chapter Thirteen, too literally:

> I met Dr Gooch the day before yesterday . . . He consulted me about studying Schelling, in consequence of having read my Biographia Literaria —& asked me whether *Robinson* was not the writer of the dissuasive Letter!!! It is so like him, I suppose.

The omission in a work such as the present undertaking of the relation of Coleridge's theory and techniques (which strive through the unity of poetry and philosophy to assert a creative theory of mind) to both German Romantic aesthetics and to modern critical theory such as that of Derrida, the preoccupation of Theodor Adorno with method and style, and of Walter Benjamin and other Marxists and Structuralists, can only be justified by the admission that the connections are pervasive and important enough (contrary to the general belief that Romanticism is somehow ahistorical) to require something more systematic and thorough than a mere chapter or an occasional statement of parallels and similarities. The basic concept in Romantic aesthetics of the work of art as an object of constantly progressing and changing significance (dependent for its determinations upon a perceiving mind which is also developing, and whose project of reading indeed is precisely to develop its critical consciousness through a critique of its own perceptual acts of organizing and assimilating the poem) is the most immediate and obvious connection with modern critical theory. The importance in Romantic art of the engagement of the reader with the text expresses another similar preoccupation, especially as the notion emerges of the work of art as fundamentally fragmentary and incomplete, with gaps and faults. The idea of language (and art) as potentially a prison of familiarity links with the concept of the necessity in art for defamiliarization and shock techniques.

There are also no doubt many differences, though they are not always as great as they may appear at first glance. Coleridge more than any other Romantic except Blake was passionately concerned with the social and political influences upon the artistic consciousness, and with the discovery of basic principles common to the various disciplines, as were Adorno and Benjamin: even though they denied the notion of 'first principles' from an epistemological point of view, they were committed to the unity of philosophy and sociology, for example—for the necessity for a constant interaction of theory and empirical research. Nor was the romantic commitment to idealism of the sort that is rejected by Adorno or Benjamin. Romantic idealism was tendentious and purposeful as a polemic against eighteenth-century materialism. It rejected the notions that the mind is passive and reality is stable and independent of it, or, in aesthetic contexts, that the work of art has a fixed and determinate meaning or truth apart from the experience of and engagement with it. Romantic idealism was not dogmatic (though interpretations of it are), for it never fell into the illusion of an alternative stability of mind as a structure unchanging and determinate, and this is the major criticism of modern critical theory against conventional idealism, that it reifies mind as the reality. (For a lucid account see Raymond Williams, *Marxism and Literature* (Oxford: 1977), though his account (as for example of Plato) often makes no distinction between dogmatic expositions of idealism, and genuinely dialectical idealism.)

Where differences between the Romantic aesthetic and modern criticial theory seem more substantial, one must wonder whether Romanticism does not offer a valuable critique of some of the narrownesses and superficialities to which any new movement is vulnerable. For example, the Romantic commitment to the phenomenon of inspiration in artistic creation does not, as it is often claimed, minimize the effect of social and cultural influence; it rather takes into account an intense and undeniable experience of the empirical consciousness and seeks to integrate it into a theory of art. Modern critical theory often denies experience which demands explanation, however much a fabric of appearance as opposed to reality that experience may be. Nor does the Romantic emphasis upon the work of art as an organic whole contradict a more socio-historical criticism; it rather fosters such recognition of the integral, organic involvement of art in its social and cultural context. For though each work of art may be a whole in so far as it has a structural unity, it is also a 'true part' of a larger whole, and cannot be taken out of its relation to that whole without altering it and minimizing it. That larger whole may be its literary context, or even the whole of society in its broadest sense.

No one who is familiar with Blake, Shelley, or Coleridge can doubt their commitment to the idea that art is intimately related to the society that produces it. On the other hand, their broad aesthetic vision was able also to take account of the individual experience; and indeed the tension between society and the individual was a predominant theme in the poetry. Nevertheless, modern critical theory no doubt provides an opportunity to reinterpret in new terms the illusions to which each era is subject in its own particular forms and guises, and in that sense it may provide an invaluable perspective upon the Romantic aesthetic for the modern reader–critic. It seems certain, however, that although the terminologies and formulations vary in the extreme, the concepts, distinctions, and polemics in which modern critical theorists and Romantics were engaged are astonishingly similar. This similarity is a sober reminder that the theory of change itself requires, dialectically at least, a concept of continuity.

NOTES

Introduction

1. Dorothy Emmet in 'Coleridge and Philosophy', *Writers and their Background: S. T. Coleridge*, ed. R. L. Brett (London: 1971), 195–220, and George Whalley in 'On Reading Coleridge', also in Brett, 1–44, show a fine sensitivity for the sort of philosophizing at which Coleridge excelled. Emmet says, for example, 'he is most illuminating in the occasional throw-away remark . . . few professional philosophers have seen as far as Coleridge into the powers of the human mind' (197, and see 220). Whalley sees Coleridge as 'tentative and exploratory', and finds as much or more value in such openness as in the formulated conclusions of more conventional or systematic philosophizing (2).

2. See *BL* I ch. ix 94 and n, and L. Werkmeister, 'The Early Coleridge: His "Rage for Metaphysics"', *The Harvard Theological Review* 54 (1961), 99–123; see also *The Letters of Charles Lamb*, ed. with those of Mary Lamb, by E. V. Lucas, 3 vols (1935), I 123–4, and II 190 on Coleridge's early enthusiasm for metaphysics. See *The Complete Works of William Hazlitt*, ed. P. P. Howe, 21 vols. (1930–4), vii 117–18, and xvii 107–8, on Coleridge's early passion for philosophizing. Further, one of Lamb's most well-known accounts of Coleridge expounding upon 'the mysteries of Iamblicus and Plotinus' occurs in 'Christ's Hospital Five and Thirty Years Ago', *Essays of Elia*. In a letter to Ludwig Tieck (*CL* IV 750–1), Coleridge also admitted to sharing Tieck's admiration for Jacob Boehme's *Aurora* when a schoolboy. More generally, see John Beer, 'Ice and Spring: Coleridge's Imaginative Education', *Coleridge's Variety*, ed. J. B. Beer (London: 1974), 54–80.

3. See *BL* I ch. ix 95 and 242n, for the following succession of 'philosophical idols' from Southey's *Life*: Hartley, Berkeley, Spinoza, Plato, and Boehme; the last of whom 'had some chance of coming in' when Southey last talked to Coleridge. The implication of a succession of idols is no less incorrect than this hypothetical order would have been. See also Hazlitt's listing in his article on Coleridge in *The Spirit of the Age* (1825).

4. On Coleridge's reading of Fichte, see Daniel Stempel, 'Revelation on Mount Snowdon', *Journal of Aesthetics and Art Criticism* 29 (Spring 1971), 371–84. The first sustained readings of Kant and Fichte in 1800 led Coleridge to the mystified criticism that both seemed to be expounding a 'theory of Dreams'; see marginal notes to Fichte, *Grundlage der gesammten Wissenschaftslehre* BM *MS* C 126 f 13(1) and Kant, *Critique of Pure Reason*, BM C 126 i 9. Coleridge later criticized Kant for his failure to see the necessity for three powers in a metaphysics of nature, and in the same breath he criticized Schelling for an *inadequate* 'importation' of a third power. This late marginal note occurs in Kant's *Metaphysische Anfangsgründe der Naturwissenschaft*, BM *MS* C 126 n8. Coleridge also criticized Kant and Fichte quite early for their

'stoic morality' and their abstraction of duty to the detriment of love and imagination in moral acts. Here he seems entirely consistent with, if more sophisticated than, his position of anti-Godwinism in the 1795 Lectures (see discussion below). On this stoic morality see e.g. Kant's *Grundlagung zur Metaphysik der Sitten*, and cf. *CL* IV 791 December 1812 and *CN* III 4017 on duty.

Coleridge's most significant criticism of Kant's metaphysics involved his own commitment to ideas as constitutive and not merely regulative, as Kant publicly described them. The extensive Tennemann marginalia on the *Geschichte der Philosophie* are full of these fascinating and lengthy 'completions' of Kant. See *P Lects* notes for a sample of these marginal notes. But see also Elinor Shaffer, 'Metaphysics and Culture: Kant and *Aids to Reflection*', *Journal of the History of Ideas* 7 (1970), 297–313 on Coleridge's later relation to Kant's thought.

5. For discussion see Thomas McFarland, *Coleridge and the Pantheist Tradition* (Oxford: 1969), 169–79, for a somewhat different account of Coleridge's shaking off of Hartley. McFarland seems to find no traces, in 'The Eolian Harp', for example, of inconsistency or waverings from Hartley toward Cudworth and a more active theory of mind (171). For a different view see C. B. Martin, 'Coleridge and Cudworth', *Notes & Queries* 13 (May 1966), 173–6, who places Coleridge's release from Hartley much earlier, and sees readings of Cudworth in 1795–6 as having been of decisive importance. McFarland places his entire stress for Coleridge's rejection of Hartley on religious grounds, saying that 'with Coleridge the emotional need for Christianity always came before the intellectual need for philosophy, but where one went, the second was sure to follow' (170). Thus he takes almost no account of influences from the Cambridge Platonists, the mystics, or Kant and Plato during the 1793–1801 period. Nor does he take into consideration personal experiences, both as a father and husband and friend, or as a poet; all of these would have been vital to Coleridge, and the basis of his religious feeling. They are considered here as important factors in the development of his thought. See below for further discussion.

6. On the divine attributes see *Lects 1795 (CC)* 208–9, and nn. See also *BL* I ch. x 114 and 136–7 for Coleridge's uncertainties during this time with regard to theological issues and their incompatibility with his philosophical position. For discussion see Stephen Prickett, *Romanticism and Religion* (Cambridge: 1976), and also Basil Willey, 'Coleridge and Religion', *Writers and their Background: S. T. Coleridge*, ed. R. L. Brett (London: 1971), 221–43.

7. See Dorothy Waples, 'David Hartley in *The Ancient Mariner*', *Journal of English and Germanic Philology* 35 (July 1936), 337–51, for an interesting view of Hartley's influence on the poetry of the period.

8. See W. Schrickx, 'Coleridge and the Cambridge Platonists', *A Review of English Literature* 7 (1966), 71–90, and George Whalley, 'The Bristol Library Borrowings of Southey and Coleridge, 1793–8', *Library* (September 1949) 114–31.

9. See my 'Berkeley's Ironic Method in *The Three Dialogues*', *Philosophy and Literature* 4 (Spring 1980), 18–32.

10. But it is also clear that German higher criticism of the Bible was having an influence on Coleridge; see Elinor Shaffer, '*Kubla Khan*' and the Fall of Jerusalem (Cambridge: 1975).

11. See Stephen Prickett, *Romanticism and Religion* (Cambridge: 1976), for the interrelation of Coleridge's poetic, philosophic, and religious commitments, and of course McFarland, *op. cit.*, 169–79 especially.

12. For a general account of Coleridge and Kant, see René Wellek, *Kant in England* (Princeton: 1931), an account which takes a quite different view from this one. Wellek's Chapter Three seems particularly misleading on Coleridge's differences from Kant. See also A. O. Lovejoy, 'Coleridge and Kant's Two Worlds', *Essays in the History of Ideas* (Baltimore: 1948). See footnote 18 below.

13. See Stephen Prickett, *Coleridge and Wordsworth: The Poetry of Growth* (Cambridge: 1970) for an analysis of the way in which such opposites lead to organic unity in Coleridge's poetry.

14. See *CL* I 267, December 1796, and *CN* I 182, October 1796. And see below the discussion in the chapter on 'Frost at Midnight' for the sources and transformations of 'toys', 'playthings', etc.

15. The connections of Locke or Newton (or Condillac) with Hartley occurred in the 1790s in favourable terms; but after 1801, the connection continued, all three falling into disfavour. See e.g. *CL* IV 670, 1816 for a later concise summing up: 'I have endeavoured to explain myself at large on that distinction between the Reason and the Understanding, which I deem of such vital Importance—& with this some leading points of my scheme of philosophy, as contrasted with the Mechanic, Locke, Hartley and Condilliac System.' See also *CL* IV 760 and *CN* I 634 f56. In 1820 Coleridge chastizes those 'who have learnt the exclusive origination of the *omne scibile* in the Senses from Locke and the detail of the process from Hartley.' *CL* V 88. See also *CL* VI 715 for another coupling of Locke and Hartley. But of course Coleridge had criticized Newton as early as November 1796; see above pages 5 and 11.

16. *CL* II 709 to Poole, March 1801, written after discussing Newton, whom Coleridge had a few pages earlier in his letter to J. Wedgwood coupled with Hartley, *CL* II 686.

17. Basil Willey, *Nineteenth Century Studies* (London: 1949), 7. Note the contrasting view of the editors of *Lects 1795 (CC)* lv, who seem to have interpreted Willey's intention differently, an indication perhaps that Willey's statement is somewhat ambiguous.

18. *BL* I, xxx, in the introduction by Shawcross; Shawcross however does not venture to mention any date as definite as this. G. N. G. Orsini, in *Coleridge and German Idealism: A Study in the History of Philosophy* (Carbondale, Illinois: 1969) has given a general account of Coleridge's response to the Germans, but his interpretations and conclusions often seem unfounded and misleading. A more reliable source than either Orsini or Wellek is McFarland, *op. cit.*, or, more indirectly on Coleridge's thought, Owen Barfield, *What Coleridge Thought* (London: 1971). Alice Snyder, in *The Critical Principle of the Reconciliation of Opposites* (Ann Arbor: 1918), also shows a finer grasp of Coleridge's idealism, no doubt partly derived from her close familiarity with his late, unpublished philosophical manuscripts, and his *Treatise on Method*, which she edited (Constable: 1934); the manuscript is in the British Library (Egerton 2825 and 2826). Elisabeth Winklemann's *Coleridge und die Kantische Philosophie* (Leipzig: 1933), also repays study.

Chapter One

1. 'Kubla Khan', *PW* I 295–8.

2. The composition of the verse and the preface of the poem are thought to have been separated by perhaps as much as nineteen years; the dating of the preface is even more difficult than that of the poem, for the poem was certainly written between 1797 and 1799. The preface was probably composed only just before the 1816 publication with 'Christabel' and 'Pains of Sleep'. On the dating of the poem dozens of articles have been written; but of especial interest is E. K. Chambers's 'Some Dates in Coleridge's Annus Mirabilus', *Essays and Studies* 19 (1933), 85–111 and 'The Date of Coleridge's *Kubla Khan*', *Review of English Studies* 11 (1935), 78–90. Elizabeth Schneider, in *Coleridge, Opium and Kubla Khan* (Chicago: 1953), 153–237, is surely mistaken in dating 'Kubla Khan' as late as she does; H. M. Margoliouth, in 'Wordsworth and Coleridge: Dates in May and June 1798', *Notes & Queries* 198 (August 1953), 352–4, indicates a more plausible date of about 1 June 1798. However, October 1797 seems the most likely date for a number of reasons, not to mention Coleridge's own comments on two separate occasions (see below page 22 for the *Crewe Manuscript* preface version). See also *CL* I 349–52 to Thelwall for a number of comments which encourage acceptance of autumn, 1797 as the date of composition. While the apparent gap in years between the composition of verse and preface may seem an argument against the close interaction of the two, not only the nature of the interaction, which does not depend upon a proximity in time of composition, but also the existence of the *Crewe Manuscript* with its preface version, which grew into the published version, would militate against such an argument.

3. In few of the well-known studies of 'Kubla Khan' is the preface discussed as of literary significance, nor is its aesthetic relation to the poem considered. Elinor Shaffer, in *'Kubla Khan' and the Fall of Jerusalem* (Cambridge: 1975), sees the importance of the preface as an expression of a theory of inspiration, but discusses it more in relation to higher criticism of the Bible in Germany in

the 1790s. Irene H. Chayes, in '*Kubla Khan*' and the Creative Process', *Studies in Romanticism* 6 (Autumn 1966), 1–22, offers a brief but suggestive account.

Coleridge's contemporaries differed in their responses to the meaning of the preface. Thomas Love Peacock insisted the preface should be received with a 'certain degree of scepticism' (*Works*, ed. H. F. B. Brett-Smith and C. E. Jones (1934) viii 290). Henry Alford recorded a similarly sceptical comment by Wordsworth in *Life of Alford*, ed. Alford (1873), 62.

4. The stanzaic structure of the poem differs from edition to edition. The *Crewe Manuscript* has only one major division, occuring between lines 36 and 37; *1829* has three stanzas, with no new stanza after line 36; *1834* is ambiguous, line 36 coming at the bottom of the page may suggest a fourth stanza. Even with these variations in mind, the reader usually senses major division between the first 36 and the last 18 lines.

5. R. H. Fogle, in 'The Romantic Unity of *Kubla Khan*', *College English* 22 (1960), 112–16, argues for the unity of the poem as advancing through a reconciliation of opposites to a unified whole. See also D. F. Rauber on 'The Fragment as Romantic Form', *Modern Language Quarterly* 30 (1964), 212–21. E. H. Meyerstein, in 'The Completeness of *Kubla Khan*', *Times Literary Supplement* (30 October 1937), 803, discusses the unity of the poem and its genre as a short Pindaric Ode, with two main divisions only.

6. According to Leigh Hunt, Lord Byron was 'highly struck' with Coleridge's recitation of the poem in 1816, *Autobiography of Leigh Hunt*, ed. E. Blunden (1928), 345.

7. Coleridge had presented his work under other auspices before, such as Nehemiah Higginbottom (author of a series of sonnets in the *Monthly Magazine*, November 1797), as he pointedly explained in the *Biographia* (see *BL* I, ch. ii, 17–19, on this and other (anonymous) contributions). Elizabeth Schneider suggests that Coleridge may have been the author of two articles attributed to a 'Professor Heeren of Göttingen' appearing in the *Monthly Magazine* of January 1800, a gesture of irony if it were truly Coleridge's work. Is 'Heeren' possibly a play on 'Herr' and on the German practice of piling up titles before a name? See Schneider, *Coleridge, Opium and Kubla Khan* (Chicago: 1953), 289ff.

Kierkegaard is the most obvious related example of an author creating personas for the sake of ironic communication. Shelley often attached prefaces in the form of advertisements to his poems, sometimes echoing the preface to 'Kubla Khan' in tone and style, and in the creation of a persona. See e.g. the advertisement to 'Epipsychidion'.

8. This note is attached to the *Crewe Manuscript*, now in the British Library, dated 1810 according to George Watson, in *Coleridge the Poet* (London: 1966), 119. See John Beer's edition of *Coleridge Poems* in the Everyman paperback (London: 1963) 164, for a discussion of the *Crewe Manuscript*.

9. The explanation usually advanced for why Coleridge wrote the preface suggests that the preface was a gesture of self-defence for not having finished the poem. See e.g. G. Yarlott, *Coleridge and the Abyssinian Maid* (London: 1967), 128, for a fairly representative account: '[the preface was written in] self-defence, anticipating the charge of obscurity which the poem's acknowledged imperfection of organization would produce . . .' 'Acknowledged' by T. S. Eliot perhaps, but see footnote 11. See also Lowes, who, it would seem, had promulgated this basic position some forty years earlier, in *The Road to Xanadu* (London: 1927), chapters 18, 19, 20, and especially pages 412–3. Elizabeth Schneider expresses a similar assessment; see Schneider, *op. cit.*, 26ff.

10. Lowes, *op. cit.*, 358, reminds us that 'in ancient tradition the stately pleasure-dome of Kubla Khan itself came into being, like the poem, as the embodiment of a remembered vision in a dream'. Lowes thinks this point insignificant enough to be relegated entirely to a footnote. But this is just the sort of point Coleridge would have seen fit to turn to his own use by creating a *poem* designed in a dream as an analogue of the Khan's palace or dome, an analogue expressly designed to draw the reader's attention away from the obvious *content* of the poem and toward the composition and reading of the poem. P. Collier's report (*Sh C* ii 47) suggests that Coleridge was aware of the legend that the Khan's plan for a palace had originated in a dream. Coleridge's own comments elsewhere suggest a thorough awareness of the pregnancy of the dream as a metaphor for poetic composition. A marginal note to Eichorn's *Einleitung in das Alte Testament* (Leipzig 1787), iii 38 is pertinent to the preface:

> From the analogy of Dreams during an excited state of the Nerves, which I have myself experienced, and the wonderful intricacy, complexity, and yet clarity of the visual Objects, I should infer the [spontaneity and inspired character of Ezekiel's vision of God]. Likewise, the noticeable fact of the words descriptive of these Objects rising at the same time, and with the same spontaneity and absence of all conscious Effort, weighs greatly with me, against the hypothesis of Pre-meditation, in this and similar Passages of the Prophetic Books.

And see e.g. *CN* III 4410: 'We are nigh to waking when we dream, we dream.' (cf. Freud who interprets the dream within a dream as closest to reality.) The visionary in the epilogue may be in some such situation. Note in connection with this the statement in *Literary Remains*, ed. H. N. Coleridge (London: 1836–9), I 173: 'A poem may in one sense be a dream, but it must be a waking dream'. That 'one sense' is perhaps best indicated by another comment, in *Misc C*, 36: 'You will take especial note of the marvellous independence and true imaginative absence of all particular space or time in the Faery Queen . . . It is truly . . . of mental space. The poet has placed you in a dream, a charmed sleep, and you neither wish, nor have the power, to inquire where you are, or how you got there.' This freedom from the conscious dictates of space and time characterizing the unconscious and art is mentioned also by A. R. Jones quoting H. House in 'The Conversation and other Poems', *Writers and their Background: S. T. Coleridge*, ed. R. L. Brett (London: 1971), 99: 'We are also conscious of an "extraordinary sense of the mind's *very being*, in suspense, above time and space", that "arises in the poet himself in the act of composition".'

11. Critics from Elizabeth Schneider to George Watson have discounted the notion that the poem was literally composed in a dream. See George Watson, *op. cit.*, 120, and Schneider, *op. cit.*, 22ff and 45. Yarlott and Lowes seem to assume the dream account to be meant literally only, without any symbolic or ironic significance. See Yarlott, *op. cit.*, 128 and Lowes, *op. cit.*, chapters 18, 19 and 20. John Beer points out that however the poem was composed, it is not a 'meaningless reverie [as many have assumed] but a poem so packed with meaning as to render detailed elucidation extremely difficult.' Beer, *Coleridge the Visionary* (London: 1959), 202. Eliot's view that the poem lacks the organization needed to complement the inspiration is set to rest by the elucidation of the connections amongst the imagery in Beer, *op. cit.*, chapters 7 and 8. See Eliot, *The Use of Poetry and the Use of Criticism* (London: 1933), 146.

12. An anonymous contributor to the *Times Literary Supplement* (16 February 1962), says that this omission from the *Crewe Manuscript* 'places the whole matter of the circumstances in which 'Kubla Khan' came into existence in a different, more sober light.' See also *CN* I 278 on a Mr Porson.

13. Lowes briefly notes this point, but does not seem to attach any importance to it. He, moreover, seems to identify the 'I' of the epilogue with a tartar youth; see Lowes, *op. cit.*, 408. Elizabeth Schneider recognizes the contrast between the body and epilogue of the poem, but only concludes from that that the poem is an unfinished fragment! See Schneider, *op. cit.*, 247–8. George Watson interprets the break as a distinction between fancy and imagination. See Watson, *op. cit.*, 124–6. Lowes correctly, I believe, divides the poem up into four sections, in the stanzaic divisions of 1816, but makes no claim that the fourth is different from the other three. See Lowes, *op. cit.*, 406. In Yarlott, *op. cit.*, 147ff, no distinctions between the parts are drawn at all in any conscious sense, nor is there any significant discussion of how the epilogue content relates to the lines 1–36, or why it varies in narrative perspective, content, and style.

14. The title of the work is actually *Purchas his Pilgrimage*, though Coleridge's version sometimes appears on the bindings of editions and as E. H. Coleridge has pointed out in the notes, the lines which Coleridge quotes as his source are quite different from the lines in the *Pilgrimage*.

15. Lowes, *op. cit.*, 362ff, suggests that a passage in *Purchas* does at least mention damsels and youths and songs. 'Abyssinian' and 'dulcimer' are traceable to more obscure sources, through Abyssinian is discussed later by Purchas. The damsels and youths were inmates of the Khan's palace, however, a point which serves to connect the singing damsel even more closely with the Khan's activities, as will be discussed; see page 26, and see note 17.

16. Many critics since have disagreed with Lowes's reductive assumption that the 'I' of lines 37–54 is a tartar youth. Most postulate him as the archetypal

poet, and cite sources as ancient as Plato's *Ion* to mark the connection between poetry, madness, and the corresponding imagery of honey dew and milk, and the flashing eyes and floating hair. See e.g. Yarlott, *op. cit.*, 148ff, who too simply equates the 'I' with Coleridge and not the poet *par excellence* as well. George Watson, *op. cit.* 122 sees him as the latter, as does Schneider, in 'The Dream of '*Kubla Khan*', *PMLA* 60 (1945), 800. John Beer offers the most satisfactory account of the 'I' as visionary, artist, or genius: 'the apotheosis of all the 'divine men' who had haunted Coleridge's youthful imagination'. Beer, *op. cit.*, 261ff. He is not Coleridge, but Coleridge's ideal of absolute genius (as contrasted with commanding genius: see 226–7); not Coleridge him*self* but only Coleridge as he transcended himself:

> To have a genius is to live in the universal, to know no self but that which is reflected not only from the faces of all around us, our fellow creatures, but reflected from the flowers, the trees, the beasts, yea from the very surface of the sands of the desert. A man of genius finds a reflex to himself, were it only in the mystery of genius.

> (*P Lects* 179)

17. That the damsel sings of 'Mount Abora' seems to exclude her from being the singer of lines 1–36. But in nearly all of the important passages traced as sources for the River Alph, a mountain was present, from which the river sprang. Thus the river and the mountain are always closely associated in the landscape, so that to sing of Mount Abora would be to sing of the river as well. For the most important mountain–river connection see Beer, *op. cit.*, 221: 'This river, as soon as it issues out from between the cleft of the mountain . . .' See also 220, for another connection: '. . . the River Barrady breaks out from between the Mountains: it's Gardens extending almost to the very place', and 257 for the religious and inspirational associations of the mountain. Lowes, *op. cit.*, 361, offers other sources in which the river issues from a mountain. See especially 372 for a description of a mountain full of water that is forced out at the foot to become the river. Still more importantly for the connection, Lowes, 373, traces the name Abora not to a mountain but to the names of two rivers, Abola and Astaboras. Lowes concludes, '. . . Mount Amara—its name merged with the name of the river that flowed by the Mountains of the Moon' (376). See further 382. And see the *Crewe Manuscript* for the variant 'Mt Amara'.

John Beer further associates the maid with the Khan's world by uncovering the explicit sexual and female connotations of the walls and towers and gardens, and their sources in the *Song of Solomon* (see *ibid.* 270–1). Thus not only might the maid's song be construed as the song of lines 1–36, but the landscape description would be of the 'damsel with a dulcimer' described allegorically.

18. Thus the pun on 'air' as melody. Cf. 'The Eolian Harp' line 32 and see below page 78. For Coleridge on music as 'articulated breath' see *CN* III 4022.

19. See e.g. *LS (CC)* 29, for Coleridge on the imagination as that 'reconciling and mediatory power, which incorporating the Reason in Images of the Sense, . . . gives birth to a system of symbols, harmonious in themselves, and

consubstantial with the truths, of which they are the conductors'. Note the use of 'harmonious'. Note also the explanation in *BL* I ch. vii 86. All efforts to identify the Abyssinian maid with a specific woman in Coleridge's life seem reductive and quite contrary to the activity of imagination as a producer of *symbols*, not of allegories: see *LS (CC)* 30.

20. See Coleridge 'On the Philosophic Import of the Words Object and Subject', in *Blackwoods Magazine* 10 (October 1821), 247–50, on the given and the external.

21. Jean Paul Richter, in his *Vorschule der Aesthetik* (1804), places the idea of the poet's observation, his 'Schau' or 'Betrachtung', of his own work of art, at the centre of the theory of irony as aesthetic distance, since the artist is said to be simultaneously spectator, and vice versa. The artist's ability to maintain a third person perspective *while creating*, is a measure of his achievement of ironic self-consciousness. Thomas Mann would seem to agree: see 'The Art of the Novel', 88–9: 'the sense of art itself . . . an all-embracing crystal clear and serene glance, which is the very glance of art . . . a glance of the utmost freedom and calm and of an objectivity untroubled by any moralism. This was the glance of Goethe . . .'

22. George Watson says 'Kubla Khan' is 'wonderfully of a piece', *op. cit.*, 120. John Beer also argues with detailed analysis for the completeness of the poem, *op. cit.*, 275. On the poem's metrical unity, see A. C. Purves, 'Formal Structure in *Kubla Khan*', *Studies in Romanticism* 1 (Spring 1962), 187–91.

23. A further reason for thinking that Coleridge's description of the dream and the 'images [which] rose up before him as *things*' was a metaphor of poetic composition, is to found in his letters to Southey and Davy, and Godwin as well, which Lowes, *op. cit.*, 66, points to as descriptions of eidectic imagery. Coleridge seems to have been unusually adept at this ability to seem actually to see scenes before one as external, independent perceptions, at the same time that one is aware that they are purely mental productions. But see also the Eichorn marginal note quoted above, footnote 10.

24. See e.g. the anecdote about reading Plato in *BL* ch. xii 160–1 or the letter from a friend in *BL* I ch. xiii. Both chapters are full of recipes for reading imaginatively. The gloss to 'The Ancient Mariner', it will be argued below, is a fine instance of a parodied reading situation.

25. Yeats writes about the paradoxical relation of active and passive in creative experience:

> The purpose of rhythm, it has always seemed to me, is to prolong the moment of contemplation, the moment when we are both asleep and awake, which is the one moment of creation, by hushing us with an alluring monotony, while it holds us waking by variety, to keep us in that state of perhaps real trance, in which the mind liberated from the pressure of the will is unfolded in symbols.

From 'The Symbolism of Poetry', *W. B. Yeats, Selected Criticism*, ed. N. Jeffares (London: 1964), 48. Yet Yeats never underestimated the conscious role of the poet. See Beer, *op. cit.*, 203–4 for Yeats's appreciation of the balance between instinct and intention.

26. Coleridge describes this peculiar passive, receptive state of the conscious mind in *BL* ch. xii 166–7, in his quotation from Plotinus, and in his metaphor of the air-sylph or the chrysalis.

27. For Coleridge's use of 'thingify' see *CL* IV 885 to Derwent Coleridge, November 1818: '. . . to think is to thingify'. The entire passage on logic is relevant.

28. See Shelley, 'The Defence of Poetry', 517:

> Poetry is not like reasoning, a power to be exerted according to the determination of the will. A man cannot say, "I will compose poetry." . . . for the mind in creation is as a fading coal, which some invisible influence, like an inconstant wind, awakens to transitory brightness; this power arises from within, like the colour of a flower which fades and changes as it is developed, and the conscious portions of our natures are unprophetic either of its approach or its departure.

Shelley then goes on to make observations expressly relevant to the loss of vision of the visionary, and relevant to Coleridge: 'Could this influence be durable in its original purity and force, it is impossible to predict the greatness of the results; but when composition begins, inspiration is already on the decline, and the most glorious poetry that has ever been communicated to the world is probably a feeble shadow of the original conceptions of the poet.' Shelley further notes a point lending support to the hypothesis that Coleridge's dream account is a metaphorical rendering of the poetic process of composition: 'I appeal to the greatest poets of the present day, whether it is not an error to assert that the finest passages of poetry are produced by labour and study. The toil and the delay recommended by critics, can be justly interpreted to mean no more than a careful observation of the inspired moments, and an artificial connexion of the spaces between their suggestions by the intertexture of conventional expressions; a necessity only imposed by the limitedness of the poetical faculty itself.' And see the important passage on judgement and instinct in *CL* IV 898n to C. A. Tulk, 17 December 1818. See also Coleridge's *Shakespearean Criticism*, ed: T. M. Raysor, 2 vols. (London: 1930), I 197–8, and *BL* II 'On Poesy or Art', 258. And see *Coleridge's Literary Criticism*, ed. J. W. Mackail (London: 1921), 186.

29. See W. J. Bate and John Bullitt, 'The Distinction between Fancy and Imagination in Eighteenth Century English Criticism' *Modern Language Notes* 69 (1945), 8–15, for sources which could well have influenced Coleridge's early thinking.

30. Most critics see the Khan's activities as unrepresentative of artistic creation,

because he seems to decree, measure, and quantify. See John Beer's analysis in terms of the commanding genius distinguished from the absolute genius, *op. cit.*, 216–17 and 226–7. George Watson agrees that the poem has levels concerned with aesthetic process (*op. cit.*, 122), but his claim that the first thirty-six lines of the poem are results merely of the faculty of fancy is inconsistent with the richness of the images and their power as symbols invoking universals. He seems to make the poem into a mere allegory.

31. See Shelley's 'The Defence of Poetry', *op. cit.*, 496. For Coleridge on the degeneration of truth see the appropriate passage in *CN* I 119 dated only vaguely as 1795–6: 'Truth is compared in scripture to a streaming fountain; if her waters flow not in perpetual progression, they stagnate into a muddy pool of conformity & tradition. Milton.' The Khan at least showed wisdom in building his dome by a streaming fountain of truth.

32. See further *AR*, aphorism 1, and *The Friend (CC)* I, 110.

33. See Yarlott, *op. cit.*, 133 on the Khan shutting out nature. And see also 131ff for a general discussion of the Khan's 'art' as opposed to truly inspired art. Yarlott makes an interesting comparison of Kubla's garden with the dell, marriage, and domesticity generally; see 151. See Beer, *op. cit.*, 222–3 for similar observations, and his additional insight that the Khan's garden of earthly paradise and the sun-worship of the poem suggest the pantheistic tendencies which always conflicted with Christianity in Coleridge's thought.

34. The landscape of 'Kubla Khan' seems to reflect late seventeenth and early eighteenth century interests in gardening as a metaphor for the cultivation of genius. Shaftesbury, and earlier, Sir William Temple, had all written using the garden as a metaphor for genius. The metaphor became more interesting as writers set up the dichotomy between the carefully landscaped garden (geometric garden), the 'chinese' garden (less obviously manicured), and the wild, natural garden. Finally the garden was contrasted with nature itself, and this contrast reflected the changing attitude toward the nature of genius and the relation of instinct to judgement. The poetry of the eighteenth century also reflected the development of the concept of genius in the imagery, Thomson, and later Chatterton, amongst others, relying more and more upon natural scenery, which culminated in the romantic landscapes of the Gothis novels and romantic poetry.

35. The poem also suggests to many critics a level of creation at the cosmico-religious level; thus Elinor Shaffer's relating of 'Kubla Khan' to higher Biblical criticism, and Dorothy Mercer's relating the poem to Jacob Boehme and the redemptive process in 'The Symbolism of *Kubla Khan*', *Journal of Aesthetics and Art Criticism* 12 (1953), 44–65. The connection of the poem with *Paradise Lost*, *Song of Solomon*, and *Ezekiel* enriches the religious dimension. For a different, more pagan, interpretation, see C. I. Patterson, 'The Daemonic in *Kubla Khan*', *PMLA* 89 (1974), 1033–42.

36. Thus the visionary is distinct from the Khan only in that he possesses the Abyssinian maid—he is artist inspired, while the Khan is perhaps artist, or maker, without inspiration, at least from the visionary's point of view. It is the Khan's dome and garden which are 'unfinished' for the spectator: they lack the completing inspiration of imagination. Boundaries seem arbitrary and not expressive of any integral part/whole relationship or of any inter-action with nature and with the materials out of which the boundaries are built. It is true, as most critics maintain (Yarlott, *op. cit.*, 145–6, Beer, *op. cit.*, 246 but see Watson, *op. cit.*, 123 and 128 for a contrasting view), that the visionary's 'dome in air', the 'shadow dome' and the Khan's 'pleasure dome' are all different. But they are different only as maid, visionary, and Khan are different: as aspects of the self and, as Blake would put it, as different levels of vision. Or they illustrate the changing function of imagery, from description of an external landscape, to symbolic of the internal organizing mind. It is necessary to stress however that the Khan's activities, his gardens, may also be a model of imaginative, vital art, as well as of degenerate art. This apparently contradictory two-fold significance best expresses the nature of art and metaphor as potentially degenerative from the point of view of spectator and artist. Thus visionary and Khan may have identical roles as artists, or they may be seen as opposite—the Khan as artist, the visionary as spectator wishing to complete for himself by imaginative response the un-finished dome. Thus the poem represents vividly the aesthetic situation of spectator striving to recreate for himself the work of art—the dome—by means of imagination—the damsel.

37. Watson, *op. cit.*, 123, recognizes the ambiguity of the contained or con-taining imagery and landscape. Yarlott assumes reductively that the ancient forests are encompassed by the Khan's walls, but not assimilated into the garden effectively. A recognition by Yarlott of the enclosure ambiguity would, however, strengthen his case that art which shuts out or fails to assimilate nature is only artifice. See Yarlott, *op. cit.*, 137.

38. Contemporary reviewers of 'Kubla Khan' did not see it this way. *The Eclectic Review*, 2nd series 5 (1816), 565–72, announced that the poem should never have been published. Hazlitt said it was 'nonsense' in the *Examiner* 440 (2 June 1816), 348–9. The most favourable response was to estimate the poem as 'not wholly discreditable', as 'Christabel' was said to be, *Anti-Jacobin Review* 1 (1816), 632–6. More recently, T. S. Eliot felt called upon to protest against 'the exaggerated repute of *Kubla Khan*', *The Use of Poetry and the Use of Criticism* (London: 1933), 146.

Chapter Two

1. The text referred to throughout is that of *PW* I 186–209. The *Lyrical Ballads* version is given in *PW* II 1030 ff.

2. There are so many psychologically-based interpretations of 'The Ancient

Mariner' that in the context of this analysis it would be a digression to take account of many of them. E. E. Bostetter's 'Nightmare World of *The Ancient Mariner*', *Studies in Romanticism* 1 (Summer 1962), 241–54 and his *The Romantic Ventriloquist* (Seattle: 1963) are two of the least satisfying and most reductive of the psychological types of criticism. George Whalley's 'The Mariner and the Albatross', *University of Toronto Quarterly* 16 (July 1947), 381–98, interestingly and perceptively discusses the biographical and psychological connections in the poem; and see David Beres, 'A Dream, a Vision, and a Poem,', *International Journal of Psycho-Analysis* 32 (1951), 97–116.

3. In the 1800, 1802, and 1805 editions of *Lyrical Ballads*, the poem was entitled 'The Ancient Mariner. A Poet's Reverie'. The spelling of the title had been modernized and the notion of a reverie added, and may be significant for the meaning of the dream in 'Kubla Khan'.

4. Such coalescence is one of the primary characteristics of irony, in addition to its 'selection' of readers (see also Chapter Three). Both devices suggest connections with the theories of the German Romantic Ironists, such as Karl Solger, Friedrich Schlegel, Ludwig Tieck, and others. See Ingrid Strohschneider-Kohrs, *Romantische Ironie in Theorie und Bestaltung, Hermaea*, 6 (Tübingen: 1960). The connections with Coleridge are not of the sort which Alois Brandl suggests in *Samuel Taylor Coleridge und die englische Romantik* (Berlin: 1886); his claims of German influence on 'The Ancient Mariner' and other works are rather dubious and often ill-founded, as most critics agree. E. H. Zeydel is a more reliable and informative source; see his *Ludwig Tieck and England. A Study of the Literary Relations of Germany and England during the early Nineteenth Century* (Princeton: 1931). Tieck was well known to Coleridge only some twenty years after the poem was written.

5. Irene H. Chayes, in 'A Coleridgean Reading of *The Ancient Mariner*', *Studies in Romanticism* 4 (Winter 1965), 81–103, does not show her usual perceptiveness in her treatment of these three elements, which she virtually dismisses as of no great structural interest.

6. Humphry House, in *The Clark Lectures* (London: 1953), 85ff briefly discusses the Wedding Guest context, but does not seem to see either it or the gloss as functioning aesthetically or structurally. At page 111, he rather hastily rejects Robert Penn-Warren's suggestive comment (in 'A Poem of Pure Imagination: Reconsideration', *Kenyon Review* 8 (Summer 1946), 391–427) that the poem is about poetry; at that time the phrase still carried some power of communicating meaning. Lately it seems to have become a worn-out or dead formulation. See Penn-Warren's extended interpretation of 'The Ancient Mariner' in his edition of the poem (New York: 1946).

7. The following account is not meant to exclude other functions of the Wedding Guest context. See e.g. M. L. D'Avanzo, 'Coleridge's Wedding Guest and Marriage Feast: The Biblical Context', *University of Windsor Review* 8 (Fall 1972), 62–6.

8. Freud, in *Beyond the Pleasure Principle* (1920), describes such a repetition syndrome as one of the primary instincts which man must acknowledge.

9. On the threshold metaphor, see Angus Fletcher, 'Positive Negation', *New Perspectives on Coleridge and Wordsworth*, ed. G. H. Hartman (New York: 1972), 133–64. J. L. Borges's story 'The Man on the Threshold' is another interesting fictional account of the threshold experience as a mirroring of perception, and more specifically, of reading.

10. See John Beer, *Coleridge the Visionary* (London: 1959), 15: '. . . the tragedy of the romantic hero is that he should still aspire towards any sort of certainty.'

11. H. Brown, in 'The Gloss to *The Rime of The Ancient Mariner*', *Modern Language Quarterly* 6 (September 1945), 319–24, makes the interesting point that the gloss distances the reader from the story; but he doesn't push his argument to its logical conclusion. For it is by gaining distance from his own responses, mistaken for the meanings in the text, that the reader is enabled to see the reading analogy in the gloss framework.

12. On the distinction, e.g., between thought and thing, see Coleridge's 'On the Philosophic Import of the Words OBJECT and SUBJECT', *Blackwood's Magazine* 10 (October 1821), 247–50. Elsewhere he also discusses the difficulty of establishing the boundary between these opposites and of accounting for them as facts of experience in a theory of reality (in *CN* III 3605 f117^V, and 4351 f22). Coleridge, like Schelling, could not accept the dualist position of the absolute boundary between (or reality of) thought and thing, as is clear everywhere in his writings. See e.g. his distinction between contraries and opposites in *CN* II 2502, 2631, 2832, and III 4326, and see *The Friend (CC)* I 94 for an account of the necessity that true opposites must at ground be homogeneous (a very Blakean position). Further, the *Philosophical Lectures* stress this homogeneity, see e.g. 371–87, and lecture two. But Coleridge departed from Schelling in that he denied polarity or opposition as a characteristic of the absolute itself, which he insisted must be one and entire; see *CL* IV 874–6, and *CN* III 4445, 4449–50. See also *P Lects* 390–1 and *CN* III 4424 for Schelling's relations to Zoroaster, Plotinus, Proclus and others.

13. The best of the few critical accounts of the gloss is Lawrence Lipking's fascinating article 'The Marginal Gloss', *Critical Inquiry* 3 (Summer 1977), 609–656; Lipking discusses Coleridge's 'The Ancient Mariner' amongst many other works and authors, such as Joyce.

14. The most impressive expression of the analogy of a mental landscape and a psychological sea-journey is Huxley's first few pages of *Heaven and Hell*. Though indirect, they offer a better account of the significance of the drama of 'The Ancient Mariner' than almost any critical study of the poem. The supernaturalism of the poem, like the despecification of time/space indicators, acts with equal force to locate the poem's action not in the external, natural world, but in the world of imagination: the reader's mind *qua* perceiver, for

instance. Thus there is an explicit tension between the gloss and the poem's supernaturalism, a contrast which should serve to strike the reader as demanding some explanation.

15. I. A. Richards's *Coleridge on Imagination* (London: 1934) is still one of the best accounts of Coleridge's theory, but for a more recent account see R. L. Brett, 'Coleridge's Theory of Imagination', *English Studies* 2 (1949), 75–90, or my own discussion in *Sources, Processes and Methods in Coleridge's Biographia Literaria* (Cambridge: 1980), chapter eight.

16. See L. C. Knights, 'Idea and Symbol: Some Hints from Coleridge', *Coleridge: A Collection of Critical Essays*, ed. Kathleen Coburn (Englewood Cliffs, N. J.: 1967), 112–22.

17. See also Coleridge's letter to Bowles, quoted on page 60.

18. See Shelley's 'Defence of Poetry' for similar views on moralizing in poetry. This distinction between a moralizing gloss and a verse markedly free of such gestures may suggest the need for a reconsideration of some critical interpretations which stress the ethical elements of the poem without distinguishing the gloss from text. See e.g. E. M. W. Tillyard, in 'Coleridge: The Rime of the Ancient Mariner', *Poetry and its Background*, ed. Tillyard (New York: 1970), 66–86, or J. V. Baker, *The Sacred River* (Baton Rouge, La: 1957), 178 ff.

19. But see P. M. Adair, *The Waking Dream* (London: 1967), for an account of the poem as a struggle between pantheism and personal religion. There is probably much truth in this view—it certainly is consistent with our knowledge of Coleridge's philosophical and religious thought. But it doesn't add greatly to an understanding of how the poem functions in experience or signifies to the reader. Moreover, as with the moralistic criticism of the poem, the religious dimension is complicated considerably when one considers the gloss as a non-authoritative posture; thus it is necessary for the reader constantly to be on his guard not to allow the gloss and verse to become intertwined into a single point of view.

20. Coleridge's criticism of the Greek poets in contrast to the Hebrew poets is an interesting elucidation of Plato's own criticism of the poets in the *Ion* and other dialogues, and in the *Republic*. Coleridge further explains himself when he writes on Milton:

I was much impressed with this in all the many Notes on that beautiful Passage in Comus from 1. 629 to 641—all the puzzle is to find out what Plant Haemony is—which they discover to be the English Spleenwort—& decked out, as a mere play & licence of poetic Fancy, with all the strange properties suited to the purpose of the Drama—They thought little of Milton's platonizing Spirit—who wrote nothing without an interior meaning. 'Where more is meant, than meets the ear' is true of himself beyond all writers. He was so great a Man, that he seems to have considered Fiction as profane, unless where it is consecrated by being emblematic of some Truth/

(*CL* I 866, to William Sotheby, 1802)

21. For an insight into what 'gloss' meant for Coleridge, see the wavering between 'gloss' and 'feign' in the 'Triumph of Loyalty', and between 'gloss' and 'paint' in 'The Night-Scene', *PW* II 1071, lines 310f, and ibid., I 422, lines 52f.

Chapter Three

1. The text of 'The Eolian Harp' is that of *PW* I 100–102. The date of first publication was 16 April 1796, in *Poems*, and in that edition the date of composition was given as a subtitle as follows: 'Composed August 20th, 1795, At Clevedon, Somersetshire'. Since Coleridge was not married until 4 October, he must have leased the 'Cot' some weeks in advance and gone for a viewing of it perhaps with Sara, if the biographical implications in the poem are accurate. In all subsequent editions, however, the date of composition was omitted, leaving only 'Composed at Clevedon, etc.'

2. On the importance of the active appreciation of nature in the poem, see H. J. W. Milley, 'Some Notes on Coleridge's Eolian Harp', *Modern Philology* 36 (May 1939), 359–75.

3. On radiation as an appropriate symbol of imagination see John Wright, *Shelley's Myth of Metaphor* (Athens, Georgia: 1970), chapter iv.

4. For Blake on personification as the distinguishing mark of imaginative activity see, for example, a letter to Thomas Butts, 2 October 1800, in William Blake, *Complete Writings*, ed. G. Keynes, 804–5.

5. Coleridge would already have been familiar with the concept of opposition in union, through, for example, Boehme, Plato, Bruno, Plotinus, Origen, etc. See Barfield, *What Coleridge Thought*, 187–8 and 214n.

6. For a development of this idea, see A. F. Gaskins, 'Coleridge: Nature, the Conversation Poems, and the Structure of Meditation', *Neophilogus* (Gronigen) 59 (1975), 629–35.

7. See Jill Rubenstein, 'Sound and Silence in Coleridge's Conversation Poems', *English* 21 (Summer 1972), 54–60, for a more general account. And see also P. A. Magnuson, 'The Dead Calm in the Conversation Poems', *The Wordsworth Circle* 3 (Spring 1972), 53–60.

8. For Coleridge on the Imagination as 'hovering' between opposites, see *Coleridge on Shakespeare*, R. A. Foakes (London: 1971), 82.

9. See *The Statesman Manual*, *LS (CC)* 29–30 and 79. *CL* I 349 and 354 express in prose the sort of yearning for wholeness that lines 44–49 strive to elucidate.

10. On Coleridge's rejection of dualism see the *P Lects* 371–87. And see *BL* I ch. viii 88–9, *CN* III 4397 and 4412. Some of his most interesting rejections of dualism occur in the marginalia to Kant's *Metaphysische Anfangsgründe der Naturwissenschaft*, and the *Logik*.

11. See also *CN* II 2937 of autumn 1806 for a continuing interest in the connections of the eolian harp and poetry: 'Aolian Harp motive for opening the Sash; & at once lets in music & sweet air; purifies & delights, moral Eloquence —Poetry—'. See also *BL* I ch. vii 81, on a similar criticism of the image as of mind or consciousness, instead of spiritualized body.

12. R. C. Wendling, in 'Coleridge and the Consistency of *The Eolian Harp*', *Studies in Romanticism* 8 (Autumn 1968), 26–42, admits the artificiality of the diction here, but explains it away as faith intruding into the imaginative realm.

13. The 'Jasmin and Myrtle' occurs several times in other poems, such as in the delightful poem 'Reflections on Having Left a Place of Retirement' (1795), and *PW* 106, perhaps less obtrusively conventional in function.

14. See e.g. C. B. Martin, 'Coleridge and Cudworth: A Source for *The Eolian Harp*', *Notes & Queries* 13 (May 1966), 173–6, which discusses the poem as already a sign of Coleridge's gradual release from the 'mechanical philosophy'.

15. Especially in Chapter Twelve, but even in Coleridge's more abstruse and later speculations, the final settling upon the 'Will as deeper than Reason' indicates his commitment to the principle of mind as self-originating. See e.g. *Aids to Reflection* 'Comment CIXc' and the long footnote attached. And see *CN* III 3676, 1810: 'Freedom (i.e. Arbitrium, Free Will)—the *verbal* Definition of—The faculty of absolutely beginning any state . . . the *real* definition; the faculty of Causality thro' or by Thought alone—or Thought actually causative.'

16. See e.g. *The Statesman's Manual LS (CC)* 20, 31, and 91, and see *The Friend*, *(CC)* I 65 and 432. In *CN* III 3320 the spring and fountain are related, which makes the preface to 'Christabel' relevant, where tanks and fountains are contrasted. And consider that the spring as a metaphor is especially rich in its synthesis of the mechanical and the organic.

17. The editors of the *Lects 1795 (CC)*, do not make as much of this double reference of 'atheism', and on that basis they seem not to assume any ambiguity in the footnote to 'The Eolian Harp': it is presumably to them the *athée* who is cold and lacks a sense of the ravishing. See *Lects 1795 (CC)* 158, footnote 3.

18. On pantheism and Christianity in Coleridge's thought see Thomas McFarland, *Coleridge and the Pantheist Tradition* (Oxford: 1969).

19. Blake engages in such ironies in both his language and his illuminations. The one most apt for comparison with this poem is the emerging face of Urizen out of the tree in the illustration of 'The Lamb', a delightful caricature of Sara's act: 'thy more serious eye a mild reproof/Darts, O Beloved Woman!' The *eye* of Urizen in the emerging face hidden in the tree perfectly corresponds to the line in terms of the function of the hidden face in the drawing and the function of Sara as hidden censor in the poem. Nor should the pun on 'eye' as ego be lost, suggesting the internal, analogous conflict between imagination and a censoring understanding.

20. See *CN* I 41, 1795–6, for an explanation of why Coleridge might have been persuaded, against his feelings, to marry. This excerpt compares with Keats's letter on 'Soul-making', the unhappiness and the world generally being a school for the human heart:

> Misfortunes prepare the heart for the enjoyment of Happiness in a better state. ~~The pains~~ Life & sorrows of a ~~good man~~ religious & benevolent man ~~art the~~ is as its April Day—(his pains & sorrows fertilizing rain)—the Sunshine blends with every shower—and look! how lovely it lies on yonder hills!

Compare *CN* I 17, 1795–6:

> From the narrow path of Virtue Pleasure leads us to more flowery fields, and then Pain meets & chides our wandering—
> —Of how many pleasures, of what lasting Happiness is Pain the Parent & Woe the Womb!

21. The union of thought and feeling is a synthesis Coleridge speaks of time and again as the only means to wisdom. See e.g. *CN* III 3362, 3246, and 3490, and see *CL* II 1034.

22. For some of Coleridge's most interesting associations of poetry and music see *CN* III 4022, 4337, and especially 4319, which has detailed bearing upon 'The Eolian Harp', both for its comments on music and for its relevance to lines 26–33. The notebook entry is dated December 1816, and these lines appeared first in the 1828 edition. They seem to be the result of such musings on light, sound, and music as are evident in this long, abstruse, and philosophical passage. See M. H. Abrams, 'Coleridge's *A Light in Sound*', *Proceedings of the American Philosophical Society* 116 (1972), 458–76; and see Richard Haven 'Coleridge and Jacob Boehme: A Further Comment', *Notes & Queries* 10 (May 1963), 183–7. A careful analysis of prose jottings in comparison with such lines as 26–33 might give an insight into the sources of romantic poetry in the intellectual struggles of these poets better than any critical study could hope to achieve. And it would certainly help to show that the conciseness and brevity of poetry hides, or at least condenses, much exciting philosophical speculation. See also *CL* IV 750–1, to Ludwig Tieck, 4 July 1817, for sound–light associations.

23. That is, a region 'deeper than Reason itself', but not contrary to reason. See *The Statesman's Manual, LS (CC)* 67 and n 2. The note is a marginal comment of Coleridge's.

Chapter Four

1. The text of 'Frost at Midnight' is from *PW* I 240–42.

2. On the exotic versus the domestic see Chapter Five on 'This Lime-Tree Bower'; the contrast is expressive of the degeneration of language and perception. 'Frost at Midnight' has its exotic elements in the primitive fire–water imagery connecting its origins with the same projected 'Hymns' that are supposed to have had important links with 'The Ancient Mariner'. The informing doctrine of pre-existence also adds exoticism to the poem's overt childhood myth; see below.

3. The absence of an active level may account for the lack of attention to this aspect of the poem in such well-known discussions as that of Humphry House, *The Clark Lectures* (London: 1953), or R. H. Fogle's 'Coleridge's Conversation Poems', *Tulane Studies in English* 6 (1955), 108–110.

4. See the variation given by E. H. Coleridge, in *PW* I 241:

> Ah me! amus'd by no such curious toys
> Of the self-watching subtilizing mind . . .

or

> Ah there was a time,
> When oft amused by no such subtle toys
> Of the self-watching mind, a child at school . . .

5. See above introduction, pp. 11–12, and for Coleridge on the meaning of such 'representation' see *LS (CC)* 113 and *CN* III 3602, 3605. M. G. Sundell, in 'The Theme of Self-realization in *Frost at Midnight*', *Studies in Romanticism* 7 (Autumn 1967), 34–9, fails to refer the theme to the conscious composition or to the reader as active participant.

6. For a possible source or influence on this stanza see Cowper, 'The Task', IV, lines 291–5:

> Nor less amused have I quiescent watch'd
> The sooty films that play upon the bars,
> Pendulous, and foreboding, in the view
> Of superstition, prophesying still,
> Though still deceived, some stranger's near approach.

7. See Robert Langbaum, 'Frost at Midnight', in *The Poetry of Experience*, ed. Langbaum (New York: 1957), 45–6 for a lucid discussion of the relation of present and past and the use of time in the poem.

8. See F. Kaplan, 'Coleridge's Aesthetic Ministry', in *Miracles of Rare Device* (Detroit: 1972), 44–61.

9. For discussion of this passage see John Beer, *Coleridge the Visionary* (London: 1959), 247.

10. See *ibid.*, 153–4, on the ambivalence of ice and snow imagery.

11. 'Identity in difference' was Coleridge's formulation for the idea or law of polarity, as e.g. in *The Friend (CC)* I 94. There are many notebook references to 'synthesis or indifference of opposites', as e.g. *CN* II 2502, 2631, 2832, and *CN* III 4326, 4333, 4351, 4378 and 4418 f13. This definition of identity in difference also acted as a definition of metaphor, and the capability of the imagination generally. See e.g. *BL* II ch. xiv 12.

12. Entries in the notebooks suggest that Coleridge was early interested in theories of language. See e.g. *CN* I 866–7 and 918. See also I 1387. The eighteenth-century theorists who viewed poetry and metaphors as ornamental were for example, Isaac Watts and John Locke. See Locke's *Essay Concerning Human Understanding* (Oxford: 1924) 86. Or see Isaac Watts, *Logick: or the Right Use of Reason in the Enquiry after Truth* (London: 1736) 64–5. See J. Isaacs, 'Coleridge's Critical Terminology', *Essays and Studies by Members of the English Association* 21 (1936), 86–104, for Coleridge on language.

Chapter Five

1. The published text is from *PW* I 178–81; the letter is from *CL* I 334–6.

2. See *CL* I 334 n 3, and see *The Poetical Works of Samuel Taylor Coleridge*, ed. J. D. Campbell (London: 1893), 591 on the Lloyd version.

3. These six lines are an alteration of the manuscript version, but they are still different from the published version, for it deletes the hylozoic lines, 'A living Thing/That acts upon the mind' (lines 23–4). Compare *CN* I 200 n on hylozoism and Cudworth.

4. See however the footnote to 'Lines at Shurton Bars', *PW* I 99–100, on flashing flowers at sunset in July and August. It seems to relate to the shining purple heath flowers in these lines, and has similarities with the flashing and luminescence of the water snakes.

5. Shelley, 'The Defence of Poetry', 519. It seems appropriate to borrow Shelley's terms since he was greatly influenced by Coleridge.

6. Compare *CN* I 1449 f 4ᵛ and 1448, August 1803, for an interesting later connection with these lines.

7. A similar point is implied in R. C. Wendling, 'Dramatic Reconciliation in Coleridge's Conversation Poems', *Papers on Language and Literature* 9 (Spring 1973), 145–60.

8. See J. D. Boulger, 'Imagination and Speculation in Coleridge's Conversation Poems', *Journal of English and Germanic Philology* 64 (October 1965), 691–711, for some hints about this level.

9. See Anya Taylor on the effect of fictionalizing and magic in 'Magic in Coleridge's Poetry', *Wordsworth Circle* 3 (Spring 1972), 76–84.

Bibliography

Abrams, M. H. 'Coleridge's "A light in sound".' *Proceedings of the American Philosophical Society* 116 (1972), 458–76.

Adair, Patricia M. *The Waking Dream*. London: 1967.

Adorno, Theodor. *Negative Dialektik*. Frankfurt: 1966.

Minima Moralia. Frankfurt: 1951.

Alford, Henry. *Life of Alford*. Ed. Alford. London: 1873.

Allsop, Thomas. *Letters, Conversations and Recollections of S. T. Coleridge*. London: 1936.

Appleyard, J. A. *Coleridge's Philosophy of Literature: the Development of a Concept of Poetry 1791–1819*. Cambridge, Mass.: 1965.

D'Avanzo, M. L. 'Coleridge's Wedding-Guest and Marriage Feast: The Biblical Context'. *University of Windsor Review* 8 (Fall 1972), 62–6.

Baker, J. V. *The Sacred River: Coleridge's Theory of the Imagination*. Baton Rouge, La.: 1957.

Barfield, Owen. *Saving the Appearances: A Study in Idolatry*. London: 1957.

What Coleridge Thought. London: 1971.

Barth, J. R. *Symbolic Imagination*. Princeton: 1977.

Bate, W. J. and Bullitt, John. 'The Distinction between Fancy and Imagination in Eighteenth Century English Criticism'. *Modern Language Notes* 69 (1945), 8–15.

Beer, John. *Coleridge's Poetic Intelligence*. London: 1977.

Coleridge the Visionary. London and New York: 1959.

'Ice and Spring: Coleridge's Imaginative Education'. *Coleridge's Variety*. Ed. Beer. London: 1974. 54–80.

'Poems of the Supernatural'. *Writers and their Background: S. T. Coleridge*. Ed. R. L. Brett. London: 1971. 45–90.

Benjamin, Walter. *Illuminations*. Ed. Hannah Arendt. London: 1970.

Beres, David. 'A Dream, a Vision, and a Poem'. *International Journal of Psycho-Analysis* 32 (1951), 97–116.

Berkeley, George. *Works*. Ed. A. A. Luce and T. E. Jessop. 9 vols. London: 1948–57.

Blake, William. *Complete Writings*. Ed. G. Keynes. London: 1966.

Bostetter, E. E. 'Nightmare World of "The Ancient Mariner"'. *Studies in Romanticism* 1 (Summer 1962), 241–54.

The Romantic Ventriloquist. Seattle: 1963.

Boulger, J. D. 'Imagination and Speculation in Coleridge's Conversation Poems'. *Journal of English and Germanic Philology* 64 (October 1965), 691–711.

Brandl, Alois. *Samuel Taylor Coleridge und die englische Romantik*, Berlin: 1886.

Brett, R. L. 'Coleridge's Theory of Imagination'. *English Studies* 2 (1949), 75–90.

Brooks, Cleanth. 'Irony and "Ironic" Poetry'. *College English* 9 (1948), 231–7.

Brown, H. 'The Gloss to The Rime of the Ancient Mariner'. *Modern Language Quarterly* 6 (September 1945), 319–24.

Chambers, E. K. 'Some Dates in Coleridge's Annus Mirabilus'. *Essays and Studies* 19 (Winter 1965), 81–103.

'The Date of Coleridge's "Kubla Khan"'. *Review of English Studies* 11 (1935), 78–90.

Chayes, I. H. 'A Coleridgean Reading of the Ancient Mariner'. *Studies in Romanticism* 4 (Winter 1965), 81–103.

'"Kubla Khan" and the Creative Process'. *Studies in Romanticism* 6 (Autumn 1966), 1–22.

Cudworth, Ralph. *The True Intellectual System of the Universe*. Ed. John Harrison. 3 vols. London: 1845.

Derrida, Jacques. *Of Grammatology*. Trans. G. C. Spivak. Baltimore and London: 1974.

Eliot, T. S. *The Use of Poetry and the Use of Criticism*. London: 1933.
Emmet, Dorothy. 'Coleridge and Philosophy'. *Writers and their Background: S. T. Coleridge*. Ed. R. L. Brett. London: 1971. 195–220.

Fletcher, Angus. 'Positive Negation'. *New Perspectives on Coleridge and Wordsworth*. Ed. G. H. Hartman. New York: 1972. 133–64.
Fogle, R. H. 'The Romantic Unity of Kubla Khan'. *College English* 22 (1960), 112–16.
'Coleridge's Conversation Poems'. *Tulane Studies in English* 6 (1955), 108–10.
Freud, Sigmund. *Jenseits des Lustprinzips*. Leipzig: 1920.

Gaskins, A. F. 'Coleridge: Nature, the Conversation Poems, and the Structure of Meditation'. *Neophilogus* (Gronigen) 59 (1975), 629–35.
Godwin, William. *An Enquiry Concerning Political Justice*. London: 1793.

Hartley, David. *Observations on Man*. Introduction: T. L. Haguelet. 2 vols in 1. Gainesville, Fla.: 1966.
Haven, Richard. 'Coleridge and Jacob Boehme: A Further Comment'. *Notes & Queries* 10 (May 1963), 183–7.
Hazlitt, William. *The Complete Works*. Ed. P. P. Howe, 21 vols. 1930–4.
House, Humphry. *Coleridge, the Clark Lectures, 1951–2*. London: 1953.
Hume, David. *Treatise of Human Nature*. Ed. C. Mossner. Baltimore: 1969.
Hunt, Leigh. *Autobiography*. Ed. E. Blunden. London: 1928.
Huxley, Aldous. *Heaven and Hell*. New York: 1954.

Isaacs, J. 'Coleridge's Critical Terminology'. *Essays and Studies by Members of the English Association* 21 (1936), 86–104.

Jones, A. R. 'The Conversation and other Poems'. *Writers and their Background: S. T. Coleridge*. Ed. R. L. Brett. London: 1971. 91–122.

Kant, Immanuel. *Critique of Judgment*. Trans. James C. Meredith. Oxford: 1952.
Critique of Pure Reason. Trans. Norman Kemp-Smith. London: 1929.
Kaplan, F. 'Coleridge's Aesthetic Ministry.' *Miracles of Rare Device*. Detroit: 1972. 44–61.
Keats, John. *Letters of John Keats, 1814–21*. Ed. H. E. Rollins. 2 vols. Cambridge, Mass.: 1958.
Knights, L. C. 'Idea and Symbol: Some Hints from Coleridge'. *Coleridge: A Collection of Critical Essays*. Ed. K. Coburn. Englewood Cliffs, N. J.: 1967.

Lamb, Charles. *The Letters of Charles Lamb*. Ed., with those of Mary Lamb, by E. V. Lucas. 3 vols. London: 1935.
Langbaum, Robert. 'Frost at Midnight'. *The Poetry of Experience*. Ed. Langbaum. New York: 1957. 45–6.
Lipking, Lawrence. 'The Marginal Gloss'. *Critical Inquiry* 3 (Summer 1977), 609–56.
Locke, John. *Essay Concerning Human Understanding*. Ed. P. H. Nidditch. Oxford: 1975.
Lovejoy, A. O. 'Coleridge and Kant's Two Worlds'. *Essays in the History of Ideas*. Baltimore: 1948.
Lowes, J. L. *The Road to Xanadu: A Study in the Ways of the Imagination*. 2nd ed. Cambridge, Mass. and London: 1930.

McFarland, Thomas. *Coleridge and the Pantheist Tradition*. Oxford: 1969.
Magnuson, P. A. 'The Dead Calm in the Conversation Poems'. *The Wordsworth Circle* 3 (Spring 1972), 53–60.
Margoliouth, H. M. 'Wordsworth and Coleridge: Dates in May and June 1798'. *Notes & Queries* 198 (August 1953), 352–4.
Martin, C. B. 'Coleridge and Cudworth'. *Notes & Queries* 13 (May 1966), 173–6.

Mercer, Dorothy. 'The Symbolism of "Kubla Khan" '. *Journal of Aesthetics and Art Criticism* 12 (1953), 44–65.
Meyerstein, E. H. 'The Completeness of *Kubla Khan*'. *Times Literary Supplement* (30 October 1937), 803.
Milley, H. J. W. 'Some Notes on Coleridge's Eolian Harp'. *Modern Philology* 36 (May 1939), 359–75.

Orsini, G. N. G. *Coleridge and German Idealism*. Carbondale, Illinois: 1969.

Patterson, C. I. 'The Daemonic in *Kubla Khan*'. *PMLA* 89 (1974), 1033–42.
Peacock, T. L. *Works*. Ed. H. F. B. Brett-Smith and C. E. Jones. London: 1934.
Penn-Warren, Robert. *The Rime of the Ancient Mariner. With an Essay by Robert Penn-Warren*. New York: 1946.
Plato. *The Collected Dialogues of Plato*. Ed. E. Hamilton and H. Cairns. Princeton: 1961.
Prickett, Stephen. *Coleridge and Wordsworth: The Poetry of Growth*. Cambridge and New York: 1970.
Romanticism and Religion. Cambridge: 1976.
Priestley, Joseph. *Hartley's Theory of the Human Mind*. London: 1775.
Purchas, Samuel. *Purchas His Pilgrimage*. London: 1617.
Purves, A. C. 'Formal Structure in *Kubla Khan*'. *Studies in Romanticism* 1 (Spring 1962), 187–91.

Rauber, D. F. 'The Fragment as Romantic Form'. *Modern Language Quarterly* 30 (1964), 212–21.
Richards, I. A. *Coleridge on Imagination*. London: 1934.
Ed. *The Portable Coleridge*. London and New York: 1950.
Richter, Jean Paul. *Werke*. Ed. N. Miller. 6 vols. Darmstadt: 1959–63.
Rubenstein, Jill. 'Sound and Silence in Coleridge's Conversation Poems'. *English* 21 (Summer 1972), 54–60.

Schneider, Elizabeth. *Coleridge, Opium and Kubla Khan*. Chicago: 1953.
'The Dream of *Kubla Khan*'. *PMLA* 60 (1945), 800.
Schrickx, W. 'Coleridge and the Cambridge Platonists'. *A Review of English Literature* 7 (1966), 71–90.
Shaffer, Elinor. *'Kubla Khan' and the Fall of Jerusalem*. Cambridge: 1975.
Shelley, Percy Bysshe. *The Complete Poetical Works of Shelley*. Ed. N. Rogers. 2 vols. so far published. Oxford: 1972–5.
'The Defence of Poetry', *Selected Poetry and Prose of Percy Bysshe Shelley*. Ed. C. Baker. New York: 1951, 494–522.
Snyder, Alice D. 'The Critical Principle of the Reconciliation of Opposites as Employed by Coleridge'. *Contributions to Rhetorical Theory* 9 (1918), 1–56.
Stempel, Daniel. 'Revelation on Mount Snowdon'. *Journal of Aesthetics and Art Criticism* 29 (Spring 1971), 371–84.
Strohschneider-Kohrs, Ingrid. *Romantische Ironie in Theorie und Gestaltung. Hermaea* 6. Tübingen: 1960.
Sundell, M. G. 'The Theme of Self-realization in "Frost at Midnight" '. *Studies in Romanticism* 7 (Autumn 1967), 34–9.

Taylor, Anya. 'Magic in Coleridge's Poetry'. *Wordsworth Circle* 3 (Spring 1972), 76–84.
Tillyard, E. M. W. 'Coleridge: The Rime of the Ancient Mariner'. *Poetry and its Background*. Ed. Tillyard. New York: 1970. 66–86.

Waples, Dorothy. 'David Hartley in *The Ancient Mariner*'. *Journal of English and Germanic Philology* 35 (July 1936), 337–51.
Watson, George. *Coleridge the Poet*. London and New York: 1966.
Watts, Isaac. *Logick: or the Right Use of Reason . . .* London: 1736.
Wellek, René. *Kant in England*. Princeton: 1931.

Wendling, R. C. 'Coleridge and the Consistency of *The Eolian Harp*'. *Studies in Romanticism* 8 (Autumn 1968), 26–42.
    'Dramatic Reconciliation in Coleridge's Conversation Poems'. *Papers on Language and Literature* 9 (Spring 1973), 145–60.
Werkmeister, L. 'The Early Coleridge: His "Rage for Metaphysics" '. *The Harvard Theological Review* 54 (1961), 99–123.
Whalley, George. 'The Bristol Library Borrowings of Southey and Coleridge, 1793–8'. *Library* (September 1949), 114–31.
    'The Mariner and the Albatross'. *University of Toronto Quarterly* 16 (July 1947), 381–98.
    'On Reading Coleridge'. *Writers and their Background: S. T. Coleridge*. Ed. R. L. Brett. London: 1971. 1–44.
Wheeler, K. M. 'Berkeley's Ironic Method'. *Philosophy and Literature* 4 (Spring 1980), 18–32.
    Sources, Processes and Methods in Coleridge's Biographia Literaria. Cambridge: 1980.
Willey, Basil. *Nineteenth Century Studies*. London: 1949.
    'Coleridge and Religion'. *Writers and their Background: S. T. Coleridge*. Ed. R. L. Brett. London: 1971. 221–43.
Williams, Raymond. *Marxism and Literature*. Oxford: 1977.
Winklemann, Elisabeth. *Coleridge und die Kantische Philosophie*. Leipzig: 1933.
Wright, John W. *Shelley's Myth of Metaphor*. Athens, Ga.: 1970.

Yarlott, G. *Coleridge and the Abyssinian Maid*. London: 1967.
Yeats, W. B. 'The Symbolism of Poetry'. *Selected Criticism*. Ed. N. Jeffares. London: 1964.

Zeydel, E. H. *Ludwig Tieck and England. A Study of the Literary Relations of Germany and England during the early Nineteenth Century*. Princeton: 1931.